THAT DEVIL'S TRICK

Manchester University Press

That devil's trick

Hypnotism and the
Victorian popular imagination

William Hughes

Manchester University Press

Published by Manchester University Press
Altrincham Street, Manchester M1 7JA
www.manchesteruniversitypress.co.uk

British Library Cataloguing-in-Publication Data
A catalogue record for this book is available from the British Library

Library of Congress Cataloging-in-Publication Data applied for

ISBN   978 0 7190 7483 7   hardback

First published 2015

Typeset
by Carnegie Book Production, Lancaster
Printed in Great Britain
by TJ International Ltd, Padstow

For my Father,
John Henry Hughes
(1927–1973)

Contents

Acknowledgements

ACADEMIC WRITING may well be a solitary activity for the most part, though it is necessarily the product of a professional and a social existence as well. Many individuals, from all walks of life, have encouraged me in the writing of this, the seventeenth book which I have completed as author, editor or co-editor, and this small notice is a meagre acknowledgement of the support I have received during the research and writing of *That Devil's Trick*.

I must express my gratitude, first and foremost, to Gillian Wheeler for her unswerving support during difficult times. Writers tend also to thank their publishers as something of an afterthought in the last paragraph. I won't do that, for my gratitude to Matthew Frost, my true friend as well as my publisher, deserves its rightful place in this first paragraph. In something of a similar vein I would like to thank Meredith Carroll and Kim Walker, also of Manchester University Press, for their tolerance and consideration.

Many other friends and colleagues have likewise afforded, at various times and during often ridiculously late hours, the luxuries of sage advice, constructive criticism, credible whisky, strong coffee and, on more than one occasion, brotherly love, relief and truth. I must express my gratitude to the following friends, therefore, some of whom may well feel surprised to see their names in print in this work: Carol Burns and Brian Killey, Jnr; Nick Freeman (University of Loughborough); Ruth Heholt (University College Falmouth); Nigel Kingcome (University College Falmouth); Jarlath Killeen (Trinity College, Dublin); Sorcha Ní Fhlainn (Manchester Metropolitan University); Ben Fisher (University of Mississippi); Andrew

Smith (University of Sheffield); Sir Christopher Frayling (Churchill College, Cambridge); Catherine Wynne (University of Hull); Paul Murray; David Punter (University of Bristol); Catherine Spooner (University of Lancaster); Ellen McWilliams (University of Exeter); Colin Edwards (Bath Spa University); Vic Sage (UEA, Norwich); John Strachan (Bath Spa University); Sam George (University of Hertfordshire); Tracy Brain (Bath Spa University); Roy Foster (University of Oxford); Steve May (Bath Spa University); Gavin Cologne-Brookes (Bath Spa University); Jerrold Hogle (University of Arizona); Alison Younger (University of Sunderland); Colin Younger (University of Sunderland); Jillian Wingfield (University of Hertfordshire); Mark de Fleury (Bath Spa University); Catherine Robinson (Bath Spa University); Anne Lambton (University of Sunderland); Marie Mulvey-Roberts (University of the West of England); John Newsinger (Bath Spa University); Lana Hula (Bath Spa University); Tom Read (Bath Spa University); Emmalynne McEvoy; Sonja Zimmermann; Roger Sales (UEA, Norwich); Clare Fleck (Knebworth House); and, from Trowbridge, Don Farmer; John Cadby; Brian Weston; Ray Honey; Stephen Nuttall; Mark Manning; David Hipperson; and the late Bill Beaven.

Finally, I'd like to express the deep love and gratitude I feel to my uncle, Tom Hughes, and to all of my cousins. I finally have my family back again.

William Hughes
Trowbridge, Wiltshire, 14 February 2014

Preamble

Animal magnetism – a farce?

> Amateur theatricals are all very well in private places. Charles, and John, and Frederick, are then 'at home', and have none but their friends to look on at their odd performances, which of course, though they laugh at, it is all 'in confidence'.[1]

O N   A   C H I L L   N O V E M B E R   E V E N I N G   in 1848, a select audience gathered in the Banqueting Hall of Knebworth House, the Hertfordshire home of Sir Edward Bulwer-Lytton, to witness a charitable performance of Elizabeth Inchbald's *Animal Magnetism: A Farce in Three Acts*. The play was arranged and produced by the popular author Charles Dickens. Among the actors – all amateurs – were Dickens himself, who took the role of the Doctor, jealous guardian to a young girl amorously pursued by John Leech, the *Punch* caricaturist, in the guise of the Marquis de Lancy. These two male leads were supported by Dickens's illustrator, George Cruikshank, who acted the part of Jeffrey, the Doctor's comic manservant; and by Mark Lemon – founding editor of *Punch* and a contributor to both the *Illustrated London News* and Dickens's *Household Words* – who played La Fluer, valet to the Marquis de Lancy. The other roles, including those of the Doctor's ward, her maid and various gallants, were taken by associates of the fashionable author and his host.[2]

Though undoubtedly graced by a celebrity cast of literati well experienced in amateur dramatics, this lively comedy of disguise, deception and sexual intrigue, enacted by a handful of players in a single interior set, seems at first sight hardly a topical drama for the mid-nineteenth century. Having been

first produced in 1788 at the Theatre Royal, Covent Garden, in the presence
of its author, *Animal Magnetism* was neither a new nor even a recent play.[3]
In context, it appears curious that a gala evening such as this – arranged to
raise donations for the endowment of a Curatorship of Shakespeare's House
in Stratford-upon-Avon – failed to attract an original drama by Dickens,
or even a revival of Bulwer-Lytton's popular 1840 drawing-room comedy,
Money. Indeed, *Animal Magnetism* appears to have been sufficiently ephemeral
so as not to receive so much as a bare acknowledgement in John Forster's
recollection of the evening in the once-authoritative *Life of Charles Dickens*
(1872). The only title on the programme explicitly recalled by Forster in
his biography of the author is that of *Every Man in His Humour*, apparently
the main entertainment of the evening, and an appropriate enough choice
given that Shakespeare himself had acted in Ben Jonson's comedy in 1598.[4]

An eighteenth-century farce such as *Animal Magnetism* may thus appear
an odd choice for an evening dedicated to a sixteenth-century dramatist
and presented by a group of men associated with the depiction, in word
and image, of thoroughly nineteenth-century issues. Its presence on the
programme might well have been motivated simply by the need to maintain
the jovial atmosphere of the evening by deploying a work that required
few props and no changes of scene. Low comedy such as farce draws upon
the atemporality of ridiculous situations, interpersonal confusion and –
frequently – bawdy or suggestive dialogue, rather than the precise detail
of historical or contextual knowledge. Even acknowledging this, however,
Animal Magnetism cannot be regarded as a play in any way exceptional among
the English comedies of the late eighteenth century. Falling from public
favour in the first quarter of the nineteenth century, it was not regularly
revived in the Victorian era in the way that other comedies, such as Richard
Brinsley Sheridan's *The Rivals* (1775) or *The School for Scandal* (1777), were.
Dickens alone seems to have judged *Animal Magnetism* worthy of repeated
production, prefiguring its presentation at Knebworth with a charitable
performance at the Haymarket Theatre, London, in 1848 and a number of
provincial engagements in the same year.[5]

Animal Magnetism was also repeated at Knebworth in 1850, with Augustus
Leopold Egg – the painter of detailed and morally symbolic works such as
the triptych *Past and Present* – replacing Cruikshank in the role of Jeffrey.[6]
In 1857 Dickens revived the play again, albeit with a Spanish rather than
French setting, in a production that cast the novelist Wilkie Collins in the
role of one of the two menservants.[7] On that occasion, *Animal Magnetism*
was played in association with Collins's own melodrama of trance and

telepathy, *The Frozen Deep* – a production in which Dickens, Lemon and Egg also acted.[8] An amateur production always, in these few revivals, *Animal Magnetism* appears to be an odd but consistent recurrence in Dickens's amateur-dramatic repertoire, a work that presumably holds a personal interest for its director or producer that may not necessarily be readily evident to an audience, however indulgent.

There is a sense, however, in which Inchbald's eighteenth-century farce *might* be regarded as a work not unduly anachronistic for consideration by a mid-nineteenth century audience. The specific plot device through which the play's sexual duplicities are enacted is grounded in an intellectual and medical doctrine popular in the 1780s, the animal magnetism of the title. An eighteenth-century precursor to the many medical disciplines and practices which were, by 1848, laying competing claims to the increasingly respectable title of hypnotism, the theoretical dogma of animal magnetism was controversial even at the time of the play's conception.[9] Though the medical efficacy of animal magnetism – that is, the diagnostic, curative and clairvoyant theory initially popularised by the Austrian physician Franz Anton Mesmer – had been institutionally dismissed by successive enquiries under authorities as diverse as the French monarchical and revolutionary governments and the British Medical Association, the controversy that was associated with both its claims and the activity of its practitioners persisted well into a nineteenth century arguably as rich in disputable pseudosciences as it was in scientifically credible advances. If Mesmer's original conception of animal magnetism, with its vision of an intangible, universal and manipulable fluid, was largely discredited and clinically discarded by 1848, the common language through which animal magnetism was both conveyed and disputed retained a residual power that unavoidably shaped the reception of subsequent practices such as hypnotism. Animal magnetism, or mesmerism as it was often called, was arguably an unavoidable linguistic – and thus conceptual – correlative of *any* form of later trance-based curative, anaesthetic or diagnostic practice, whatever its formal appellation. As the hypnotist J. Milne Bramwell noted, in a book published long after the magnetic theory had been discredited, 'the influence of Mesmer continued to be widely felt: numerous observers in different countries produced phenomena resembling those he had shown, and explained them in much the same way'.[10] The controversy that surrounded animal magnetism, likewise, was apt to attach itself to its successors, however much they diverged intellectually from the fluid-based dogma of the eighteenth-century physician.

To recall animal magnetism within the drama or fiction of the nineteenth century was thus to invoke by implication a rich cultural tapestry in which the specificities of multiple professional practices vied for attention with the vagueness of popular imagery, where the controversies of the 1780s freely interchanged with those of the succeeding century, and where the sincere practitioner was at times congruent with the charlatan in a linguistic field that consistently deployed the same imagery for both. In short, during the nineteenth century the dogmas of animal magnetism, however loosely understood, persisted not merely as a memory of the past but also in a contextual relation to contemporary representations of both clinical professionalism and medical charlatanry. Indeed, because the assumptions and terminology of animal magnetism remained associated with later theories of the mind and body, Inchbald's play was perhaps potentially more farcical in 1848 than it had been even sixty years earlier, at the height of its novelty.

For Dickens, though, there may have been a yet more personal context which motivated his abiding interest in Inchbald's *Animal Magnetism* and its presentation of eighteenth-century mesmerism. Dickens himself claimed a facility in magnetic practice. This much is evidenced by a letter sent by him to John Forster whilst the author was on holiday at Bonchurch on the Isle of Wight in 1849. John Leech, Dickens's co-player at Knebworth some ten months earlier, had become 'very ill with congestion of the brain' having 'been knocked over by a bad blow by a great wave on the forehead'. Though Leech had been 'very heavily bled', presumably by a local surgeon or apothecary, he had apparently become 'seriously worse' in Dickens's opinion.[11] Thus, as Dickens recalls:

> I proposed to Mrs Leech, to try magnetism. Accordingly in the middle of the night I fell to; and, after a very fatiguing bout of it, put him to sleep for an hour and thirty-five minutes. A change came on in the sleep, and he is decidedly better. I talked to the astounded little Mrs Leech across him, when he was asleep, as if he had been a truss of hay ... What do you think of my setting up in the magnetic line with a large brass plate? 'Terms, twenty-five guineas per nap.[12]

Dickens's light-hearted conclusion only partially masks his apparent conviction that *this* act of mesmerism at least had provided not merely a type of temporary anaesthetic relief to the 'alarming state of restlessness' hitherto suffered by his unfortunate friend but also an improvement in his condition upon waking.[13] Though no specific detail is advanced as to what specific technique the author had utilised in order to induce the patient's trance, it is clear that some prolonged or 'fatiguing' effort was involved on the part of the amateur magnetist.

If the account rendered in Dickens's private letter is to be believed, therefore, this was no self-conscious administration of a placebo to a gullible and tired friend, and no deliberate fraud enacted against the 'astounded' witness. Apparently, also, Dickens's mesmeric intervention was an act which embodied no egotistical bravado beyond an ironic suggestion that a successful author might exchange his celebrated literary practice for an uncertain medical one. To all intents and purposes, if Dickens's account is taken at face value, the author's actions in that private space upon that September evening were sincere, altruistic and, withal, successful. Their recollection in both letter and biography, however, differs diametrically from the markedly less than favourable presentation of mesmerism embodied in the script of Inchbald's *Animal Magnetism*. Dickens's likely involvement in the selection and production of that specific play on more than one occasion thus again seems rather curious. It may well be that the play was proposed each time as being nothing more than a lively distraction, but it still seems unlikely that a writer so familiar with the power of ridicule would have embraced so consistently a farce directly relevant to a practice for which he appears to have entertained nothing other than sincere and inquisitive regard.

The choice seems even odder, given Dickens's friendship with Dr John Elliotson, Professor of Medicine at London University and Senior Physician to the North London Hospital. As well as being something of a medical consultant to literary celebrities – he enjoyed the professional patronage not only of Dickens but of William Thackeray and Wilkie Collins also – Elliotson was apparently a charitable figure as favourable to his poorer clients at the hospital as to wealthier visitors attending his Conduit Street consulting rooms.[14] Elliotson's alleged identity with the unnamed Physician of *Little Dorrit* (1856–7), who 'went, like the rain, among the just and unjust, doing all he could' cannot be conclusively proved, though his association with Thackeray's Dr Goodenough in *The History of Pendennis* (1848) appears to be long accepted.[15] Forster's assessment of Elliotson as one 'whose name was for nearly thirty years a synonym with us all for unwearied, self-sacrificing, beneficent service to everyone in need' is indicative at least of one side of the doctor's public reputation.[16]

Dickens and Elliotson had become involved in a charitable publication in 1844, and had also travelled together in the countryside near Geneva in 1846.[17] The author had dined with the Professor on the occasion of the latter's resignation from the faculty of University College, a move prompted by institutional unease regarding Elliotson's public experiments with mesmerised patients.[18] This dining invitation, which Dickens recalled in a letter to George Cruikshank, is especially significant in context.[19] Dickens, according to Forster, had 'always sympathised ... with Dr Elliotson's mesmeric investigations', and with Cruikshank – another participant in the Knebworth amateur theatricals – had twice attended demonstrations of magnetic practice at the North London Hospital.[20] These mesmeric experiments, though, were to be the focus of the other – less desirable – component of Elliotson's public reputation, that of a physician who, if not actually a quack himself, was the dupe of both fraudster practitioners and wily patients who exploited the contemporary vogue for spectacular public displays of mesmeric practice. Dickens, it must be stressed, maintained his friendship with Elliotson during and after the controversy that saw the Professor not merely estranged from the faculty of University College Hospital (as the North London Hospital had by then become) but the subject of disparaging editorial comment in *The Lancet* and other professional publications on the occasion of his delivering the annual Harveian Oration in 1846.[21]

There is, undeniably, a sense in which *Animal Magnetism* may be said to satirise the often spectacular behaviour exhibited by both eighteenth-century magnetists and their mesmerised patients. But the medical practitioners depicted in Inchbald's script – and no doubt the individual interpretations actually acted by Dickens and Leech during the production of the play – do *not* resemble qualified Victorian physicians, such as Elliotson, who deployed magnetism in the ostensibly clinical context of the hospital or the consulting room. The professional status of Inchbald's Doctor, indeed, is questionable. The Doctor's first appearance upon the stage is characterised by his indignation at having been censured by a presiding medical faculty who 'have refused to grant me a diploma – forbid me to practice as a physician, and all because I don't know a parcel of insignificant words'.[22] It is clear, indeed, from Inchbald's script, that the Doctor is as inept in conventional therapeutics as he is in the obviously false magnetism later taught to him by the equally ignorant valet, La Fluer. The Doctor admits that though 'a dozen or two of my patients have died under my hands' yet 'I have this morning nine visits to make'.[23] Lisette, his ward, replies, with obvious irony:

Very true, Sir, a young ward has sent for you to attend his guardian

– three nephews have sent for you to attend their uncles, very rich men – and five husbands have sent for you in great haste to attend their wives.[24]

The real focus of *Animal Magnetism*, arguably, is thus not mesmerism itself but rather the gullibility of those who regard it from a position of ignorance. These figures – typified by Inchbald's incompetent Doctor – are apt to apprehend magnetism as a panacea not so much for human illness in general as for their own misfortune specifically, whether this latter be financial impecuniosity or a lack of success in amorous adventures. This is most certainly the case in *Animal Magnetism*.

Such individuals amongst the uneducated public are ready prey for the quack mesmerist who may promise unlikely but desired benefits through the exercise of his alleged art. However, quack mesmerists are also – because of their strident claims to proficiency within magnetic science – the only available external study resource for those experimentally engaged in the development of mesmerism as a curative rather than simply profitable activity. The sincere metropolitan medical researcher may thus easily be equated with the quack lecturer upon a provincial platform merely because his presence has at some stage been observed at such a performance – often, ironically, by *another* medical practitioner equally curious about, but less convinced by, the claims of animal magnetism.[25] Elliotson may well have been deceived by the manipulations of some of his working-class magnetic subjects, as the medical press frequently insisted following University College Hospital's institutional rejection of his public mesmeric experiments in 1838.[26] As Dickens no doubt would have asserted, though, the gentlemanly and charitable doctor would have been far less easily swayed by the claims of those who practised mesmerism for strictly pecuniary motives.[27]

Itinerant and quack mesmerists, operating outside of the formal control of the various colleges and bodies which regulated British medicine as a profession, were certainly still in evidence in the mid-nineteenth century. These practitioners consistently attracted the disdain of the medical press, as much for their presumption to professionalism as for the often grotesque details presented as emblematic of their actual practice. A letter to the *Provincial Medical and Surgical Journal* dated 16 February 1843 is representative of many similar dismissals. The writer intimates, with some evident irony regarding the social origins of his subjects:

I lately attended a lecture upon animal magnetism given by *two gentlemen*, one of whom had been apprentice to a carpenter, and the other had formally gained, as I am informed, an honest livelihood as a marker in a billiard-room. In the present instance ignorance and impudence went hand in hand to the amusement of most of the audience, who now talk of the evening with some little shame, as if they had been witnessing the jugglery of some miserable country fair.[28]

If the writer's closing sentence is implicitly scathing with regard to the taste here exhibited by 'the good folks of Kent', he is more pointedly insistent that 'similar scenes have been patronised by such a man as Dr Elliotson'.[29] The statement, of course, begs the implicit question as to whether Elliotson himself might have been conscious of 'some little shame' when reflecting upon whether his own presence had added a veneer of gravitas to a performance – and a doctrine – here deemed ridiculous by a lay audience as well as an educated clinical observer.

Dickens could thus produce *Animal Magnetism* with no likelihood of offending his medical friend simply because the play could not be readily interpreted as a satire either upon Elliotson or his magnetic experiments. Elliotson's ability in *conventional* therapeutics was never questioned by the professional bodies with which he was associated, and, though his non-mesmeric practice was often innovative and controversial – he pioneered, for example, the use of the stethoscope and the deployment of quinine – it remained grounded in the physiological medicine practised by his contemporaries.[30] Again, in Inchbald's play the celebrated Dr Mystery – an oblique portrayal of Mesmer – does not actually appear, his role being usurped by the opportunist La Fluer. La Fluer, it might be added, is not a lower-class pretender to medical professionalism but a mere tool in a romantic adventure, and one whose knowledge of mesmerism is demonstrably as superficial as that of the incompetent Doctor he deceives.[31] Produced in a Victorian context, Inchbald's play is a comedy of ironic ignorance, truly a farce, and certainly not an immediate satire on either nineteenth-century revisions of Mesmer's doctrine or its best-known practitioner in contemporary England. The focus of the farce, in 1848 at least, would appear to be the gullibility of the layman rather than the malpractice of the professional.

Given Dickens's taste for the grotesque and his central role in the drama, the production raises the further question, indeed, as to how much the dignified, frock-coated lecturer Elliotson could be made to resemble not merely the sham practitioner La Fluer but also the theatrical figure of Franz Anton Mesmer. This latter, according to an 1851 account by the physician Herbert Mayo, was wont to 'slowly and mysteriously' circulate amongst his patients 'affecting one by a touch, another by a look, a third by passes with his hand, a fourth by pointing with a rod'.[32] Such fripperies are not easily associated – at least in the indulgence that often colours obituary retrospect – with a gentleman who on his decease was described as one of the 'oldest and most distinguished members' of the medical profession.[33]

In its revivals in London, at Knebworth, and across the English provinces, *Animal Magnetism* – an eighteenth-century text – and animal magnetism – an eighteenth-century doctrine – are crucially ensheathed in a network of nineteenth-century contexts. This network embraces discourses pertinent to the expression of historical and contemporary magnetic practice. It recalls popular and clinical appreciations of the perceived validity and effectiveness of the practice during two adjacent periods in the history of magnetism, and it embodies also the intensity of formal and informal debate between sincere believer and sceptical derider. Exemplified in Dickens's individual dramaturgy, this imbrication of the language of the former century with the consciousness of the latter is arguably typical of the British experience of animal magnetism and its conceptual descendents.

Unlike its French counterpart, British interest in animal magnetism is predominantly a nineteenth- rather than an eighteenth-century phenomenon. Certainly, it has long been held that the Viennese doctor's arrival in Paris was keenly anticipated. One nineteenth-century account intimates that Mesmer 'reached Paris in the month of February, 1778, whither the fame of his miracles had gone before him, and where many persons were expecting him with impatience'.[34] Derek Forrest, writing 170 years later makes much the same point when he argues that

> Mesmer's reputation ... had preceded him to Paris. Traveller's tales and newspaper accounts of remarkable cures led to a general expectation that Parisians were soon to benefit from this mysterious therapy.[35]

Once established in fashionable Parisian society, Mesmer and his practice became the subject of both idle gossip and serious debate in drawing rooms and salons, and were discussed extensively across the pages of articles, pamphlets and books.[36] No such intensity of either interest or polemic was evident upon on the other side of the English Channel, however. Robin

Waterfield, in *Hidden Depths: The Story of Hypnosis* (2002), intimates that 'magnetism was known in Britain before the nineteenth century, but it seems to have aroused little interest'.[37] Forrest argues further, however, that prior to the 1837 visit by the Baron Dupotet – the so-called 'Fourth Pope of Animal Magnetism' and a nominal follower of Mesmer who had practised at the Parisian Hôtel Dieu – 'Britain had remained largely unaffected by the French mesmeric furore'.[38]

The latter judgement appears somewhat hasty, if not harsh. Certainly, articles and announcements in the eighteenth-century British press evidence an awareness of Continental mesmerism, as Waterfield suggests in passing.[39] Popular newspapers acknowledged the existence of French and Belgian societies premised upon 'the tenets of Mesmer', even where they denounced as 'impostors' the oath-bound 'adepts' who 'pretend to a knowledge of all the profound mysteries of magnetism'.[40] A translated edition of the French Royal Commission's report on Mesmer's practice was likewise advertised to anyone who cared to consult its negative conclusions regarding the efficacy (and indeed existence) of animal magnetism as theorised by Mesmer, though – as Forrest intimates – the opinions of Benjamin Franklin and his learned associates may well have 'received little notice' in Britain at the time.[41]

Possibly more significant, though, are the few newspaper references which acknowledge the presence of a fledgling magnetic industry on British shores. Indeed, English-language instruction in mesmerism was actually available in London in the year in which Inchbald's *Animal Magnetism* was first produced, though the 'New System of the World' promulgated at Golden Square appears to be intimate to an alternative induction by the 'College for Instructing Pupils in Mesmer's Philosophy of Animal Magnetism', based at Hatton Garden, Holborn.[42] The Reverend J. Bell, named in association with both conclaves, is intimated as being a member of Mesmer's 'Philosophical Harmonic Society at Paris', and may well be the translator or author of the advertised 'first Number of the New System of the World, in the English and French languages, price 2s, 6d.'.[43] Bell claimed to be 'the only person authorised by the Society to Teach and Practise Magnetism in England'.[44] If this latter assertion suggests that Bell possibly feared the commercial rivalry of other practitioners not authorised by the Parisian school in which he had been instructed, those not committed to magnetism were less convinced as to the place mesmerism actually occupied in British culture at the time. Horace Walpole, for example, suggested that 'Animal Magnetism has not yet made much impression here' in 1784, only four years prior to Bell's advertisements.[45] Robin Waterfield is probably also correct in suggesting that the French Revolution was to seriously inhibit the further dissemination of Continental magnetic literature within Britain.[46]

What is clear, therefore, is that magnetism as a theory was known in late eighteenth-century Britain, and that its reputation in France may have been, for a limited number of wealthy initiates, supplemented by actual observation or practical experience upon English shores. *Detailed* knowledge of what might actually happen at a British magnetic séance, however, was less readily available to those unwilling or unable to pay the (usually unspecified) fees associated with instruction: as one advertisement tellingly noted, 'Any Lady or Gentleman of respectability that wish to be instructed in any of these classes of science, may know the terms of teaching, &c., by sending or applying'.[47] The stress on 'respectability' here is almost certainly significant. Magnetism in its eighteenth-century British incarnation would appear to have been at times marketed through the appeal that an association with 'The foreign Princes and Ladies, who are members of this science, that are now in England' might bring to the parvenu.[48] '[T]he initiating of students' by such colleges was arguably as much a matter of induction into an allegedly prestigious social circle as it was to a hermetic science.[49] For these reasons, magnetism was not a mass movement within any British social class or intellectual profession, and did not enjoy the immense periodical presence which mesmerism had achieved in Paris. British magnetism at the eighteenth-century *fin de siècle* was almost certainly more than the very slight presence envisaged by both Forrest and Waterfield, but it was still at best a shadowy reflection of the popular interest it had become in France.

The obscure nature of British magnetism has, however, shaped the manner in which historians of hypnotism have regarded the relationship between the last two decades of the eighteenth century and the mid-nineteenth-century heyday of British magnetic practice. Rather than acknowledging in detail the evidence that *is* there – the advertisements for expensive inductions and arcane publications, the invitations to public lectures and private demonstrations, and the indignant dismissal of such things by an often Francophobe British press – historians of hypnotism have characteristically dwelled upon the Parisian experience before proclaiming the genesis (usually in the 1840s) of a seemingly unprecedented 'Mesmeric Mania' or 'Mesmeric Campaign' in Elliotson's London.[50] In such surveys, it is as if the fifty years between 1788 and 1838 (the year of Elliotson's departure from

University College Hospital) had exhibited no distinct trace of mesmerism in the British popular and clinical consciousnesses, no published writing by which both the residual and the innovative might be said to engage with each other over the territory of animal magnetism. Instead of this rich field of distinctively British practice and interpretation, the reader of historical studies of hypnotism is all too often presented with a rather artificial linearity, an intellectual and epistemological process that links Mesmer and his Continental associates with Elliotson and his British contemporaries as if eighteenth-century dogma was absorbed in the original French by all concerned. Elliotson's successors and contemporaries – most notably James Esdaile and James Braid – are rhetorically distanced in such accounts from the earlier debate, so that the many conceptual descendants of magnetism – practices and theoretical disciplines with names as diverse as odylism, somnambulism, lucid sleep, Braidism, human hibernation, trance, phreno-magnetism, phrenohypnotism and, of course, hypnotism – gain a semblance of distinction, a suggestion of discrete conceptual boundaries that may not have been so distinct and concrete to their practitioners.

This demarcation is further enforced by a characteristic dependence upon a somewhat narrow – even selective – body of evidence that favours the debate as enacted in mainstream clinical journals such as *The Lancet* and *British Medical Journal* rather than that associated with the popular and non-specialist publications which disseminated it beyond the medical profession. Such accounts may lack the experimental apparatus associated with the assertion of credible clinical proofs and refutations, but they are a reflection of what animal magnetism and its successors actually *meant* to the vast majority of interested observers. Accessible to the non-specialist as they were, popular writings such as these were to significantly shape the opinions of non-clinical commentators and writers of fiction. Again, they may well have also informed the broader leisure-time reading of those with a clinician's grasp of the debate upon animal magnetism. Distanced to a greater or lesser extent from the personal polemic and contemporaneity of clinical debate, such writings arguably contributed to the retention of earlier magnetic ideas and phraseology in the nineteenth-century popular consciousness, and demonstrably perpetuated both well into the high Victorian era and its *fin-de-siècle* coda.

Literary critics have in recent years readily responded to the fact that the vast majority of English-language fictional portrayals of magnetic or hypnotic phenomena were produced in the nineteenth – rather than the eighteenth – century. These critics appear, laudably, to accept the common ground and the shared language that lie between the pseudoscience of mesmerism and the aspiring science of hypnotism.[51] Historians of hypnotism, however, have been less inclined to consider the perplexing possibility that the hypnotic practice of the nineteenth century does not entirely depart from the magnetism of the eighteenth, and that the languages and characteristic gestures of both are sufficiently congruent to tincture any new development with the colour of a rediscovery. As one popular medical guide opined as late as 1901, 'The oldest hieroglyphics indicate that the production of mesmeric phenomena was known to the ancient Egyptians long before any book was written'.[52] So, too, was mesmerism known to those – practitioner and layman alike – who nominally perceived its ostensible successor, hypnotism. Novelty is thus always underpinned by a degree of familiarity, resemblance suggests relationship, and meaning is never absolutely fixed into a temporality associated with the time of publication. Inevitably, in the rhetoric both of fiction and of medicine, curative hypnotism may seemingly always exchange places freely with stagy mesmerism, and the charlatan exchange his showy garments – however temporarily – for the sober mantle of the clinician.

That Devil's Trick is not a 'history' of magnetism and hypnotism in the tradition of scholarly but accessible works such as Alison Winter's *Mesmerized: Powers of Mind in Victorian Britain* (1998), Derek Forrest's *Hypnotism: A History* (2000) or Waterfield's *Hidden Depths: The Story of Hypnosis* (2004). Though it acknowledges the mutability of magnetic and hypnotic practice, and the apparent chronological transition between the dominance of the fluid theory of Mesmer and that of the more conventional physiological practice of Braid and his successors, the central conceit of *That Devil's Trick* is one of co-existence and retention rather than evolution and succession. Because of the conventional mode of history that structures hypnotism as a successor to (but not necessarily a conceptual descendant of) mesmerism, the terms 'magnetism' and 'hypnotism' cannot satisfactorily be used interchangeably.[53] However, in *That Devil's Trick*, the former is regarded as being unavoidably integral to the latter, constituting a correlative at some times, a corrective at others. In this respect, *That Devil's Trick* goes somewhat against the grain of those twentieth-century works that declaim a disciplinary separation through which magnetism is envisaged as a mere pseudoscience and hypnotism a pioneering form of proto-psychology. The boundaries thus established between the two are at best questionable and at worst misleading. Indeed, the possibility that magnetism – or even the evocatively named mesmerism – were still actively promulgated and practised at the end of the nineteenth century is not disprovable. There is no discrete age of animal magnetism, no unequivocal era of hypnotism, no *absolute* separation between the two that can be satisfactorily enforced through either chronological or conceptual criteria. This is *not* to say that magnetism and hypnotism are essentially the same thing. There *are* perceptible differences of technique and epistemology, but these differences are persistently challenged in both medical and popular culture because the similarities between the two practices are capable of being so consistently recalled.

That Devil's Trick differs further from conventional histories through its contention that popular accounts of magnetic and hypnotic practice constitute a comparable form of evidence to those derived from clinical publications. The latter have a restricted (that is, a predominantly professional) audience, and thus a necessarily limited influence. The former are not merely more widely disseminated as mass media but also represent a telling index of how magnetism and hypnotism appear in the non-clinical gaze. The retention of clinically outmoded techniques and apparently disproven theories in such popular accounts may perpetuate the magnetic past in the popular mind, thus questioning further the assertions of authoritative clinical statements. *That Devil's Trick* is not a simple history of hypnotic practice, therefore, but rather a study of how the nineteenth-century popular mind – the public rather than clinical mind – envisaged, elided and expressed both magnetism and hypnotism. Alison Winter is without doubt the pioneer in the acknowledgement of more popular sources in charting the demarcation of the endurance of mesmeric practice across the nineteenth century: *That Devil's Trick*, in many respects, supplements and addresses the script of *Mesmerized* through access to a considerably more dense body of detail derived from the most widely disseminated publications in the British metropolitan and provincial press.

The fluid nature of that popular mind, of course, may also be discerned in generically fictional as well as specifically journalistic depictions of both mesmeric practice and magnetic epistemology. These fictional accounts are, like their journalistic counterparts, characteristically free from the professional discipline imposed elsewhere by clinical definitions which strive to separate allegedly progressive practices from earlier incarnations now deemed residual or regressive. The interventions into the ongoing discourse on magnetism made by some authors of nineteenth-century fiction are necessarily acknowledged in *That Devil's Trick*, though it must be emphasised that the current volume should not be considered as a critical work cast in the mould of, for example, Maria M. Tatar's *Spellbound: Studies on Mesmerism and Literature* (1978), Daniel Pick's *Svengali's Web: The Alien Enchanter in Modern Culture* (2000) or the detailed individual essays which make up the 2006 collection *Victorian Literary Mesmerism*, edited by Martin Willis and Catherine Wynne. Readings of what Tatar terms 'the linguistic texture' of fiction implicitly place an emphasis upon the author's contextual and contemporary knowledge, his research and his interpretation.[54] *That Devil's Trick* effectively supplements such studies by conveying, possibly for the first time, the widely disseminated cultural archive of images, reputations and fears through which the reading public may have approached the mesmeric fictions of its day. In emphasising the pervasive nature of a popular press, the volume acknowledges the predispositions and prejudgements that may be embodied in a popular audience. Such things colour, mobilise and contextualise their consumption of both fiction and stage melodrama. As Alison Winter suggests, 'By the 1840s, most Victorians would have had some idea of what went on in a mesmeric séance'.[55] It might be further suggested that those same Victorians would almost certainly have entertained a body of knowledge on that topic which far exceeded the superficial imagery of entranced subjects and potentially predatory mesmerisers. This popular and enduring cultural archive is the focus of the current volume. Its written contexts as reproduced in *That Devil's Trick*, drawn as they are from widely circulated popular reportage, may thus be judiciously applied by literary critics to an extensive range of mesmeric fictions far exceeding those examples enumerated in the current volume.

That Devil's Trick opens and closes with brief readings of two popular fictional texts separated by almost a century. If the preliminary discussion of Inchbald's *Animal Magnetism* may serve to indicate how the conventions of the eighteenth century were still potent in the Victorian era, the concluding references to George du Maurier's *Trilby* (1894) and Paul Potter's 1895 stage adaptation of the novel demonstrate how those clichés were further adapted in the light of the development of mesmeric, and nominally hypnotic, practice. Between these two exemplars of mesmerism in fiction and drama may be found an at times equally imaginative version of the practice and practitioners of animal magnetism as reproduced in newspapers and popular journals between the eighteenth-century *fin de siècle* and that of the nineteenth century.

Such sources, with their wide dissemination at all levels of literate and semi-literate society, inform the three chronological chapters at the heart of *That Devil's Trick*. The first of these, 'The Epoch of Mesmer', concentrates initially upon how British readers perceived the work of Mesmer, his followers and his imitators on the Continent of Europe in the first three decades of the nineteenth century. This chapter represents the first substantial study not merely of British attitudes towards Mesmer after the initial rise of mesmerism but also of the tangible public knowledge of the techniques and technologies deployed first in Paris and latterly in London. These latter are traced from Mesmer's *baquet* by way of the metallic tractors of the American Elisha Perkins, which enjoyed a brief vogue in the United Kingdom at the turn of the nineteenth century, to distinctly British deployments of Galvanism and the Leyden jar. The independent development of a specifically British mesmerism is then charted from the rise of the first indigenous practitioner in the British Isles, the Irish physician John Bonnoit de Mainaduc. From Mainaduc the chapter moves to consider the influence of one of Mesmer's immediate disciples, the Marquis de Puységur, upon the later British practitioners whose work forms the subject of the second chapter, 'Medical Magnetism'.

Chapter 2 charts the transition of mesmerism from its initial theatres of the salon and the drawing room into the regular hospital system. The chapter opens with an extensive reading of the influential career of Baron Dupotet, popularly known as 'the English pope of animal magnetism', a French savant who, having practised mesmerism at the Parisian Hôtel Dieu, was accepted on to the wards of the Middlesex Hospital and, later, of University College Hospital. It considers in detail how mesmerism was practised in the United Kingdom from the late 1830s using a variety of popular sources both favourable and polemical, before analysing the sexual allegations which were to be associated with the Baron's practice. These caused him to be compared with the controversial eighteenth-century English doctor James Graham, inventor of the Celestial Bed, an ingenious aid to conception which employed a magnetic system analogous to mesmerism. From Dupotet, the chapter then moves to consider the adoption of magnetism by Richard Chenevix and John Elliotson, both of whom enjoyed considerable reputations as practitioners of conventional physiological and chemical medicine. Chenevix is a significant but strangely understudied figure in the history of British mesmerism; Elliotson is better known, though critical interest in his work has been largely confined to the controversy surrounding his public displays of the apparently entranced O'Key sisters at University College Hospital. That controversy has been played out in histories of mesmerism largely with reference only to professional assessments of Elliotson's work, with a particular emphasis upon attacks made upon the Doctor in *The Lancet*. *That Devil's Trick* contrasts these with reports in the non-medical press, and provides an innovative insight into how the non-professional might have regarded one of the most spectacular medical controversies of the early nineteenth century.

Elliotson's departure from University College Hospital is usually regarded in mesmeric histories as the effective termination of his activity in British practice. Chapter 3 corrects this mistaken assumption, by advancing a detailed reading of the Doctor's involvement with the London Mesmeric Infirmary, a well-funded institution patronised by the nobility which, none the less, faded quietly into obscurity around 1870. The chapter also considers the work of two other exponents of the deployment of mesmerism as an aid to surgery. The work of the Scot James Braid is analysed in its attempt to codify hypnotism as a physiological practice quite distinct from the fluid epistemology of mesmerism. The chapter's consideration of popular accounts of surgery under mesmerism at the mid-century leads the analysis from Braid to Elliotson, Topham and Esdaile. The latter's work in India, and the systematic study which recorded Esdaile's anaesthetic experiments in India are also revealed in unprecedented detail, as is his brief intervention into military surgery.

The Conclusion briefly charts the hitherto obscure final years of British mesmerism. Its reading of the Victorian *fin de siècle* embraces not merely the representation of mesmeric practice on the stage and in fiction but considers, with reference to contemporary reports of the work of Jean-Martin Charcot in the British popular press, the reasons why such an interest might have arisen when magnetic practice was in such a profound decline.

That Devil's Trick is a highly detailed and innovative study. It has departed from the sources of evidence usually deployed in histories of mesmerism, and has adopted instead the ephemeral and yet pervasive archive that is popular reportage. It might be, perhaps, a methodological pointer as to how the other pseudosciences of the Victorian period could best be revealed in all their richness and variety.

Notes

1 Anon., 'Haymarket Theatre – Amateur Performance', *Caledonian Mercury*, 22 May 1848, p. 4, cols 4–5, at col. 4.

2 Frederic George Kitton, *Charles Dickens by Pen and Pencil* (London: Frank T. Sabin, 1890), 3 vols, Vol. 1, p. 124.

3 Inchbald, indeed, was almost a forgotten dramatist. Though her 'once-popular comedy *Wives as they Were and Maids as they Are*' had been revived at the Haymarket in 1848, it was considered an absurdity by reviewers and not part of the repertoire of 'our legitimate drama'. See Anon., 'Theatres and Music', *John Bull*, 13 May 1848, 311–12, at p. 312, col. 1.

4 John Forster, *The Life of Charles Dickens* (London: Chapman and Hall, 1892), p. 398.

5 Anon., 'Haymarket Theatre – Amateur Performance', p. 4, col. 4. The reviewer is notably scathing regarding the 'entertainment' provided by the preceding performance of *The Merry Wives of Windsor* and drily remarks that 'Mrs Inchbald's *Animal Magnetism* [was] resorted to as a restorative at the conclusion'.

6 See Charles and Mary Cowden Clarke, *Recollections of Writers* (London: Sampson Low, Marston, Searle & Rivington, 1878), pp. 296–333, reprinted in Philip Collins, ed., *Dickens: Interviews and Recollections* (London: Macmillan, 1981), Vol. 1, p. 92. For details of the provincial tour, in which *Animal Magnetism* was produced alongside both *Every Man in His Humour* and *The Merry Wives of Windsor*, see Kitton, *Charles Dickens by Pen and Pencil*, Vol. 1, p. 112.

7 Kitton, *Charles Dickens by Pen and Pencil*, Vol. 1, p. 124.

8 See Wilkie Collins, 'Introductory Lines (Relating the Adventures and Transformations of *The Frozen Deep*)', in Wilkie Collins, *The Frozen Deep* and *Mr Wray's Cash-Box*, ed. William M. Clarke (Stroud: Alan Sutton, 1996), 3–5; Anon., 'Notes on the Life of Augustus L. Egg', *Reader*, 44 (31 October 1863), p. 516.

9 See, for example, the sardonic coda to Anon., 'Extract of a Letter from Paris, April 23 [1787]', *The World and Fashionable Advertiser*, 4 May 1787, p. 4, col. 1.

10 J. Milne Bramwell, *Hypnotism: Its History, Practice and Theory* (London: Alexander Moring, 1906), pp. 3–4.

11 Charles Dickens to John Forster, 24 September 1849, quoted in Forster, *The Life of Charles Dickens*, p. 389.

12 Charles Dickens to John Forster, 24 September 1849, quoted in Forster, *The Life of Charles Dickens*, pp. 389–90 (original ellipsis).

13 Charles Dickens to John Forster, 24 September 1849, quoted in Forster, *The Life of Charles Dickens*, p. 389.

14 Peter Ackroyd, *Dickens* (London: Sinclair Stevenson, 1990), p. 244; Catherine Peters, *The King of Inventors: A Life of Wilkie Collins* (London: Secker and Warburg, 1991), p. 257.

15 Charles Dickens, *Little Dorrit*, ed. John Holloway (Harmondsworth: Penguin, 1980), p. 768; Humphry Rolleston, 'Irregular Practice and Quackery', *The Canadian Medical Association Journal*, 17/5 (May 1927), 501–8, at p. 504, col. 1.

Pendennis is dedicated to Elliotson, the dedication recording how the physician 'would take no other fee but thanks'.

16 Forster, *Life of Charles Dickens*, p. 236. J. E. Cosnett, 'Dickens and Doctors: Vignettes of Victorian Medicine', *British Medical Journal*, 305 (19–26 December 1992), 1540–2, at p. 1542, col. 2.

17 See Forster, *The Life of Charles Dickens*, pp. 236, 322–3. The charitable publication was a volume by a carpenter, John Overs, entitled *Evenings of a Working Man, Being the Occupation of His Scanty Leisure* (London: T. C. Newby, 1844). Written and published to ensure a modest income for Overs's family following the author's impending demise from consumption, the volume was prefaced by Dickens and dedicated to Elliotson.

18 See Derek Forrest, *Hypnotism: A History* (London: Penguin, 2000), p. 165.

19 Charles Dickens to George Cruikshank, 28 December 1838, reprinted in Madeline House and Graham Storey, eds, *The Pilgrim Edition of the Letters of Charles Dickens* (Oxford: Clarendon Press, 1965–2002), 12 vols, Vol. 1, p. 480.

20 Forrest, *Hypnotism*, p. 143.

21 *The Lancet*, 13 June 1846, p. 662. Dickens, indeed, took an interest in Elliotson's finances shortly before the Professor's death: see Forrest, *Hypnotism*, p. 191.

22 Elizabeth Inchbald, *Animal Magnetism, A Farce in Three Acts, as Performed at the Theatre Royal, Covent Garden* (Dublin: P. Byron, 1777), p. 9.

23 Inchbald, *Animal Magnetism*, pp. 9, 10.

24 Inchbald, *Animal Magnetism*, p. 10.

25 See, for example, the editorial to the *Provincial Medical and Surgical Journal*, 31 July 1844, pp. 269–70.

26 *The Lancet*, 15 September 1838, pp. 873, 876.

27 Such sentiments, indeed, are implicit in the comments regarding Elliotson's apparent sacrifice of personal fortune and professional income alike in the causes of altruism and principle which conclude his long obituary in a provincial newspaper. See Anon., 'The Late Dr Elliotson', *The Bury and Norwich Post, and Suffolk Herald*, 11 August 1868, p. 2, col. 5.

28 H. Imlach, 'Animal Magnetism', *Provincial Medical and Surgical Journal*, 4 March 1843, p. 458, col. 2 (original italics); cf. F. S. Burman, 'More Mesmeric Impostors', *Provincial Medical and Surgical Journal*, 4 November 1843, 101–2.

29 Imlach, 'Animal Magnetism', p. 458, col. 2.

30 Anon., 'Dr Elliotson', *The Morning Post*, 3 August 1868, p. 3, col. 5.

31 See, for example, La Fluer's woeful attempt to define the universal fluid when inducting the Doctor into the magnetic practice popularly associated with Dr Mystery. Inchbald, *Animal Magnetism*, p. 12.

32 Herbert Mayo, *On the Truths Contained in Popular Superstitions, with an Account of Mesmerism* [1851] (Westcliff-on-Sea: Desert Island Books, 2003), p. 92.

33 Anon., 'Obituary', *The Examiner*, 8 August 1868, pp. 508–9, at p. 508.

34 Anon., 'Animal Magnetism', *Fraser's Magazine*, 1/6 (July 1830), 673–84, at p. 675, col. 2.
35 Forrest, *Hypnotism*, p. 17.
36 Forrest, *Hypnotism*, pp. 27–8.
37 Robin Waterfield, *Hidden Depths: The Story of Hypnosis* (London: Pan, 2004), p. 157.
38 Forrest, *Hypnotism*, pp. 122, 125. Forrest is quoting Alexandre Erdan, though the footnote to the quotation on p. 122 does not give a precise page reference.
39 Waterfield, *Hidden Depths*, p. 157.
40 Anon., 'Extract of a Letter from Paris, April 23 [1787]', p. 4, col. 1.
41 'Animal Magnetism' [advertisement], *St James's Chronicle, or the British Evening Post*, 16 December 1784, p. 3, col. 4; Forrest, *Hypnotism*, p. 125.
42 'New System of the World' [advertisement], *The World*, 26 May 1788, p. 1, col. 2; 'College for Instructing Pupils in Mesmer's Philosophy of Animal Magnetism' [advertisement], *The Morning Herald*, 7 June 1788, p. 1, col. 2.
43 'New System of the World' [advertisement], p. 1, col. 2.
44 'Lectures' [advertisement], *The Morning Post and Daily Advertiser*, 10 November 1786, p. 1, col. 1.
45 Quoted in *The Academy*, 139/1 (25 February 1882).
46 Waterfield, *Hidden Depths*, p. 158.
47 'College for Instruction in Elementary Philosophy' [advertisement], *The World*, 26 June 1788, p. 1, col. 2.
48 'College for Instructing Pupils in Mesmer's Philosophy of Animal Magnetism' [advertisement], p. 1, col. 2.
49 'College for Instructing Pupils in Mesmer's Philosophy of Animal Magnetism' [advertisement], p. 1, col. 2.
50 Waterfield, *Hidden Depths*, p. 157; Forrest, *Hypnotism*, p. 169.
51 Consider here, for example, one of the most recent studies of mesmerism in the age of hypnotism: Hilary Grimes, 'Power in Flux: Mesmerism, Mesmeric Manuals and du Maurier's *Trilby*', *Gothic Studies*, 10/2 (2008), 67–83.
52 Edward Bliss Foote, *Dr Foote's Home Cyclopedia of Popular Medical, Social and Sexual Science*, Twentieth Century Revised and Enlarged Edition (London: L. N. Fowler, 1901), p. 829.
53 Note here Alison Winter's lucid tabulation of the scholarly debate upon mesmerism in *Mesmerized: Powers of Mind in Victorian Britain* (Chicago: University of Chicago Press, 1998), p. 10.
54 Maria M. Tatar, *Spellbound: Studies on Mesmerism and Literature* (Princeton: Princeton University Press, 1978), p. xi.
55 Winter, *Mesmerized*, p. 2.

I

The epoch of Mesmer

The history of mesmerism falls conveniently into three
epochs marked by the names of three men who have taken
a leading part in studying and practicing it. The first epoch
is that of Mesmer, the second that of Braid, and the third
that of Charcot.

Quarterly Review (July 1890)[1]

THE MERE NAMES of the great exponents of any theory or doctrine
can never adequately contain the theories and practices they rhetorically claim as their own. The veracity of such claims, the implicit integrity
that links an individual with the processes and practices that bear his or her
name in the public domain, is arguably subject to constant interrogation.
This is true even at those times when ostensibly pioneering individuals
– the biographical co-ordinates of derivative generic appellations such as
mesmerism or Braidism – appear to have become successfully established
as stable landmarks in the systematic definition of the phenomena they
nominally encompass. The demarcated, but still linear, history advanced by
the anonymous contributor to the Quarterly Review, above, is thus potentially
as fragile as the three individual reputations it alludes to. The history of
mesmerism may not always be so clear cut, so easily divisible into eras
whose characteristics can be typified through the application of an evocative
name alone.

Other commentators, writing both before and after the mesmeric
genealogy envisaged by the Quarterly Review, were on occasion notably

unconvinced by the claims to originality which had, in their day, already accrued to the names of Mesmer and Braid. In 1843, a mere twenty-eight years after his death, Mesmer was depicted by *The Penny Satirist*, a popular newspaper, as the mere discoverer of ancient knowledge, and 'not the inventor of the treatment that goes by his name'.[2] In 1887, twenty-seven years after the death of Braid, the slightly more salubrious pages of *The Leisure Hour* opined that 'there was nothing new in Braid's discovery' of hypnotism.[3] The account rendered by the *Quarterly Review* some three years later is, perhaps, a little less blunt with regard to the achievements of Mesmer and Braid, merely intimating in passing that the former 'undoubtedly felt' the influence of contemporary theories of the mind, and the latter, though initially trained by another practitioner, produced clinical phenomena 'precisely similar to those of Mesmer'.[4] Its conclusions regarding Charcot – still active, in 1890, at the Salpêtrière – are, however, reminiscent of the dismissals of Mesmer and Braid by *The Penny Satirist* and *The Leisure Hour*. 'Charcot', the article suggests, 'rediscovered mesmerism exactly 100 years after the original discoverer'.[5]

For the *Quarterly Review* to proclaim Charcot a mere revivalist rather than a true pioneer is for it to paradoxically undermine the progressive model of history through which its survey of a century of mesmerism has hitherto been channelled. In the non-specialist gaze associated with popular publications such as newspapers and monthly journals, Mesmer, Braid and Charcot may all seemingly be viewed as participants in the traditions established by others as much as they are pioneers in their own right. In such publications there is characteristically none of the precision associated with clinical periodicals engaged in demarcating similar chronologies. The latter's conventional reliance upon observation and detail would characteristically enforce the subtle differences between practitioners, and thus perpetuate methodological subdivisions such as magnetism, mesmerism, Braidism or hypnotism, even where the nomenclature of one of these may be appropriated for a time to cover the whole conceptual field. The same is not true of non-clinical accounts of mesmerism, which would seem to perpetuate the imprecision of the whole in order to aid both the readership's continued recognition of a familiar practice and its characteristic problems and controversies. In the case of the chronology advanced by the *Quarterly Review*, the evocative concept of mesmerism perversely survives this attempt to fragment it into meaningful, successive and discrete epochs because none of the three practitioners named may popularly be considered to have either satisfactorily explained its inconsistencies or comprehended entirely its abiding mysteries. As the article concludes, 'None of the modern theories cover all the ground, nor would they explain the essence of the thing even if they did'.[6] The 'essence of the thing' is its evocative continuity rather than any Absolute that might make for an explanation which terminates its perpetual newsworthiness or ongoing controversy. This is arguably the central difference between clinical (or practitioners') accounts of mesmerism and those advanced in the popular press. The former strive to demarcate, the latter are inclined to perpetuate. For non-clinical accounts of mesmerism, the issue normally is less one of 'proving' the possibility of the phenomena, and more a matter of evoking the debate that has formed the constant companion to mesmerism.

That debate far exceeds the question of the demonstrable existence of mesmeric phenomena that preoccupied the mainstream British medical journals of the mid-nineteenth century. The ethical dimensions of mesmeric practice are arguably less dependent upon mesmerism itself than they are premised upon the simple belief in magnetism held by those who wield, and those who yield to, its alleged or proposed powers. Upon this belief hang the predominant preoccupations of popular reportage and fiction, as well as the secondary concern of the medical establishment. The ethical behaviour of practitioners, and the responsibility and integrity associated with those who submit to, or are placed, under mesmeric control, are central to those persistent allegations of abuse, quackery and charlatanism, and diminished responsibility which allow a phenomenon originally scheduled as a medical panacea to fall within the purlieu of criminal law and abnormal psychology.

Though those issues preoccupy both popular and clinical accounts of mesmerism from the mid-nineteenth century, and are central also to the unease evoked by those Victorian fictions which deploy the magnetist as a central character, their roots lie in the eighteenth century. The figure of Mesmer, part doctor and part showman, an altruistic practitioner and a grasping charlatan, is arguably the paradigm upon which later perceptions of the magnetist are premised. Mesmer is, as it were, the perfect embodiment of the contradictions associated with both the theory and the movement that came to bear his name throughout the nineteenth century.

Historians of hypnotism have, as a consequence of their conventional drive towards constructing a linear history of practice from the eighteenth century to the present, tended to evoke Mesmer solely through summaries of eighteenth-century accounts of his demeanour, behaviour or practice. He was, according to Robin Waterfield, 'a man of contrasts', who by 1781 had achieved 'a reputation as a crank' through his 'arrogant and paranoid' reactions to criticism and investigation.[7] Derek Forrest, in his considerably more detailed account of the same historical period, depicts Mesmer as 'fat but muscular' and 'not a man to be easily overlooked', but concludes after quoting from the doctor's own writing that he was 'an arrogant man who was making inordinate claims for his discovery and who appeared to be suffering from a persecution complex'.[8] Mesmer, in both accounts, is a figure bound up very much in his French contemporaries' hostile response to both his claims and his mannerisms. But Mesmer is also, however, a discrete though minor figure in nineteenth-century British consciousness, a practitioner whose attitudes and techniques continued to be reported and interpreted both in their own right and in conjunction with later developments in mesmerism and hypnotism. All three epochs envisaged by the *Quarterly Review* are thus, in a sense, simultaneously a single epoch pervaded by Mesmer in the guise of the practitioner as well as in his functional role as pioneer or first populariser. To read mesmerism in a truly nineteenth-century context, therefore, it is necessary to consider Mesmer himself as the nineteenth century both envisaged and interpreted him. Mesmer's place in the British popular consciousness of the nineteenth century, indeed, is arguably somewhat different to the positioning which he has historically received at the hands of historians of hypnotism.

'Mesmer, in a coat of lilac silk': The wizard, the doctor and the consulting room

In twentieth-century histories of hypnotism, Franz Anton Mesmer is more often deployed in the manner of a rhetorical device than advanced in the guise of a historical figure. His perceived character is customarily presented in these ostensibly historical accounts in such a way as to enforce a necessary distinction between the spectacular phenomena of unregulated eighteenth-century magnetism and more recent professional therapeutic practice. The obvious contrast between the unprovable, fluid-based, magnetism of Mesmer and modern, theoretically premised and experimentally supported, psychological explanations for hypnotic states ought, surely, in itself to be sufficient for this rhetorical purpose. However, the singular figure of Dr Mesmer, typified by elaborate clothing, exaggerated or mystical gestures and eccentricities of manner, almost without exception accompanies and undermines any modern exposition of his theory. In this way, an apparent distance is progressively established between this egotist showman, the 'Doctor Mystery' of his day, and the more recognisable institutional figures of the sober, black-suited late Victorian physician and the white-coated twentieth-century clinician.

George Owen's 1971 account of a mesmeric séance in the rue Montmartre, Paris, is not atypical. It bears no specific date, lacks any reference to contextual documentation or scholarly publication, and presents the whole occasion as a sort of speculative drama, where those present form an audience which is gradually incorporated into the cast, and where the plot leads inevitably to a climactic denouement or, to borrow from Mesmer's terminology, a crisis. Of Mesmer's patients, Owen writes:

> Listening to music, they awaited the effects, often dramatic, of the magnetism. Mesmer, in a coat of lilac silk and carrying an iron wand, would walk among the patients, accompanied by d'Eslon and assistants chosen for their youth and comeliness. He would touch the bodies of the patients with the wand, or 'magnetize' them with his eyes, fixing his gaze on theirs ... the process was repeated until the subject was 'saturated with the magnetic fluid' and was transported with pain or pleasure.[9]

Raymond E. Fancher's colourful 1979 account of what may well be the same magnetic séance has similar implications. Fancher writes:

> The lighting was dim, and Mesmer, in an adjoining room, played soft music on his glass harmonica. When the stage was properly set, he emerged, dressed in a flowing lilac-colored robe, and began pointing his finger or an iron rod at the various patients. Some of them invariably began to experience tinglings and peculiar bodily sensations which quickly passed into a crisis state. Soon other patients followed suit.[10]

Both of these accounts explicitly evoke the atmosphere of the theatre rather than that of the clinic. Each is a public performance – and, with its music, a melodrama almost – but both may implicitly function in the manner of a farce when presented to a modern reader who, sceptical or otherwise, understands contemporary therapeutic hypnotism to be a sober practice conducted in private and without undue indignity.[11] In the tradition of farce, delusion is infectious, and once one patient succumbs to the crisis, others follow, each having their several entrances and exits as they are carried offstage to the 'adjoining, and clearly marked, *chambre de crises* ("crisis room") where they received individual attention'.[12]

The undated, unreferenced but still apparently representative séance is a feature characteristic of the mocking polemic that still influences the perception of Mesmer in twenty-first-century scholarly accounts of the Parisian phase of his work. Recent scholarly histories of hypnotism, if anything, lean even more towards the imaginatively fictional, rather than unadornedly historical, treatment of Mesmer and his practice. If Mesmer's garment quietly evolved from a simple '*coat* of lilac silk' to a more mystically inflected 'lilac-colored *robe*' in just eight years, Robin Waterfield's 2002 account of yet another (or possibly still the same) séance makes utterly explicit the forced equation of mesmerism, stagecraft, conjuring and charlatanism. The Preface to *Hidden Depths*, Waterfield's epic history of hypnosis, opens – tensely – thus:

> It is 1784. You are in a dimly lit salon in a mansion in a prosperous section of Paris. The room is presided over by a tall, slightly overweight man dressed in a purple cloak trimmed with lace and embroidered with occult symbols. Other sigils decorate the walls and heavy velvet curtains cover the windows, allowing just the odd ray of sunlight in to strike the thickly carpeted floor, and hardly a sound penetrates from the street outside. Melodious piano music can be heard softly from another room.[13]

There is a slight hint of the ridiculous here, the adiposity of the man sitting uneasily next to the power conveyed by the pointed use of 'presided'. That power, though, is itself constructed as questionable, a dubious occultism evoked in the Age of Enlightenment. Waterfield emphatically notes that 'The *wizard* ... is none other than Franz Anton Mesmer', as if to underline that the presiding figure is not clothed in the functional garb of a doctor, just as the room does not display the trappings of a clinician's working environment.[14] In many respects, he who presides here is a fellow – if not the original – of Inchbald's celebrated Dr Mystery, the doctor *as* mystery, the curative art as mystification. As if to place the matter beyond question, Waterfield expands somewhat upon the crisis-experience of the patients which was more economically advanced by earlier commentators such as Owen and Fancher.

> The atmosphere in the room grows very intense. Occasionally Mesmer or one of his assistants prowls around the room. He inspects the woman next to you, passes his hands behind her back without touching her, points the wand at her, and she goes into convulsions. Her body begins to jerk, and her breathing is shallow and uneven; a flush comes over her face and neck. Finally she collapses gently to

the floor, coughing up phlegm. Assistants calmly come and take her away to another room, which you can see is lined with mattresses and soft silk drapes. Mesmer follows to attend to her, now that she is on the road to health.[15]

The reader, he or she who sits next to the woman who is eventually removed in a state of mesmeric crisis, is implicitly unmoved by all of this theatre, and observes without the commitment of belief or participation. That reader, indeed, may even be engaged in interpreting certain details in sexual terms – the 'prowling' of the magnetists, the spasmodic jerking and other symptoms which suggest orgasm, the mattress ready to receive the supine body of the woman all take the account into ambiguous rhetorical territories beyond medical discourse.[16] What *is* observed, however, is not curative mesmerism as such but its spectacle. It is the mummery of a past century that is evoked in such accounts, the devices by which the credulous may be manipulated so that they become only marginally less ridiculous to twentieth- and twenty-first-century eyes than Mesmer himself.

Nineteenth-century eyes, though, were inclined for the most part to view Mesmer and his practices somewhat differently – and nineteenth-century authors were often less openly hostile to this figure from recent history than they were sometimes to contemporary medical practitioners. Owen's account, which may well have influenced the tone of its successors, is without doubt derived from one of these. Alfred Binet and Charles Féré published a history of mesmerism, *Le Magnétisme animal*, in France in 1887 and a translation was made into English in the same year.[17] Binet and Féré's account is somewhat more subdued than Owen's. In the translation, Mesmer's salon is depicted as being nothing more than 'a large hall, hung with thick curtains, through which only a soft and subdued light was allowed to penetrate'.[18] A 'melodious air, proceeding from a pianoforte or harmonicum, placed in the adjoining room' added atmosphere to an environment where, otherwise, 'Absolute silence was maintained'.[19] The detail of Binet and Féré's depiction of Mesmer himself, again, closely anticipates Owen's account, though the implications of drama *as theatre* are notably absent in the former. Binet and Féré note that

> Mesmer, wearing a coat of lilac silk, walked up and down amid this palpitating crowd, together with Deslon and his associates, whom he chose for their youth and comeliness. Mesmer carried a long iron wand, with which he touched the bodies of the patients, and especially those parts which were diseased; often laying aside the

wand, he magnetized them with his eyes, fixing his gaze on theirs, or applying his hands to the hypochondriac region or the lower part of the abdomen … he renewed the process again and again, until the magnetized person was saturated with the healing fluid, and was transported with pain or pleasure, both sensations being equally salutary.[20]

In Binet and Féré's late-Victorian account, Mesmer lacks the obvious paraphernalia of charlatanry and showmanship which with he was invested in the second half of the twentieth century. The lilac (or purple) garment, which bears a variety of evocative names, is a constant feature in all of these accounts, and one which has been spectacularly misinterpreted. An earlier description of the doctor, incorporated in an 1837 article entitled 'Animal Magnetism' in *Leigh Hunt's London Journal* advances a few telling details omitted from later accounts. The setting is, inevitably, a mesmeric séance, and Mesmer enters 'clothed in a long-flowing robe of lilac coloured silk, richly embroidered with golden flowers, and holding in his hand a long white wand'.[21] This is clearly not 'a purple cloak trimmed with lace and embroidered with occult symbols', but a somewhat more innocuous garment utterly appropriate to the time and location. Mesmer is wearing an unexceptional house coat or *robe de chambre*, the fashionable indoor dress of a dandified eighteenth-century gentleman. He is not habited as a nineteenth-century stage conjurer, nor indeed as a priest in some new religion.

Similarly – if nineteenth-century commentators are to be believed – it appears that Mesmer also furnished his chambers in fashionable Parisian style rather than with the symbols of cabalism or the occult arts. The detail advanced in descriptions written in the nineteenth century seldom, if ever, aspires to the dubious elaborateness that characterises Waterfield's imaginative séance. *Leigh Hunt's London Journal*, for example, cleverly suggests, and then rhetorically dissipates, the supposedly mystic trappings of Mesmer's salon. The anonymous writer opens by evoking a state of calm and controlled contemplation:

The house which Mesmer inhabited was delightfully situated. His rooms were spacious and sumptuously furnished, stained glass and coloured blinds shed 'a dim religious light', mirrors gleamed at intervals along the walls, a mysterious silence was preserved, delicate perfumes floated in the air, and occasionally the melodious sounds of the harmonica or the voice came to lend their aid to his magnetic powers.[22]

The phrase 'a dim religious light' is a quotation from Milton's reflective and somewhat melancholic ode, 'Il Penseroso'.[23] From this point in the journal's account, however, there may be discerned an immediate and lasting change of tone:

> His *salons* became the daily resort of all that was brilliant and *spirituel* in the Parisian fashionable world. Ladies of rank, whom indolence, voluptuous indulgence, or satiety of pleasures, had filled with vapours or nervous affections – men of luxurious habits, enervated by enjoyment, who had drained sensuality of all that it could offer, and gained in return a shattered constitution and premature old age – came in crowds to seek after the delightful emotions and novel sensations which this mighty magician was said to dispense. They approached with imaginations heated by curiosity and desire; they believed because they were ignorant; and this belief was all that was required for the action of the magnetic charm.[24]

Other writers were equally insistent that Mesmer was engaged in an elaborate attempt to stimulate the jaded sensuality of Parisian high society. In an 1842 article simply entitled 'Mesmerism', for example, an anonymous writer for *The Satirist, or the Censor of the Times*, was sarcastic rather than censorious in tone:

> Mesmer, the inventor of the humbug [i.e., magnetism] knew human nature tolerably well; and fixing his scene of operations at Paris he laid on his bait accordingly. He furnished his house in the most sumptuous style; the rooms were covered with mirrors and perfumed with orange scents, and soft music, blended occasionally with a fine female voice, was heard. So many attractions, combined with the piquant charm of a new delusion, took the fancy of the Parisians altogether. Patients poured in from all quarters, and the *peculiar* treatment they had to undergo established the fame of Mesmer on a secure basis.[25]

It appears to be universally acknowledged by nineteenth-century commentators, therefore, that – in the words of an 1830 article in *Fraser's Magazine for Town and Country* – Mesmer's 'apartments became fashionable; and ladies of high rank went to them for the purpose of procuring "sensations agréables"'.[26] Mesmeric séances were thus perceived as being as much concerned with immediate sensuality as they were with ongoing spiritual development.

None the less, the popular discourse of occultism – as embodied in seemingly casual phrases such as 'this mighty magician' or 'the magic of his eye' – is an abiding characteristic of nineteenth-century depictions of Mesmer.[27] Though mesmeric phenomena were at times denounced as satanic in origin by unsympathetic Christian commentators, secular writings which associate Mesmer's own practice with occultism are notably *not* preoccupied with the apparently inexplicable phenomena of witchcraft.[28] Rather, they find a focus in the hermetic and secretive culture that traditionally reserves such uncanny powers for but a few adepts. For example, 'The Medical Adviser' of *The Penny Satirist* suggested in an 1837 editorial that in Vienna, prior to his arrival in Paris, 'Mesmer assumed the airs of a magician' and that the doctor subsequently 'began to perform his cures under a veil of mystery, through which no one was able to penetrate'.[29] The focus of this remark is neither the embroidery upon Mesmer's coat nor the opacity of his velvet curtains but the self-interest that would eventually motivate his profitable restriction of the secrets of magnetism to a coterie of fee-paying and oath-bound initiates. Thus, as 'The Medical Adviser' intimates, a few years later in Paris,

> The treatment was still practised under a mysterious form, and the knowledge of the hidden parts of the system ... was communicated to adepts, who, after having paid a certain sum, were received into a kind of magical or medical free-masonry. The adepts formed several societies called 'Harmonies'.[30]

Though this may sound melodramatic to a modern readership, secretive practices of this nature were in keeping with the culture of late eighteenth-century Paris. Mesmer, in common with many of his contemporaries in conventional as well as speculative medicine, was a Freemason.[31] The model of the Masonic lodge, with its systems of initiation and advancement, and its aspirations to universal brotherhood, provided an obvious alternative mode of organisation to that which underpinned those learned societies whose members had questioned the very existence of a universal magnetic phenomenon.[32] Mesmer in the guise of Dr Mystery may be read here as the presiding master of a speculative lodge of Enlightenment values, open to both sexes and not veiled in allegory but rather cloaked in necessary – as well as tantalising – secrecy.[33]

The magnetist-as-magician, gaudily bedecked in unlikely symbols and peddling a mystic panacea, would seem to be the creation, therefore, of a twentieth-century rhetoric determined to align Mesmer with those stage practitioners who attracted ridicule even in the nineteenth century with their spectacular manipulation of entranced subjects and alleged feats of mind reading.[34] If Mesmer's patients are consistently noted for their gullibility in nineteenth-century writings on the subject, the doctor himself is as often grudgingly admired for his ability to both anticipate and respond to the tenor of his age.

Mesmer is perceptibly less ridiculous in his nineteenth-century guise than he appears in subsequent accounts, for all the broad consensus of both regarding his dress and accoutrements. Rarely, in the former accounts, is he rhetorically deployed in order to establish a boundary between the past and the present, between two explanations for what might appear the same phenomena. Mesmer does not customarily function as a defining boundary which may graphically separate dubious eighteenth-century magnetism and the apparently pioneering clinical technique of hypnotism, pioneered in the nineteenth century by Braid. That form of demarcation is, quite simply, not there in the popular mind of the first forty years of the century at least. Hypnotism, even in the mid-nineteenth century, could still be conflated with magnetism in a way that is inconceivable in the twenty-first century. Arguably, the popular mind – that which reads publications such as *Leigh Hunt's London Journal*, *The Satirist* or *The Penny Satirist* – does not distinguish between the fluid theories of magnetism and later explanations for hypnotic phenomena in the way that a medical or technical journal of the period might. In such popular works, there is no emphatic requirement to enforce a distinction between the two: mesmerism is either as legitimate as hypnotism, or equally questionable. If magnetism, and Mesmer himself, are mocked in such accounts, it is merely on basis of their own claims, rather than in the interests of those who are attempting to enforce an alternative explanation, a different and more respectable identity, for the same phenomena in the hands of later practitioners.

Baquets and batteries:
the technology of mesmerism

If Mesmer is advanced as an unlikely and grotesque figure in twentieth- and twenty-first-century accounts of magnetic practice, the technologies contextually associated with animal magnetism are likewise depicted in such works as impostures so blatant that those who gather around them can be regarded as little more than purblind dupes. The emphasis in such accounts characteristically evades any form of empathy which might justify the claims associated with these magnetic devices through access to the discursive assumptions under which they were conceived. The technologies of mesmerism are as much a product of the thought of the late eighteenth century as the glass harmonica, itself an instrument with more than a musical significance given its occasional deployment within the initiation of a mesmeric séance. The glass harmonica, though seldom encountered in the twenty-first century as a musical instrument in actual performance, generates no epistemological problems for a modern listener, given that its tonal range and practical application continue to meet the expectations of contemporary musical praxis.[35] The technologies of mesmerism, however, are problematic because they can no longer function under the presiding discourses of modern physics or medicine. These instruments are, in essence, no longer capable of being viewed as scientific or medical apparatus. Rather, they are now to be considered the occulted tools of the magician that Mesmer has rhetorically become – less evocative, perhaps, than the significantly emphasised wand, but still alien to modern intellectual sensibilities educated to disregard as mysticism or error anything which might be termed – no doubt with a suitable stress on the prejudicial prefix – a *pseudo*science.

Writing for the no-doubt educated and discerning audience associated with the British Broadcasting Corporation in the early 1970s, the cultural critic and medical historian Jonathan Miller advanced a sceptical image of those who placed their trust in the magnetic cures of a practitioner who apparently spent a significant amount of time 'stalking the salon in a magician's robe'.[36] Miller writes:

> Throughout the late 1770s and early 1780s, Mesmerism became a huge cult in Paris and throughout the French provinces. The subjects, clients or patients – it's hard to settle on the right title – grouped themselves around a tub or bucket in which, according to the Mesmeric orthodoxy, the magnetic fluid would accumulate. Gripping iron bars plunged into the fluid, the subjects experienced every type of trance, fit and transport. Every effort was made to encourage a susceptible state of mind.[37]

Miller's evocation of the susceptible collective mind gathered rather ridiculously around a 'bucket' – the size of which is teasingly unspecified – is reinforced by the implicitly empty space within this somewhat incongruous and homely receptacle. Miller, of course, has already identified the contents of the apparently lidless 'bucket' with the 'impalpable fluid' of Mesmer's doctoral dissertation, thus rendering the receptacle implicitly as empty as the heads of those grouped around it – a body of gullible and vacuous individuals whom a twentieth-century physician pointedly hesitates to classify.[38]

Miller, of course, is being rhetorical here. In his choice of words, he is admittedly advancing a literal and uncompromising translation of the French word *baquet* – the term by which the device was known at the time. The 'tub or bucket' conceived in a twentieth-century reader's imagination, however, is unlikely to resemble in size, materials or form the actual device deployed in Mesmer's eighteenth-century practice. In size, indeed, the receptacle resembled a personal bath or a small pool rather than a mere pail. An 1817 account of a Parisian séance, published in *Blackwood's Edinburgh Magazine*, makes this much clear:

> The apparatus necessary for the administration of the magnetism, and the method in which it was employed, were the following. In the centre of a large apartment was a circular box, made of oak, and about a foot or a foot and a half deep, which was called the bucket. The lid of this box was pierced with a number of holes, in which were inserted branches of iron, elbowed and moveable. The patients were arranged in ranks about this bucket, and each had his branch of iron, which by means of the elbow, might be applied immediately to the part affected.[39]

The explicit presence of a lid in the *Blackwood's* account, of course, enforces a totally different rhetorical outcome from that later envisaged by Miller. The patients in this case cannot see that the *baquet* is empty – and the writer of the article, likewise, is unable to comment upon its contents. None the less, a logical explanation is tendered by the *Blackwood's* commentator for the peculiar construction of the *baquet*:

> The interior part of the bucket was so constructed as to concentrate the magnetism; and was a grand reservoir, from which the fluid was diffused through the branches of iron that were inserted in its lid.[40]

The writer is here drawing rather heavily upon the fluid analogy associated with mesmerism. This concentration upon the 'fluid universally diffused', explicated earlier in the article through quotation from Mesmer's own memoir, rather perversely distracts the author from the parallel analogy of magnetism which he elsewhere emphasises through the anodes of the *baquet* and the specifically iron rods borne by the superintending magnetisers.[41]

The logic of the *baquet* – a logic quite clearly implied by the descriptions in the article – is not that of hydraulics, nor entirely that of magnetism, but recalls eighteenth-century electrical experimentation. Even if the work of the Italian scientist Luigi Galvani – who in the 1780s conducted neural experiments upon the severed legs of frogs – was unknown to Mesmer, he was definitely aware that Maria Theresa von Paradis, one of his Viennese patients, had previously been treated through the application of an early version of electrotherapy. A footnote to Mesmer's *Mémoire sur la découverte du magnétisme animal* (1779) intimates that this gifted but blind musician was given around three thousand electric shocks in a succession of attempts to stimulate her optic nerves.[42] Galvani's work was reported in the British popular press, and public demonstrations of his experiments were ultimately given in London in the early years of the nineteenth century. The language used in these descriptions of recognisably electrical experimentation – where the intangible power was originated not through the human body in the manner of animal magnetism but by way of a rudimentary generator or possibly a Leyden jar – is highly reminiscent of contemporary accounts of Mesmer's practice.

One 1803 report in a provincial newspaper, for example, recalls how a lecturer, 'Mr Wilkinson, Surgeon in Soho Square', 'shewed the influence of the Galvanic *fluid* on the nerves and muscles of various dead animals'.[43] Galvani's original discovery was apparently made not in the laboratory, however, but when skinning frogs' legs for culinary purposes. This

> was done in a room in which there was an electrical apparatus; during the time he had the point of his knife applied to one of the frogs, a gentleman, who stood near him, happened to draw an electrical spark from the machine; the professor immediately observed an uncommon motion of the muscles of the frog; the circumstance attracted his notice, and led him to repeat the experiment; he found, that if the electric fluid was communicated to a person near him, while he held the point of his knife over the animal, its nerves and muscles were visibly affected. This experiment urged the Professor Galvani to further enquiries; the result of which proved, that there was an electric fluid pervading the nerves and muscles of animals, which was capable of being acted upon by metallic substances of almost every description.[44]

Much of this report – particularly the invisible transference of pervasive energy from one body or another – directly parallels the discourse through which Mesmer intimated his own intangible magnetic fluid. Galvani, indeed, holds his own metallic wand, and subsequent experiments under Galvanic logic arguably provide an overlooked context which parallels, if it does not actually explain, the popular image and understanding of the *baquet*.

The *baquet* should be viewed in context not so much as a reservoir as a battery. Devices for the storage of electricity had been improvised from the late-eighteenth century, and their existence and configuration certainly formed part of nineteenth-century popular scientific consciousness.[45] Early Leyden jars, such as those available to Galvani, were water-filled glass containers, though later versions dispensed with the liquid content: both types, however, utilised metallic anodes that projected from their lids in a manner reminiscent of the iron branches observed upon Mesmer's *baquet*.[46] Mesmer himself, one nineteenth-century British chronicler of animal magnetism claimed, stated 'I have charged jars with magnetic matter in the same way as is done with electricity'.[47] Later batteries, such as the liquid-based devices associated in England with the work of Sir Joseph Banks, often superficially resembled the mesmeric *baquet* albeit in a conveniently rectangular form. Banks's battery, for example, 'consisted of four boxes, each about two feet long and four inches broad, placed so as to form a square', where an apparently later device, 'Cruikshank's trough battery', was contained 'in a box of baked wood'.[48] Projecting metallic anodes, again, would have been essential for the transfer or discharge of the accumulated electricity. Notably, one popular encyclopaedia account from 1882 explicitly conflates the experimental 'animal electricity' of Galvani with the theories of Mesmer, stating that 'after the death of Galvani, which happened in 1798, little was heard of the matter, and *animal magnetism*, as it was called, was held in contempt'.[49]

Though the transmission of electric current might most efficiently be achieved through metallic wires, public demonstrations frequently occasioned the use of spectators as an electrical conduit.[50] A particularly spectacular public display of electrical technology was undertaken in Todmorden, a market town on the border of Lancashire and Yorkshire, in 1837, in which a Leyden jar was charged with atmospheric electricity for the benefit of an interested public:

> On Tuesday our townsman Mr S. E. Cottram afforded the inhabitants of this romantic vale a high treat. During the course of the day he had contrived to pass from Patmos Sunday School, the lecture-room of the society, two metallic wires to the summit of one of

the neighbouring hills; one of the wires was connected with the outside of a Leyden jar and the other was made to communicate at a given signal … with the inside of the jar when it had received a charge. Several hundred people were assembled on the stage and were greatly surprised and delighted on joining hands to receive the shock so powerful and so instantaneous, and at so great a distance from the machine.[51]

If the glass Leyden jar utilised here does not in itself resemble Mesmer's wooden *baquet*, the (no doubt directed) behaviour of the good citizens of Todmorden *is* reminiscent of how those seeking a cure by animal magnetism disported themselves around the evocative reservoir in Mesmer's Parisian salon. The pseudonymous 'G', writing in *Blackwood's Edinburgh Magazine*, makes this much clear in his depiction of one such gathering around the *baquet*:

A cord passed round their [the patients'] bodies, connected the one with the other. Sometimes a second means of communication was introduced, by the insertion of the thumb of each patient between the forefinger and thumb of the patient next him. The impression received by the left hand of the patient was communicated through his right, and thus passed through the whole circle.

Indeed, as 'G' later confirms, 'The cord which was passed round the bodies of the patients was destined, as well as the union of their fingers, to augment the effects by communication'.[52]

A closer inspection of that which lies beneath the cover of the *baquet* reveals not the vacant space implied in Jonathan Miller's account but a strange assembly of substances and vessels that neatly aligns the doctrine of animal magnetism with the more conventionally scientific theories of both electricity and iron-based magnetism. A popular science article in *The Lady's Newspaper*, dated 30 January 1847, for example, expands somewhat upon the 'circular box, made of oak' advanced by 'G' in *Blackwood's Edinburgh Journal* some thirty years earlier:

In the middle of each room in which the persons to be treated were collected was placed a large circular vessel, made of oak-wood about a foot or a foot and a half in height: the interior of this vessel was filled with pounded glass, iron filings, and bottles containing magnetised water arranged symmetrically: the cover or upper part of the vessel was pierced with numerous holes, in which were placed polished iron rods, bent and capable of being moved: this was called the *baquet* or magnetic tub. The patients were placed in successive rows around the baquet, and each one had one of the rods of iron, the end of which he applied to the part of his body which was supposed to be the seat of his disease: a cord passed around their bodies united the patients to one another, and sometimes they formed a second chain by taking hold of each other's thumbs.[53]

The closing sentence here asserts more forcefully the contextual justification for the cord and chain of thumbs: the augmentation which 'G' intimates is, in effect, a doubling of the communicative medium, and a more efficient *circulation* of the energy or force rather than its amplification. Another newspaper account, published in 1837, would seem to confirm this as a popular interpretation of the detail of earlier French practice, in British eyes at least:

> The patients ranged round the baquet in large numbers, and in several rows, received the magnetism by all these means – by the branches of iron which convey to them that of the baquet; by the cords wound round their bodies, and by the union of their thumbs, which conveys to them that of their neighbours.[54]

The internal structure of the *baquet* is calculated to ensure the satisfactory transmission of force. Iron and water, two materials closely associated with the mobility of electricity, lie within its cavity and the insulating glass (in the form of bottles and the granular medium in which these are packed) emulates the containing effect of the conventional Leyden jar. *The Lady's Newspaper*, indeed, confirms of the *baquet* that 'its interior arrangement was for the purpose of *concentrating* the magnetic fluid'.[55] An earlier account, published in 1834 in *Leigh Hunt's London Journal*, further clarifies the arrangement of the apparatus, noting that in the *baquet* 'were laid a number of bottles disposed in radii, with their necks directed outwards, well corked and filled with magnetized water'.[56] A reader in the nineteenth century would thus be led by analogy to understand that the iron rods on the *baquet* were intended to provide a tactile connection with a force in much the same way as the anodes on the Leyden jars deployed at Todmorden and in other demonstrations of conventional electricity.

The magical wand borne by the magnetiser may likewise be explained not as an occult tool but in the manner of a scientific implement. 'G', certainly, suggests that this is the case:

The persons who superintended the process had each of them an iron rod in his hand, from ten to twelve inches in length. This rod was a conductor of the magnetism, and had the power of concentrating it at its point, and rendering its emanations more considerable.[57]

The Lady's Newspaper, likewise, stated that 'The purpose of the magnetiser's rod was to concentrate to a point the fluid which issued from him, and thus to render it more powerful'.[58] Like the human finger – essentially another tool in the possession of the magnetiser – the wand represented an extremity through which concentrated power might be directed. The finger was, in a sense, simply another anode – an outlet for accumulated energy.[59]

An analogous explanation may also be associated with the regular presence of music – variously the glass harmonica, pianoforte or human voice – at mesmeric séances. Of course, such aural stimuli may contribute psychologically to the mood of expectation, as critics of mesmerism from the eighteenth century to the present have suggested.[60] However, in context, their consistent deployment may also be explained by way of the equally invisible progress of sound, as a form of directable energy, across empty space. If the physical body of a magnetiser is, like the *baquet*, a reservoir of potential magnetic energy awaiting only the pointed extremity of a rod or fingertip to direct it in concentrated and kinetic form at a specific point, so too may sound also convey magnetic energy albeit in an implicitly more diffused form. *Blackwood's Edinburgh Journal*, again, conveys this as a simple statement:

> Sound was also a conductor of magnetism; and in order to communicate the fluid to the piano forte, nothing more was necessary than to approach to it the iron rod. The person who played upon the instrument furnished also a portion of the fluid; and the magnetism was transmitted by the sounds to the surrounding patients.[61]

Cleave's London Satirist and Gazette of Variety, published twenty years' later, similarly noted that animal magnetism might be deliberately circulated 'by the sound of the piano-forte, or an agreeable voice, which diffuses it in the air'.[62] Ten years' after this, a similar interpretation was also advanced through the pages of *The Lady's Newspaper*, albeit with some equivocation:

> The magnetiser had previously charged the pianoforte with magnetic fluid; the person playing on it was incessantly giving out more; the sound conducted it to the patients. The purpose of the music was

to put the patients into a state of quiet; to give them agreeable sensations, and thus to dispose them to receive the magnetic action.[63]

Even this equivocation, though, is tempered by a reflection upon the efficacy of the process. This is not musical theatre, seemingly, but a sort of pre-operative sedative analogous to the chemical pre-medication so often deployed in surgery in the twenty-first century. The systematic function of such actions, as it were, is acknowledged even where the therapeutic process itself is a matter of dispute.

The accounts of mesmeric practice advanced at length by *Blackwood's Edinburgh Magazine* and *The Lady's Newspaper* thus expose the rather complex attitude that characterises the popular nineteenth-century response to eighteenth-century animal magnetism. Both articles conclude by acknowledging the consensus reached by regular, experimental science in its French institutional incarnation, as early as 1784. The claims advanced for mesmerism as a doctrine are untenable, according to the judgements of the two formal investigatory commissions comprised of medical and scientific men published that year, because the magnetic force itself cannot be demonstrated to have any tangible existence.[64] Indeed, as *The Lady's Newspaper* stated, citing the results of the 1784 investigation conducted into French animal magnetism:

> These commissioners report – 'That this pretended agent certainly is not common magnetism, for that, on examining the *baquet*, the grand reservoir of this wonderful fluid, by means of a needle and electrometer, not the slightest indication of the presence either of common magnetism or of electricity was afforded; that it is wholly inappreciable by any of the senses, or by any mechanical or chemical process ...'[65]

Animal magnetism is not 'common magnetism' nor is it electricity, but its ready association with these two quantifiable forces perversely facilitates the nineteenth-century's often indulgent attitude towards those who practise, and those who seek to benefit from, the alleged power of mesmerism. Popular attitudes towards mesmerism are frequently less openly mocking, less grotesque even, in nineteenth-century accounts than they are in interpretations written in the two subsequent centuries. Arguably, this is a singular consequence of a type of conceptual empathy on the part of a non-specialist readership which none the less broadly understood that electricity could be stored and discharged, and that magnetism likewise moved – or flowed – invisibly between one metallic substance and another. Indeed, the conflation of these two apparently discrete forces was not unknown during the nineteenth century. In his 'Essay on the Origin and Progress of Animal Magnetism', published in a popular science journal in 1840, for example, the Reverend Henry Christmas juxtaposed a statement by Mesmer with more recent scientific speculation:

> '*I have observed*', says he [Mesmer], '*that the magnetic matter is almost the same as the electric fluid, and that it may be propagated in the same manner as this, by means of intermediate bodies.*' It has been suspected in our own day, and, indeed, more than suspected, that magnetism and electricity are, in fact, one and the same fluid seen under different circumstances.[66]

Epistemologically, to a scientifically untrained mind, electricity, magnetism and animal magnetism are analogous in the way they are stored, moved and manipulated through concrete technologies. Thus, even if animal magnetism *is* regarded as a pseudoscience or a discredited philosophy, the reader may proceed some way towards an empathetic understanding of those who have believed – at whatever period of recent history – in its credibility. Such empathy, arguably, is not available to a modern reader.

'Innocent external remedies': Perkinism as a rival to mesmerism in Britain

Though grandiose claims are often made regarding its supposed inhibition of the spread of animal magnetism, the publication in France in 1784 of the so-called Franklin Report – more accurately, the *Rapport des commisaires chargés par le Roi de l'examen du magnétisme animal* – probably did little to inhibit mesmerism's popular appeal.[67] This report enjoys something of a privileged place within histories of hypnotic practice, and is frequently paraphrased or quoted in translation to the present day.[68] Even the pseudonymous 'G', in his 1817 survey of mesmerism, feels sufficiently confident to advise the readers of *Blackwood's Edinburgh Magazine* that:

> An exposure so complete, accomplished by men whose integrity and talents were acknowledged over the whole of Europe, speedily produced the effects that were to have been expected from it. In a few months, Mesmer and his animal magnetism were forgotten.[69]

There is something of an irony behind the closing comment, given that the *Blackwood's* article itself was explicitly prompted by the publication (one 'to be continued periodically') of 'the First Part of the First Volume of a work, entitled "Archives of Animal Magnetism", published in the commencement of the present year, in the German language'. This work is attributed to 'three medical professors in the respectable universities of Tubingen, Jens and Halle', and its appearance paradoxically illustrates that despite the supposedly wide circulation of the Royal Commission's report, animal magnetism 'has again been revived in Germany; and has obtained credit, not merely with the vulgar, but with the more intelligent classes of society'.[70] The enduring influence of the Report beyond France – and, indeed, possibly even *within* French culture generally – would thus appear questionable.

However great its influence in France, the report enjoyed only a limited circulation in the British Isles: a translation into English was published on 16 December 1784 at the price of 2s 6d, though that publication's broad appeal was, no doubt, *not* enhanced by the addition of a ponderous preface which purported to demonstrate 'a Parallel between Paracelsus and Mesmer'.[71] The popular British consciousness of magnetism, therefore, was not necessarily inhibited by the evidential processes and philosophical arguments that were offered to the educated population of France via the 1784 Report. The British mind was thus essentially free not merely to contemplate the possibility of mesmeric phenomena but to continue to associate them also, obliquely or otherwise, with analogous developments in subsequent medicine. One such 'remarkable popular delusion', recorded somewhat testily by 'G', is 'the belief in the metallic tractors of Perkins'.[72]

Perkinism is *not* mesmerism, though its doctrines and apparatus bear sufficient resemblance to those popularised by animal magnetism as to facilitate a superficial congruence between the two. The metallic (more accurately, bimetallic) tractors – whose purpose was literally to 'draw' (from the Latin *'tractus'*) the disorder from the affected part – were apparently shaped like a quartered cone, each being around 6.35 cm in length.[73] According to the system of Elisha Perkins, an electrical (rather than magnetic) fluid 'drew out the pain and cured the underlying disease', in a process rhetorically reminiscent of European mesmeric practice.[74] Perkinism does not seem to have enjoyed any significant popularity in France, though it was a topic of some interest in the United States – the country of its invention – and also in the United Kingdom, where it was widely advertised and formed the subject of public lectures and demonstrations. Indeed, British interest in Perkinism at the turn of the nineteenth century rivals – and possibly even equals – the better-known debate regarding animal magnetism recalled in most histories of hypnotic practice. This situation may be explained possibly by the relatively easy access to books about Perkinism granted by its origination in the English – rather than French – language. Demonstrations of Perkins's practice, likewise, would be conducted in American-inflected English rather than in the approximated and broken version of the language often associated with French mesmerists demonstrating on English soil.[75] The venerable British tradition of Francophobia, likewise, may have played a part in the rise of Perkinism, given the specifically Parisian fashion for mesmerism.

Certainly, though, the curative claims of Perkinism rivalled those of the panacea that was magnetism. As a 1797 advertisement for this miracle cure, efficacious against 'Gouts, Rheumatics, Erysipilas, Nervous Head-Aches, Quinseys, Epileptic Fits, Spasms, and all Inflammatory Affections', claimed:

> The extraordinary efficacy these instruments possess, of extracting the inflammation and giving relief by the combined influence of Electrical and Magnetic powers, can only be credited by those who have felt, or seen their speedy effect; yet, so simple and innocent in the operation, the patient will be convinced at sight, that no injury can ensue from it.

The claims to both authenticity of cure and authority of use for Perkins's tractors were to be established in the United Kingdom by way of much the same intellectual process that mesmerism had drawn upon in pre-Revolutionary France. An equivalent of the controlled trials which Mesmer had resisted, and to which his associate, Charles d'Eslon, had submitted at the behest of the French Royal Commission of 1784, were indeed actively solicited by Messrs Harriott and Bigelow, agents to Elisha Perkins. The advertisement continues:

> The evidences of their [the tractors'] great efficacy in America are incontrovertible, as may be seen by Certificates from Gentlemen of great medical abilities there ... The Advertisers are so confident of success in their practice, that they solicit Gentlemen of eminence in the Faculty to allow them to perform in their presence, on any of their patients afflicted with either of the above complaints, for they desire no other credit than what facts will establish.[76]

Such 'facts' might be established by the publications of both American and British specialists, their practical experience in the deployment of Elisha

Perkins's device no doubt enhanced by a prominent display of worthy academic qualifications. An advertisement printed in a London newspaper, *The Star*, on 1 December 1798, for example, announces as 'Just published, price 2s 6d':

> The Influence of METALLIC TRACTORS, in removing Rheumatism, Pleurisy, some Gouty affections, &c., &c., lately discovered by Dr Perkins of North America, and demonstrated in a series of experiments, by Professors Meigs, Woodward, Rogers, &c., &c., which opens a new field of enquiry in the modern science of Galvanism. By BENJAMIN DOUGLAS PERKINS AM, Son to the Discoverer.

If this in itself were not enough, the advertisement continues by offering the potential purchaser of both book and nostrum a further guide to this new science:

> A View of PERKINEAN ELECTRICITY, or an Enquiry into the influence of Metallic Tractors, with an Appendix, containing a variety of Experiments, by which the efficacy of this Practice is fully ascertained. By Charles C. Langworthy, Surgeon of Bath.[77]

The two books authored by Perkins and Langworthy were, clearly, not unauthorised exposés but manuals distributed with the implicit approval of the American inventor. The younger Perkins had, indeed, himself been despatched to London in order to generate sales of the tractors. Also significant was the way in which aspiring practitioners might be inducted into the use of the device. Instead of Mesmer's quasi-Masonic harmonic societies and binding oaths of secrecy, the tractors were apparently supplied with an instruction manual devoid of all mysticism and theatre:

> NB The Metallic Tractors, accompanied with plain directions, rendering the mode of application perfectly intelligible to every capacity, may now be had of Mr Perkins, No. 18, Leicester-Square, at five guineas per set. Hours of attendance at home from nine to two o'clock every day – Patients abroad visited afterwards. The tractors may also be had of Messrs Ogilvy and Son, Booksellers, Holborn.[78]

The younger Perkins was also the editor (but not the translator) of a volume published in 1799 by two Danish physicians, Johan Daniel Herholdt and Carl Gottlob Rafn. This work, *Experiments with the Metallic Tractors in Rheumatic and Gouty Affections*, was more expensive, being priced at 5s, and was probably aimed at the medical market rather than the aspiring lay practitioner.[79] In a review dated 24 October 1799, an anonymous reviewer for *The Oracle and Daily Advertiser* was quick to note the success obtained during trials made 'even under unfavourable circumstances' recorded in the first part of the work, a survey of some fifty subjects treated in Copenhagen.[80] The review is favourable towards both the book and the doctrine. Quoting at a midpoint the authors' opinion that the arguments against animal magnetism will not apply to Perkinism, the reviewer concludes 'On the whole, we have no hesitation in acknowledging, that the experiments adduced in this work, are of such a nature, and so respectably attested, as to go very far towards removing the doubts we formerly entertained of the efficacy of this novel practice'.[81]

One of the conclusions advanced by the Franklin report of 1784 was that the imagination of the receptive patient, rather than the imposition of an intangible fluid, was the likely cause of the phenomena demonstrated in association with mesmeric practice.[82] Experimental practice – which had, after all, failed to detect the presence of any electrical or magnetic charge at d'Eslon's mesmeric séances – was thus marshalled in order to verify the purported connection between the therapeutically deployed tractors and the removal of both pain and actual inflammation. Though the 1799 review in *The Oracle and Daily Advertiser* quoted merely the observations of 'One gentleman' who, having applied the tractors to his bruised horse, '*could perceive* a swelling diminish', other publications drew upon the analogy of conventional, scientifically credible, electrical experimentation in order to endorse Perkinism.[83] In an untitled news item dated 9 June 1800, *Lloyd's Evening Post* verifies the experiments conducted by Galvani's contemporary and rival, Count Alessandro Volta, through their British emulation, and thus rhetorically aligns them to the nominally electrical manipulations associated with the deployment of Perkins's tractors:

> The beautiful experiment in Galvanism, lately communicated to Sir Joseph Banks by Professor Volta; and repeated by Dr Garnet at the Royal Institution, confirms the pretensions of the advocates of Perkinism, who affected an influence of metals on the bodies of animals when externally applied. The many extraordinary facts evincing the efficacy of metallic tractors in diseases, though apparently authenticated by indisputable testimony, could not gain evidence with some, because no experiment had been hit upon to render their influence immediately perceptible, otherwise than in the removal

of the complaint. This experiment offers an instant demonstration. Humanity must rejoice in the introduction of innocent external remedies against diseases, which while they are found equally or more beneficial, do not, like all internal medicines, render the patient liable to be injured from injudicious administrations.[84]

The letter to which the article refers is almost certainly that mentioned in the *Philosophical Transactions of the Royal Society of London* for July 1801.[85] In this communication, originally written in French, Volta discusses natural and artificial organs of electricity, the former exemplified by the torpedo fish and the latter by the Leyden jar and the galvanic battery. Volta's experiments were sporadically repeated for the benefit of mixed audiences attending lectures hosted by the Royal Institution and other scholarly bodies, and these events were in turn recounted by popular works whose circulation was significantly greater than the *Philosophical Transactions*. As the *Critical Review, or, Annals of Literature*, noted in an 1801 digest of the *Philosophical Transactions* for 1800, the emphasis of Volta's investigation was specifically towards that 'electricity excited only by the simple contact of metals of a different kind'.[86] Volta's battery, with its stack of bimetallic plates separated by a brine-soaked medium, bears no physical resemblance at all to the pointed tractors of Perkins's practice – though even relatively erudite summary accounts, such as that published in the *Critical Review*, for the most part fail to emphasise this vital difference. This imprecision arguably facilitates the potential for analogy that exists between Perkinism and Galvanism, an illusory congruence that may be all the more convincing when such experiments feature, as the *Critical Review* intimates, the communication which takes place between the electrical source and the flesh of the subject. It is but a small epistemological leap between a 'galvanic apparatus' that terminates in 'two metallic rods with rounded extremities' which may be applied in order to impart a perceptible sensory shock to the ears or nose, and the pointed bimetallic tractors wielded by a Perkinean practitioner.[87] The former was almost certainly the type of equipment utilised in 1800 by Thomas Garnet, who was Professor of Natural Philosophy and Chemistry at the Royal Institution between 1799 and 1801, during the demonstration recorded in *Lloyd's Evening Post* that year. Later accounts are if anything even more vague, one non-clinical medical dictionary of 1849, for example, describing Perkinism as 'the application to diseased parts of the extremities of two *needles* made of different metals, called by him *metallic tractors*'.[88]

As the account in *Lloyd's Evening Post* rightly noted, a non-invasive therapy such as Perkinism may suggest itself as being demonstrably safer to the medical laity than either surgery or chemical medication. A similar appeal to the non-clinician may likewise be associated with animal magnetism. Mesmer, of course, found his claims rebutted by the Parisian medical faculty before, and through, the two Royal Commissions which reported on his work in 1784.[89] Likewise, Perkinism met with a decisive rebuff in England by way of institutionalised – though not centralised – opposition by medical practitioners no doubt as concerned for their own pecuniary interests as they were for the safety of the public. In essence, the action of a small number of unconnected individuals demonstrably achieved in England a result similar to that allegedly produced by a council of intellectuals formally commissioned in France.

Certainly, by the 1840s Perkinism was little more than a memory – and not a very detailed one at that. Two short articles in *The Penny Satirist*, a popular London newspaper, recall the apparently sudden demise of what had apparently been a profitable enterprise within the metropolis at least. The earlier of the two, published in 1840, would appear to be an editorial response to a reader's query regarding the nature of Perkinism. After describing the composition and deployment of the tractors, and revealing that Perkins 'was understood to have made not less than £10,000 by the sale of them, at three guineas the pair', the writer then recalls:

> The regular practitioner raised his voice against the public delusion; and it was at Bath, if we recollect rightly, that a physician named Haygarth, practised a little *ruse*, which inflicted a heavy wound upon the healing reputation of these wonderful pieces of metal. This wily son of Esculapius caused a pair of Tractors to be made of wood exactly resembling the metallic ones in size, colour, &c. With these false instruments he gravely operated upon a man in the hospital, who was seriously afflicted with a rheumatic complaint. The poor fellow, in a short time, said he thought he was a little relieved; and after a few more applications, declared that he was certainly infinitely better; and, in fact, he did walk about with tolerable ease, which he had not been able to do for many weeks previously.[90]

A later article, entitled 'Medical Delusions of the Past', published some three years' later in the same newspaper does not mention mesmerism at all, the representative delusions being the Royal touch against scrofula, the curative anointing of the weapon rather than of the wound, the administration of tar water and the use of Perkins's tractors. The article expands somewhat on the 'cures' misleadingly effected by Haygarth – who successfully administered, so it seems, not merely 'Tractors of lead and of wood' but also 'nails, pieces of bone, slate pencil, and tobacco pipe'. It mentions also the case histories associated with the use of wooden tractors by Dr Alderson, a now-forgotten opponent of Perkinism.[91] The implicit conclusion reached by both of these recollections is strikingly similar to that published by the Franklin Commission. As the earlier article intimates, 'imagination might have done something, and nature must have performed the rest'.[92] As Robin Waterfield notes, the Franklin Commission could only conclude that the phenomena observed were a result either of the patient's imagination alone or else of that desire acting in parallel with the physical pressure exercised by the mesmerist with his hand or rod – this latter being obviously reminiscent of the contact between tractor and flesh characteristic of Perkinism.[93] Though the theoretical logic behind Perkinism was not the same as that which mobilised mesmerism, the superficial resemblance between the two therapies, and the hostility directed towards them by conventional chemical and chirurgical practitioners, permitted them to be examined and dismissed in a similar manner even by the medical institutions of two, by then estranged, cultures.

'A very moderate share of the art of healing': John Bonnoit de Mainaduc and early British magnetism

The apparent decline of mesmerism in France following the publication of the Franklin Report, and the absolute collapse of Perkinism in the United Kingdom as a consequence of the actions taken by Haygarth, Alderson and others, arguably signals more than a growing cultural, as well as professional, scepticism with regard to non-orthodox medical treatments based on fluids or forces.[94] Mesmerism, as practised by Mesmer and his immediate disciples, and Perkinism as undertaken by all those who purchased the authentic tractors, shared a common commitment to medical technology. *Baquets*, glass harmonicas, wands and tractors, if not evocative tools, were useful sources of income for those developing alternative medicine as a primarily commercial venture.[95] This technology, though, was an easy target for those who had an interest in disproving the existence of the intangible force – magnetic or electrical – that was apparently contained within it or directed through it. The Leyden jar, the galvanic battery and the voltaic pile are technologies that may be subject to quantitative scrutiny accredited by, and acceptable to, the scientific institutions of the day. Near such repositories of latent energy, sensitive needles or iron filings may visibly betray the presence of a credible, even if invisible, force to the satisfaction of layman and scientist alike. When such tests are applied, without success, to mesmeric apparatus, however, the suggestion that manipulation has taken place on the part of the operator, or imagination has been exercised by the expectant patient, becomes difficult to disprove.[96] If the necessary technology is inert, the argument follows, the philosophy behind it is equally spurious.

The presence of distinctive technology, however, is not essential for the production or dissemination of animal magnetism as conceived theoretically by Mesmer. As d'Eslon asserts, animal magnetism

> is a fluid universally diffused; it is the medium of a mutual influence between the heavenly bodies, the earth, and animated bodies; it is continuous, so as to admit of no void … it is capable of receiving, propagating, communicating all the impressions of motion; it is susceptible of flux and reflux.

The *baquet*, which d'Eslon himself employed at the time of writing, was simply a means to an end, rather than an essential tool, for the communication of the fluid may be effected 'without the aid of any intermediate body'.[97] The recipient body, indeed, need be neither technological in nature nor even manufactured, as Mesmer himself pointed out as early as 1775:

> I have rendered paper, bread, wool, silk, leather, stones, glass, water, various metals, wood, men, dogs – in a word, every thing I touched – magnetic to such a degree, that these substances produced the same effects as the loadstone on the diseased.[98]

Such bodies (or technologies), as d'Eslon suggests, merely augment a fluid which exists independently of them, for animal magnetism 'is reflected by mirrors; communicated, propagated, increased by sound', and may be 'accumulated, concentrated, [and] transported' by those whose bodies are peculiarly susceptible to its power. It is almost certainly because of this conception of the magnetic force that mesmerism – which predated Perkinism and had more coherence as a philosophical movement – was successfully able to jettison the non-human components of its practice in order to reassert that the practitioner, rather than the *baquet*, was the repository of the intangible power.[99] Perkinism, with its instruction manuals and its specific priority of apparatus over operator, was not epistemologically flexible enough to effect such a great change in its conceptual existence. Perversely, the charismatic presence of the magnetist – ridiculed so much in modern histories of hypnotic practice – is the central resource upon which early nineteenth-century practitioners of animal magnetism drew in order to stabilise and perpetuate their supposedly discredited medical discipline. His role redefined, and his appearance ultimately moderated from dandyism to doctoral sobriety, the practitioner became the central figure in the new order of magnetic practice – and the focus of attention for those sceptical of the claims of animal magnetism as well as those engaged in its therapeutic deployment.

In the United Kingdom, public consciousness of animal magnetism was somewhat different from that which pertained in France, and not merely because the *baquet* appears never to have enjoyed a concrete existence on British soil. There is an element of denial, for example, in one account published in *The Lady's Newspaper* in 1853, which asserted that 'Though animal magnetism excited very great and general attention on the Continent, it never thoroughly took root in England'.[100] More recently, Alison Winter has suggested that mesmerism is something of a Victorian phenomenon in its British context:

> Taking hold in Britain so much later than elsewhere in Europe it [mesmerism] appealed to the early Victorians as a new and exciting science of life and mind. Although mesmerists had made sporadic visits to Britain before the 1830s, it was in that decade that mesmerism's British career began in earnest, with a series of experiments that consumed the attention of London in the spring of 1838, only to end some months later in spectacular discreditation.[101]

The place which mesmerism has historically occupied in British public consciousness, however, cannot be dismissed so easily. The frequency with which Parisian magnetic séances were described and recalled in the British periodical and newspaper press from the 1780s through to the mid-nineteenth century would suggest otherwise, as would the activities of those magnetists, French and British, active in London and the provinces from as early as 1785.

Reputedly the first indigenous practitioner of magnetism in the British Isles, John Bonnoit de Mainaduc, is usually dismissed in modern histories of hypnotism by way of a page or two of biographical description.[102] Trained by d'Eslon rather than by Mesmer – the latter having apparently rejected a substantial financial inducement proffered by Mainaduc – this

Irish-born physician structured his own salons somewhat on the model of Mesmer's harmonic societies, charging a fee of twenty-five guineas in order to attract a wealthy and often noble clientele, and binding his acolytes to secrecy under a financial penalty of £10,000.[103] His appearance in modern accounts of early British hypnotism is associated primarily with his financial success, this normally being conveyed through a paraphrase of part of a letter written in 1788 by the Christian writer Hannah More to Horace Walpole.[104] That letter, though, was not however entirely a piece of private correspondence, but was reproduced more than once during the nineteenth-century controversy over magnetism, no doubt as a reminder of the scepticism of an earlier age. More's letter is, indeed, an index of how Mainaduc and Mesmer were associated not merely with each other but with a whole range of other activities deemed if not superstitious then at least epistemologically questionable. More despairingly suggests:

> In vain do we boast of the enlightened eighteenth century, and conceitedly talk as if human reason had not a manacle left about her, but that philosophy had broken down all the strong holds of prejudice, ignorance, and superstition; and yet, at this very time, Mesmer has got an *hundred thousand pounds* by animal magnetism in Paris; Mainaduc is getting as much in London; there is a fortune-teller in Westminster who is making little less; Lavater's physiognomy books sell at fifteen guineas a set; the divining rod is still considered as oracular in many places; devils are cast out by seven ministers … Poor human reason, when wilt thou come to years of discretion?[105]

Clearly, to enjoy such rhetorical prominence, even in a private letter, Mainaduc would surely be something more than the derivative, minor figure he is depicted as in, for example, Forrest's *Hypnotism*.[106] Indeed, Mainaduc is a magnetic practitioner wholly worthy of closer inspection, and one not without his own freighting of personal controversy.

Mainaduc's apparently sudden conversion from conventional medical therapy to a type of practice resembling that employed by Continental magnetists did not pass without comment. In a biographical notice which made mention of the physician's father, the *European Magazine and London Review*, an organ of the Philological Society of London, noted in 1798 that the elder Mainaduc

> educated his only son (the late Dr Mainaduc) in the best manner, and under one of the best personal examples in his own behaviour,

but all in vain! The boy rambled from him at an early age, and after passing through a number of adventures, at last rested in a *magnetic doctor*; where, if he had lived, there was a probability of making his fortune. The father just lived long enough to hear of his son's establishment, which the latter accompanied by a letter of repentance and a handsome remittance, with a promise of future aids during his life.[107]

The prodigal son, in this case, would appear not to have returned home empty-handed, even if he seems otherwise repentant. Magnetic practice, though, for all its financial rewards, is presented here as a somewhat uneasy profession for a gentleman. In context, it appears but another adventure on Mainaduc's rambling path, and the account tacitly advances him as being not quite the equal of a respectable and thoroughly conventional doctor who may be presented without either italics or a magnetic prefix.

His wealth, though, may not have been entirely derived from his professional practice. Mainaduc was not merely active as a magnetic physician and teacher but was also a successful publisher on mesmeric controversy and practice. Forrest notes Mainaduc's publication of a pamphlet entitled 'A Proposal to the Ladies' in 1785, though in the same year the Irish physician also published the more substantial *Veritas, or a Treatise Containing Observations Upon, and a Supplement to, the Two Reports by the Commissioners appointed by the King of France to Examine into Animal Magnetism*.[108] Styling himself on the title page of this ponderously titled work as a conventional physician – John Bonnoit de Mainaduc MD – he not only reported the Royal Commission's response to d'Eslon's magnetism, but also appended what he claimed to be his own properly certificated 'cures performed at Calais'. The averred truths contained in *Veritas*, however, failed to convince the reviewer for the *Monthly Review*, who, having recalled the unfavourable judgement of the Franklin Commission, remarked that there is nothing 'in this treatise, that, in our opinion, impeaches in the slightest degree, the fairness or justness of their decision'.[109] Various other works also appear to have been widely advertised under Mainaduc's authorship. These include accounts of cures undertaken by Mainaduc himself, and a now-obscure volume entitled *On Animal Magnetism*, published in 1797.[110]

Mainaduc's practical teaching of what he initially termed 'Animal Magnetism' appears to have begun modestly enough in London, though with a careful emphasis on the differences that pertained between his proposed practice and that of Mesmer. An advertisement in *The Morning Herald and Daily Advertiser*, dated 24 October 1785, proclaims:

> Doctor de Mainaduc will begin his instructions as soon as a sufficient number have subscribed to form a class, in which will be included Mr Mesmer's Theory of the World, the method he taught his students by poles, baquet, bottles, water, iron conductors, &c., &c. As the theory on which this science is founded, requires attention, and the different sensations necessary for the operator to distinguish diseases by, demand instructions and practice under the professor's eye; three months will generally be found requisite for that purpose. A superficial knowledge of a science so little known in this kingdom, and of such infinite consequence, would only tend to furnish its uninstructed enemies with arguments against it, and discourage the unprejudiced from experiencing its salutary influence.

Arguably, this advertisement – despite its intimation that mesmerism is 'so little known in this kingdom' – appeals to those who know at least *something* of animal magnetism, the nature of its devices and the reputation of its founder. It flatters the reader implicitly with the suggestion that they might already have sufficient knowledge to perhaps need *less* than three months' tuition. There is an invitation to identify oneself with the unprejudiced, and Mainaduc's strategy here recalls Mesmer's own earlier efforts to obtain institutional sanction for his theory. Mainaduc advises his readers that 'Six physicians or surgeons, by applying for a ticket, will be admitted spectators of the public treatment, the patients having obligingly granted their permission'. As with Mesmer's practice in Paris, again, Mainaduc's work in London alternates between instruction, exhibition and treatment. The advertisement advises the reader that 'The hours of consultation are from Seven to Ten; and those of public treatment, from Ten to Two every morning, during which the Doctor cannot visit patients'.

The advertisement's rhetoric, though, turns in the second paragraph, where, having acknowledged 'the numberless publications which have made their appearance against this discovery', Mainaduc establishes a distinction between his own practice and the animal magnetism of the controversial Mesmer:

> The Doctor will only observe, that not one of the means mentioned by the Commissioners in their report, nor in Mr Mesmer's Aphorisms, published in Paris, by Dr Collet de Vaumorel, or in any other

book whatsoever, is employed; nor does he make use of any kind of apparatus or preparation, and to convince them his operations are not confined to any particular place, he will visit patients, and magnetise them when necessary, at their own houses.[111]

Mesmer is pointedly prefixed as 'Mr' throughout the advertisement, where Mainaduc is invariably 'Doctor'. More striking, though, is the specific eschewing of the *baquet*, iron rods and other fixtures common in Paris throughout the 1780s. Mainaduc, both magnetiser and teacher, is the emphatic centre of this medical practice, and his advertisement makes the tacit assumption that the readership will *know* exactly what 'means', 'apparatus' and 'preparation' will *not* feature in the instruction proffered within his Bloomsbury Square chambers.[112]

Mainaduc's aspirations towards establishing a discrete magnetic practice in England certainly appear to have met with a degree of success. In an advertisement published in *The World* in mid-1788, he was to again assert a firm demarcation between himself and Mesmer, and announce also to the public that not all magnetic practitioners active in England bore this teacher's imprimatur: The advertisement advises the reader:

Dr de Mainaduc, by desire of his Disciples, informs the public, that those only who can produce certificates, are to be considered as instructed by him, or capable of practising his doctrine. The science he professes, is totally unconnected with Animal Magnetism, with Electricity, and with the Theories of Mesmer, and of every other Society and Publication whatsoever. Those Gentlemen and Ladies who have not received their certificates, are requested to apply for them on Saturday next.[113]

Certainly, other British teachers of magnetism were by this time actively advertising their rival instruction, often by drawing upon Mesmer's name and the suggestion that the Viennese originator of magnetism had authorised their practice. Only ten days previous to Mainaduc's advertisement, the following announcement was featured in another London newspaper, *The Morning Herald*:

COLLEGE for instructing PUPILS IN MESMER'S PHILOSOPHY OF ANIMAL MAGNETISM, to cause Longevity, and to cure the most excruciating pangs of the Gout, Insanity, Fevers, Obstructions incident to Females, Palsies, Rheumatisms, Deafness, Diseases of the Eyes, and all disorders incident of Men, Women, and Children; for which purpose is a new Philosophical Apparatus, with great improvements, by The REV. J. BELL and S. FREEMAN MD, PROFESSORS of this NEW SCIENCE, And FELLOWS of the PHILOSOPHICAL HARMONIC SOCIETY at PARIS.[114]

'Mr Bell, a pupil to the celebrated Dr Mesmer' and 'the only one who is authorised to practise and teach in Great Britain (as his credentials and certificates from the most eminent persons ... will amply testify)', would certainly appear to have become a major rival to Mainaduc within twelve months of the latter's earliest advertisement in the London press.[115] The Reverend Mr Bell was, like Mainaduc, an active lecturer, and discoursed upon Mesmerism at Dr Brown's residence in Golden Square, charging those in attendance a rather hefty 5s for admission. A more modestly priced serial publication – entitled 'the New System of the World, in the English and French Languages' – was also offered by the clerical magnetist at 2s 6d for each issue.[116]

Bell's proposed syllabus, though, sits somewhat uneasily beside the heavily stressed Christian title whose presence, no doubt, was maintained for the reassurance of the concerned or sceptical enquirer. A more substantial newspaper advertisement, again from June 1788, advises the reader that Bell's pupils are instructed 'in three distinct classes'. The first of these 'are taught Animal magnetism, or the Doctrine of Magnetical Attraction and Repulsion, as practised by the profound Mesmer'. Those in the second class 'are taught Primitive Astronomy or Uranology'. Despite being supposedly 'founded on Newtonian principles', the derivation of this class of instruction from Mesmer's own *Dissertatio Physico-Medica de Planetarum Influxu* of 1766 is made apparent by the admission that a central focus is 'the planetary system as operating on man's body'.[117] The third class of students would appear to be engaged in a revival of alchemy, the 'Hermetic Science' taught to this cohort conveying 'the true method of transmutation of metals' with reference to Paracelsus. One wonders whether 'Any Lady or Gentleman of respectability' – as the advertisement designated its intended market – indeed ventured into the mystic realms of the hermetic class as instructed by Bell, Freeman and a third practitioner, E. Sibley AP.[118] Such fanciful aspirations, certainly, scarcely resemble the more restrained ambitions with which Mainaduc's comparatively laconic advertisements entice the potential disciple.

Mainaduc's attempts to establish and maintain a demarcation between his own practice and that derived from Mesmer would seem to have met with little success, however. An anonymous translator's note to a 1789 French account of the eccentricities of Prince Eugene of Wirtemberg, who apparently 'lived at Paris and plunged into all the follies of Mesmerism' was quick to note for the benefit of English readers that 'Mesmer was the quack-father of the modern magnetists; with whom, by the kind intervention of Mainaduc, we are now become somewhat acquainted'.[119] If this conflation of the two magnetic personalities were not enough, Mainaduc also found himself – as was also the case with several of his disciples – dogged at times by allegations of quackery.[120] A somewhat pungent letter to *Felix Farley's Bristol Journal*, written under the pseudonym of 'Gregory Gape', decries with some irony the apparent expulsion of mesmerism from superstitious, Roman Catholic France and its ready acceptance by 'a politer nation, [of] staunch Protestants; unsuspicious and ready to believe any thing a man says of himself'.[121] This provincial commentator does not spare his own regional audience the vitriol with which he loads his account of magnetism in the English capital.

> It has been asserted, too peremptorily, that a man, cannot communicate knowledge of which he is not possessed; and that Mr Mainaduc is himself possessed of a very moderate share of the Art of Healing, as many in this city can testify. One amongst a cloud of instances, is a young gentleman whom he undertook to cure of fits, if he would take up his residence in London, at the moderate compliment of ten pounds per month; after fourteen months trial he returned unaltered. The fact is admitted, but who in his sober sense ever thought Mr M. capable of removing any crabbed disorder? Does it follow from thence that he cannot teach this art to others? surely no: cannot the Scotch Doctors, who know very little of this art themselves, convey it in perfection to a man whom they never saw, at 500 miles distance, by diploma?[122]

Gape's letter attacks Mainaduc on a number of levels. Clearly, whether as a result of actual residence or merely through targeted advertising, the Irish physician has sought and treated patients in Bristol, but without significant success. A degree of greed on the practitioner's part is also inferred through the pointed inclusion of Mainaduc's tariff. Most significant of all, though, is the closing remark which hinges upon those medical bodies that are willing to grant diplomas to students who have not been personally examined by a competent referee. A question is here advanced regarding Mainaduc's qualification to practise, and its implications cover both conventional therapeutics – he is rendered as 'Mr' rather than 'Dr' throughout – and the magnetic therapy he has supposedly learned in France.[123] Though Mainaduc's ability – or even right – to teach is also questioned by this rhetorical gesture, it embeds within it one further damning interrogation of the physician's mastery of the universal and all-pervasive magnetic fluid. If the fluid itself is of this nature, why was it necessary to summon the patient to London and detain him there for fourteen months at great expense?

Mainaduc's death in 1789 did not stem the flow of disparaging remarks connected with his practice, and a review-article published in the *Edinburgh Review, or Critical Journal* for October 1806 refers again, with some irony, to the unlikely possibility that Mainaduc might project his power across geographical space.

> It is not with medicine alone that the cunning empiric performs his cures. He sometimes operates more successfully by an unusual incomprehensible legerdemain trick. Mesmer convinced thousands of the nobility, and even some men of science in Paris, that he could cure diseases without either medicine or change of diet. He placed his patients round a box full of broken glass, and made them pinch each other's thumbs, while he waved a rod of steel in the air. By employing a mysterious jargon, he even made many believe that they were capable of doing the same; and they paid him large sums for being taught this valuable art. De Mainaduc and Miss Prescott have improved upon this plan. By moving their hands, they could extract any disease out of a sick man's body; swallow it themselves, and then puff it into the air. Distance did not hinder them from operating with success. They could cure a man in India. And, though the knave De Mainaduc, with this wonderful power, died young, the art continues to be practised and paid for magnificently, and the cures are attested by coronets and mitres.[124]

Mesmer's practice is rendered strange, even ridiculous, here. The technology of the *baquet* and the wand, and the systematic nature of the hand gestures, are presented without reference to their philosophical context, and thus rendered meaningless. Likewise, the actions of Mainaduc and his lady disciple, Miss Prescott, are explained only through reference to the mummery that is Mesmer's practice.[125] The two male practitioners are elided here, despite the evident difference in how the magnetic treatment is effected, and the closing remark regarding authoritative testimony neatly elides, also, those who continue to practise magnetism and who present such documents with the vendors of quack chemical remedies who draw upon the names of the allegedly cured in order to sell more successfully to the possibly ill. As the reviewer points out elsewhere in his account of the vaccination controversy,

> This species of unintentional perjury has been very common during the last century in every part of Europe; and the more improbable the fact is, the more numerous are the affidavits, and the respectable the signatures. Clergymen, judges, and peers, are daily swearing, that they have been cured of incurable diseases: but the meanest apothecary smiles with contempt, when he reads their splendid testimonials.[126]

Though the reviewer falls short of specifically naming Mainaduc as one who has employed such testimonials to enhance trade, he *does* associate Perkins with this practice. Naming Perkins specifically as a quack, the reviewer states:

> He quickly printed, with most respectable attestations, many more cures than are now published of the failure of Vaccination. He established a Perkinean Society of gentlemen of consideration, who zealously, to this day, extol the fame of the tractors. Several worthy clergymen purchased tractors, and most patiently and charitably applied them to their poor parishioners. For a time they performed surprising cures, and thought they rescued the afflicted from the extortion of the apothecary.[127]

If Mainaduc is silently implicated in such practices, it is through a rhetorical process of condemnation by proxy and imprecision. If it may be said in this context that 'These miracles are now at an end; the gout and rheumatism rage as formerly; but Perkins has made his fortune', then it may as easily be quietly concluded that similar cynicism is likely to have motivated Mainaduc.[128]

If the testimonials and references, and the averred gentility of the practitioners associated with Mainaduc and his contemporaries, are questionable, so too, apparently, is the intensity of emotion induced by magnetic treatment. Unusually, a hostile commentator, in a book review dated 1810, likens Mainaduc's practice not to Mesmer but to Methodism, a form of evangelical Protestantism viewed with suspicion by the institutional

Anglican Church. Methodism is here manipulated into a form of quack religion, its intensity of emotional introspection being perversely associated in the reviewer's mind with the fearful sacerdotal catharsis of Roman Catholic auricular confession. The reviewer is subsequently unequivocal in his suggestion that both magnetism and Methodism are deleterious to mind and body:

> Of all morbid habits, that of watching our own sensations is one of the most unfortunate; it is by this habit that the miserable hypochondriac induces upon himself the symptoms of any disease that his fancy apprehends, and endures thereby actual sufferings from an imaginary cause; and it was upon the known effects of this habit that that the whole juggle of animal magnetism, as practised in England by De Mainaduc, was founded. But if the act of watching our bodily sensations does itself derange the body, and disturb those vital functions which are only carried on healthily and regularly as long as they are unperceived, it is not less certain that the moral economy of our nature is exposed to a like danger by that system of self-watchfulness which the Methodists require.[129]

Significantly, Mesmer is not mentioned at all in the review. The 'juggle' or deceit advanced by the review elides the rhetorical distance which customarily lies between representations of sectarian proselytising and medical malpractice. In both instances, the 'juggle' is a type of externally inspired introspection in which the self is implicitly made spiritually or physically dis-eased by a directed though unnecessary concentration upon an imagined disorder. Sinners, concentrating upon their sin, become morbidly obsessed with it, and driven to express it in the conventicles of dissenting religion. Hypochondriacs, sensitised to their symptoms and receptive of the suggestions advanced by the magnetiser, effectively conjure up their own disorder, and magnetise themselves into illness. The 'juggle' here is one in which healthy patients are effectively induced to believe in the power of one who would cure them, and make them whole. Mesmerist or Methodist, such jugglers would seem to be an imposition upon the self-sufficiency of the physiological or spiritual individual. The gaze of the magnetist being withdrawn, its power lingers on – as in the case of the fearful sinner – in the self-perpetuating fascination of introspection.

A revival of philosophical quackery:
the reputation of the Marquis de Puységur
in early-nineteenth century Britain

In his survey of hypnotic practice from the time of Mesmer to the twentieth century, Derek Forrest claims that Mainaduc's 'contribution to the theoretical development of the subject' of magnetism 'was non-existent'. Forrest does, however, advance the tantalising suggestion that Mainaduc's vision of magnetism was shaped not by his sometime teacher d'Eslon but by another of Mesmer's immediate disciples, Armand-Marie-Jacques de Chastenet, the Marquis de Puységur.[130] Puységur's relevance to early British magnetic practice, though, is not confined to his alleged influence upon Mainaduc in the eighteenth century. In many respects, Puységur demonstrably influenced the breadth of nineteenth-century British practitioners far more than he might have shaped the specific work of Mainaduc, their most-significant non-Continental forebear. Puységur was, in many respects, an evocative figure in the nineteenth-century revival of animal magnetism in both France and the United Kingdom and, though not as colourful a personality as his Viennese mentor, became an icon upon which both hostile and favourable responses to the revival of magnetic practice in England were to attach their variant opinions.

Puységur's presence in the English media was as often associated with his abstract status as an authority upon mesmerism as with the specific details of his actual practice. He was a central figure in the nineteenth-century revival of animal magnetism in France and in the movement's scientific rehabilitation. This latter was effectively enacted, following the death of Mesmer in 1815, through a formal medical commission which revisited the negative findings contained in the Franklin report of 1784. The conclusions advanced by the Academy of Medicine in Paris in December 1825 were, like those drawn by its eighteenth-century predecessor, publicised modestly in England. The British response to the 1825 report, though, is notably more polemical, and characteristically veers between the incredulous and the condemnatory. In a widely syndicated article provocatively entitled 'Revival of Philosophical Quackery', the pseudonymous 'G' quotes extensively from a translated account written by Dr Albert, a lecturer on French literature, in order to illustrate an indignant editorial surprise that

> the old humbug of that successful quack, Mesmer, which we believed
> to be completely exploded, is reviving with all its original force in

France, under the patronage of the soavans [*sic*] of the Academy of
Medicine.[131]

The 1825 report was evidenced through observations of 'experiments made
at the Hotel-Dieu, under the superintendence of Dr Dupotet, to whose
care had been entrusted a ward of patients, treated exclusively according
to this method of cure'. Puységur, as one of several 'distinguished persons',
provided a further authoritative testimony to that of 'more than thirty
doctors'.[132] If not actually clinical in itself – Puységur was the scion of a
military rather than a medical family – his work could seemingly be easily
associated with magnetic experiments made by others – such as Jules Denis
Dupotet in France and, slightly later, Dr John Elliotson in London. His
signature, as Dr Albert suggests, enjoys a sort of medical *cachet*.

Despite the explicitly clinical ambience of the report, 'G' somewhat
testily contends that 'We should not be surprised if another Abbé Paris,
Bleton, or Perkins, should soon arise with their miracles, their divining
rods, and metallic tractors'.[133] Albert is somewhat more temperate – even
favourable – in his opinions, however, and concludes simply that

> This resolution of the majority of the Academy appears to be partic-
> ularly founded on this fact, that, since the discoveries of Mesmer,
> somnambulism, the most astonishing effect of magnetism, has been
> discovered and observed. This discovery enlarges the theory of
> magnetism, changes its terms, its practice, and results, and impresses
> on it a character of a high respectability, which will henceforward
> repel all accusations tending to attribute it to the reveries of an
> imagination disordered by the illusions of empiricism.[134]

It is the discovery of somnambulism which changes not so much the discipline
of animal magnetism as the nature of the controversy surrounding it in both
France and the United Kingdom. Linked with Dupotet in Dr Albert's
statement, the discovery of somnambulism is almost invariably associated
with Puységur in other contemporary accounts of nineteenth-century
magnetic practice. The adoption of somnambulism as a popular icon of
magnetism, its vision of a lucid unconsciousness eclipsing the evocative
baquets and séances, marks an early shift in the image of the magnetist
away from the magician and towards the clinician. It provokes, further, a
reconsideration of the evidential process. For, if the *baquet* could produce
spectacle without meaning – the symptoms and crises exhibited not always
bearing a substantial relationship to any lesion or trauma apparent within

the physical body – the calmer state of somnambulism was apt to deliver to the witness verbal statements whose veracity might be tested upon the body of the subject and indeed that of the magnetiser also.

Puységur occupies a rather unstable place within the imaginative history of animal magnetism. In modern accounts his work is often viewed as a sort of watershed between mesmeric charlatanry and early psychology. In Derek Forrest's *Hypnotism*, for example, Puységur 'was to secure for himself a niche in the history of hypnotism' not merely because of his pursuit of somnambulism but also on account of his divergence from mesmeric orthodoxy. As Forrest concludes, 'Puységur's resemblance was to a modern psychotherapist – while Mesmer's was closer to a charismatic healer'.[135] For Robin Waterfield, likewise, Puységur's practice signals the first significant challenge to Mesmer's right to define both symptom and theory: somnambulism is 'a different kind of crisis altogether', and Puységur's work was to lead to a recognisable concept in modern clinical thought, 'the alternate-consciousness paradigm'.[136]

The opinion expressed by the British press in the early nineteenth century, however, was somewhat more inclined to associate Puységur with Mesmer, and additionally to undermine the apparent innovation represented by somnambulism through specific reference to certain other magnetic practices which looked to the past rather than defining the future. A survey of Continental magnetic practice, published in *The London Saturday Journal*, on 13 April 1839, for example, took pains to remind its readers that Puységur was an early disciple of Mesmer:

> During the life of Mesmer, several of the French nobles had been initiated, under his instructions, into the mysteries of animal magnetism. Among the most enthusiastic of his disciples was the Marquis de Puységur, a young nobleman, who had just inherited extensive patrimonial possessions. He had assiduously followed the instructions of his master, and had acquired considerable skill in the use of manual magnetism.[137]

The closing sentence would seem to suggest that Puységur was an orthodox, possibly even a dogmatic, enthusiast cast very much in the mould of his teacher. Only the reference to '*manual* magnetism', which suggests the use of hand gestures to induce the crisis, distinguishes Puységur from those who magnetise conventionally by way of the *baquet* and the iron rod. It is the singular act of the practitioner 'moving their hands' that links Puységur's technique to the methodology employed in London by Mainaduc and his disciple, Miss Prescott.[138] Intriguingly, though, the Irish doctor does not seem to have drawn upon the authority of Puységur in his advertisements or public statements. This would seem strange, given that Puységur seems to have at times enjoyed a personal reputation that in many respects served to dissipate the accusations of charlatanry levelled at Mesmer and many of his associates.

Puységur, indeed, is presented in a most indulgent and idealised light, even in accounts which subsequently come to take issue with his practice or his naivety. *The London Saturday Journal*, for example, depicts a bucolic outdoor gathering that hardly resembles those famously mystical scenes enacted during Mesmer's Parisian séances:

> After the death of Mesmer, the Marquis de Puységur resided upon his hereditary domains in the south of France, where he practised animal magnetism upon his own peasantry. Each evening, from spring to autumn, his vassals assembled under a large linden-tree near the marquis's residence. M. de Puységur, who had been educated in the country, was untainted with the profligacy that disgraced his order. He was a kind-hearted, benevolent man, and his feudal rule was light and paternal.[139]

The dark shadow of the *baquet*, however, seldom falls far from these imagined gatherings, even though its substitute in Puységur's practice is as pastoral as the scenes of his rural cures. In some accounts, indeed, 'the shade of his linden-tree' is specifically that of a *baquet* in all but name.[140] Quoting liberally from Charles Mackay's *Memoirs of Extraordinary Popular Delusions* (1841), a short article in *The Hull Packet*, after proclaiming Puységur 'a man of great simplicity and benevolence, raised by his wealth, above all suspicion of imposture', intimates subtly the connection between the Parisian séance and the outdoor clinic. Puységur, like Mesmer, became a victim of his own success or popularity, and like his mentor was forced to consider a mode of mass, rather than individual, therapy.

> In this emergency he hit upon a clever expedient. He had heard Mesmer say that he could magnetise bits of wood – why should he not be able to magnetise a whole tree? It was no sooner thought than done. There was a large elm on the village green at Busancy, under which the peasant girls used to dance on festive occasions, and the old men to sit, drinking their *vin de pays* on the fine summer evenings. M. de Puységur proceeded to this tree and magnetised

it, by first touching it with his hands and then retiring a few steps from it; all the while directing streams of the magnetic fluid from the branches toward the trunk, and from the trunk toward the root. This done, he caused circular seats to be erected round it, and cords suspended from it in all directions. When the patients had seated themselves, they twisted the cords round the diseased parts of their bodies, and held one another firmly by their thumbs to form a direct channel of communication for the passage of the fluid.[141]

The physical resemblance to Parisian practice is glaringly obvious here, from the ropes which stand in for the iron anodes of the conventional *baquet* to the chain of thumbs enacted by those linked together in a communicative circle.[142] As Jessica Riskin and others also note, Mesmer is popularly assumed to have himself magnetised a tree for similar purposes in Paris.[143] Puységur appears to have been fully aware of the implications of his strategy. An undated letter from the Marquis to his brother, quoted in a review article printed in *The Foreign Review* in January 1830 stated that

> I continue to make use of the happy power which I owe to M. Mesmer; and every day I bless him, for I am very useful, and produce many salutary effects on all the sick in the neighbourhood. They flock round my tree; there were more than *one hundred and thirty* of them this morning. There is a continual procession in the country. I pass two hours at my tree every morning. It is the best *baquet* possible, not a leaf of it but communicates health; all feel more or less good effects from it.[144]

Even the mode of magnetising the tree logically suggests how the first *baquet* might itself have received its final charge upon assembly, the magnetist demonstrating, as it were, the transfer of a modicum of his fluid potency into a surrogate that might be accessed without his continuous presence.

It is almost certain that a period of some forty years has been quietly condensed in nineteenth-century accounts such as those reproduced in *The Hull Packet* and *The London Saturday Journal*. Forrest and Waterfield both appear to suggest that the arboreal *baquet* at Busancy (now Buzancy) was charged with magnetic fluid around the time of Puységur's residence there in 1783 or 1784, though neither quote an account such as that rendered by *The Hull Packet* to reveal just how close to Mesmer's model the resource was.[145] Puységur's later years of magnetic practice, in which his thought diverged markedly from the theories of Mesmer, seem to have been little reported in Britain, if at all. This later period is characterised in British accounts by a vagueness which fails to suggest anything beyond a continuation of Puységur's earlier, more identifiably mesmeric, practice.[146] The anonymous preface to an 1833 reprint, in translation, of a number of letters under Puységur's hand suggests, for example, that

> He was kept two years in prison at Soissons, during the reign of terror, and had a narrow escape from the guillotine. In 1799 he was appointed Mayor of Soissons, and in this situation he rendered immense services to the poorer class of the inhabitants. In 1805 he returned to his estates of Busancy, and has, until 1816, devoted his time to the pursuit of his favourite study, Mesmerism.[147]

Even the capitalisation of the name of 'his favourite study' would suggest Puységur's attachment to an enduring mesmeric orthodoxy in the British mind: in France, where his publications needed no translation, he was associated with a more progressive revisionism. Puységur's death in 1825 rendered him unable to address such misrepresentations personally, though translated accounts of his Buzancy experiments, for the most part derived from his private correspondence in the 1780s, continued to be published in English into the 1830s.[148]

If the charge of profiting through the gullibility of wealthy clients could not be levelled against a man who primarily treated peasants without personal financial reward, the British press was quick to cast aspersions upon Puységur's own apparent naivety. He was 'generally uninformed, was weak-minded and credulous, and therefore easily induced to confound the natural with the imagined supernatural' according to *The London Saturday Journal*. In this particular British review of Puységur's practice (and its appendant association with the then-contemporary experiments conducted by the British clinical magnetist, Dr John Elliotson, in London), moreover, there is a quiet suggestion that this beneficent noble magnetist might well have been deceived by patients who were keen to deliver to him the results or outcomes which might please him most. Having constructed Puységur as 'kind-hearted [and] benevolent', the article concludes that

> He was therefore much beloved, and every peasant on his estate became eager to afford him the best opportunities of gratifying his desire. In the course of time these simple-minded rustics became sincere converts to the Mesmerian faith.[149]

The suggestion of manipulation by the patient, or the desire on the part of the subject to please the magnetist, was to be associated not merely with Puységur but also with Elliotson, who was without doubt influenced by the Marquis's practice. The relationship between magnetist and magnetised is thus significantly complicated, the allegation of trickery or collusion passing from operator to operated upon. In a sense, from this time the notion of the patient as dupe is challenged by a more suspicious view that sees the magnetised subject as somehow controlling and exploiting their supposed operator.

The actual nature of Puységur's induced somnambulism, likewise, is reported in such a way that effectively changes the perception of the function and deployment of magnetism. If Mesmer's early practice dissipated disorder through violent crisis, then the more muted phenomena associated with Puységur might be taken as a form of analgesic anaesthesia. Even here, though, an implicitly hostile press fails to grant Puységur the novelty now popularly attached to his name. *The London Saturday Journal* notes:

> Among the other effects perceived in the course of his practice, Mesmer found, that, by the application of magnetism with the hands, he could make particular persons sleep even under acute pain. When this action was found to exist in particular idiosyncrasies, it was taken advantage of to assuage the exacerbation of painful disease; and many patients afflicted with inflammation, chronic rheumatism, gout, and other painful disorders, are said to have derived relief from the sleep thus induced. Such was the state of animal magnetism at the period of Mesmer's death.[150]

Even where Puységur is deemed to have contributed a new aspect of this anaesthetic state – the condition of lucidity that differentiates magnetic somnambulism from simple unconsciousness – his discovery is treated with suspicion, associated with delusion and indeed linked to the activities of later, and unscrupulous, practitioners. *The London Saturday Journal* makes this clear:

> Many of M. de Puységur's assistants in his magnetic experiments, who underwent magnetic sleep, were observed to talk during their slumbers, and even to give rational replies to questions asked them by the magnetiser.[151]

The Hull Packet is more grudging regarding the relationship of the discoverer to the discovery, even though the account it renders says considerably more regarding the nature of the trance condition induced by Puységur's magnetism:

> His great discover, as he called it, was made by chance. One day he magnetised his gardener; and observing him to fall into a deep sleep, it occurred to him that he would address a question to him, as he would have done to a natural somnambulist. He did so, and the man replied with much clearness and precision. M. de Puységur was agreeably surprised: he continued his experiments, and found that in this state of magnetic somnambulism, *the soul of the sleeper was enlarged, and brought into more intimate communion with all nature, and more especially with him, M. de Puységur.*

'Soul', in this context, should not be comprehended in a spiritual sense. The article makes clear that it is a synonym for perception, and thus an enhanced perceptivity is imagined here, where the subject responds to the subtly exercised will of the magnetiser. The account continues:

> He found that all further manipulations were unnecessary; that without speaking or making any sign, he could convey his will to the patient, that he could, in fact, converse with him, soul to soul, without the employment of any physical operation whatever![152]

This aspect of the relationship between magnetiser and magnetised, even more so than the seeming ability of a mesmerist to command a crisis, is the root of those later polemical articles and often scandalous fictions that tease the reader with narratives of abnegated self-control and criminal interference. Though the possibility of such things had been recognised as early as 1784 – the Royal Commission had deposited a confidential report which advised as much – they were yet tempered by the practical application of the somnambulistic state as a diagnostic tool.

   Puységur, here, *is* the pioneer, for Mesmer did not develop this aspect of magnetic sleep. Even here, though, there is a disparaging note sounded, for, as *The London Saturday Journal* phrased it,

> It chanced one day, under the linden-tree, that a girl undergoing the influence of magnetic sleep, being excited to talk by the questions of the noble magnetiser, raved about some imagined internal disease with which she fancied some one present afflicted, and suggested what she stated to be the only mode of cure.

The apparent 'truth' of this diagnosis and the actuality of the outcome predicted by the somnambulist are less significant than the medical doctrine that could with ease be projected from this small incident. The newspaper columnist sees this event as little more than the action of imagination. The 'afflicted' person is not ill at all, but imagines the self successively diseased and then cured as a result of apparently authoritative diagnosis from the somnambulist. The magnetist who lends authority by his presence to the somnambulist's words, likewise, projects a theory from what he imagines to be the evidence of a cure enacted from start to finish before his eyes. So, Puységur:

> saw nothing but a new faculty possessed by magnetised 'somnam-bulists', of examining the interior of the human body, detecting disease, and indicating a remedy for it – a faculty wholly spiritual and unconnected with the universe of matter.

Puységur's lack of scientific rationality, again, leaves him open not merely to the innocent desire to please evinced by his tenants, but also to the manipulations of more cynical or deceitful manipulators. The article continues:

> The fame of the detection of this disease and its cure, spread far and wide through the province; and, as the views of the marquis on the subject were no secret, a host of impostors soon appeared, and, by their juggling, the noble disciple of Mesmer was soon convinced of the truth of that which, till then, he had considered only hypothetical: that magnetic sleep imparted to somnambulists the power of detecting and even prescribing for diseases which baffled medical skill.[153]

Magnetism, having been toppled from its assumed position in France as a panacea by the hostile report of the Franklin Commission, has subsequently presumed to assume another vital role in therapeutics, that of a diagnostic aid. The columnist for *The London Saturday Review*, however, is signally unconvinced, though his attention is not directed exclusively towards the apparently deluded Puységur. Arguably, the rhetorical focus of this article is not the career and practice of a man who died some fourteen years before but the perceived parallel with issues currently taking place within the British medical environment. The columnist is as scathing with regard to the deployment of somnambulism by later practitioners as he is regarding Puységur's readiness to interpret it as a viable diagnostic tool. The article goes so far as to schedule somnambulism as 'an effect of magnetism'

> by which thousands of wise men have been deluded, and upon which all the absurdities of spiritual or psychological magnetism have since been founded, even to the late display at the North London Hospital.[154]

The display in question was conducted by another French magnetist, the same Dr Dupotet whom Dr Albert noted as being active at that celebrated Parisian hospital, the Hôtel Dieu, in 1826. It is not a display, though, without repercussions, for its influence conclusively links nineteenth-century French magnetism with its English counterpart. Dupotet's visit to London, in many respects, is the single, most important event which facilitated the functional link between the discoveries of Puységur and the controversial practice of Dr John Elliotson. From this point, therapeutic magnetism in the United Kingdom becomes predominantly the preserve of a class of conventionally educated physicians who deploy magnetic therapy not in the salon but upon the hospital ward.

Notes

1   Anon., 'Mesmerism and Hypnotism', *Quarterly Review*, July 1890, 234–59 at p. 235.
2   Anon., 'The Medical Adviser', *The Penny Satirist*, 1 July 1843, p. 4, col. 3.
3   Anon., 'Hypnotism', *The Leisure Hour*, July 1887, p. 454, col. 1.
4   Anon., 'Mesmerism and Hypnotism', *Quarterly Review*, July 1890, pp. 236, 242, 243.
5   Anon., 'Mesmerism and Hypnotism', *Quarterly Review*, July 1890, p. 244.
6   Anon., 'Mesmerism and Hypnotism', *Quarterly Review*, July 1890, p. 258.
7   Robin Waterfield, *Hidden Depths: The Story of Hypnosis* (London: Pan, 2004), pp. 80, 85.
8   Derek Forrest, *Hypnotism: A History* (London: Penguin, 2000), pp. 17, 33.
9   Charles d'Eslon (or Deslon), physician to the younger brother of Louis XVI, was a rare enthusiast for Mesmer's theories within the institutionalised body of Parisian medical practitioners. It was d'Eslon, rather than Mesmer, whose actual practice formed the focus of the 1784 Royal Commission, headed by Benjamin Franklin. See A. R. G. Owen, *Hysteria, Hypnosis and Healing: The Work of J. M. Charcot* (London: Dennis Dobson, 1971), p. 172.
10 Raymond E. Fancher, *Pioneers of Psychology* (New York: W. W. Norton and Co., 1979), p. 176.

11 The glass harmonica (or armonica), a treadle-powered successor to earlier instruments constructed from collections of water-filled glasses, was reputedly invented by the same Benjamin Franklin who chaired the unfavourable 1784 Royal Commission charged with investigating mesmerism. A 1761 example, built in London, is in the collection of the Franklin Institute in Philadelphia: see www.fi.edu/learn/sci-tech/armonica/armonica.php?cts=benfranklin-recreation [accessed 10 February 2014].

12 Fancher, *Pioneers of Psychology*, p. 176.

13 Waterfield, *Hidden Depths*, p. xv.

14 Waterfield, *Hidden Depths*, p. xv, my italics.

15 Waterfield, *Hidden Depths*, pp. xv–xvi.

16 See, for example, Stephen J. Gould, 'The Chain of Reason vs the Chain of Thumbs', *Natural History*, July 1989, 12–21, at p. 14, col. 1.

17 In places, Owen's phrasing differs only superficially from that of the English translation of Binet and Féré's 1887 work. Compare, for example, the description of Mesmer's delegation of magnetic practice on to assistants or *valets toucheurs* and the description of the *baquet* or magnetised bath in the two works. See Owen, *Hysteria, Hypnosis and Healing*, p. 172; Alfred Binet and Charles Féré, *Animal Magnetism* (London: Kegan, Paul, Trench, 1887), p. 8.

18 Binet and Féré, *Animal Magnetism*, p. 8

19 Binet and Féré, *Animal Magnetism*, p. 9.

20 Binet and Féré, *Animal Magnetism*, p. 11.

21 Anon., 'Animal Magnetism', *Leigh Hunt's London Journal*, 3 September 1834, p. 182, col. 3.

22 Anon., 'Animal Magnetism', *Leigh Hunt's London Journal*, 3 September 1834, p. 182, col. 3.

23 John Milton, 'Il Penseroso' in L. D. Lerner, ed., *The Penguin Poets: Milton* (Harmondsworth: Penguin, 1953), 71–6, at p. 75.

24 Anon., 'Animal Magnetism', *Leigh Hunt's London Journal*, 3 September 1834, p. 182, col. 3.

25 Anon., 'Mesmerism', *The Satirist, or, The Censor of the Times*, 11 September 1842, p. 291, original italics.

26 Anon., 'Animal Magnetism', *Fraser's Magazine for Town and Country*, 1/6 (July 1830), 673–84, at p. 676, col. 1.

27 Anon., 'Animal Magnetism', *Leigh Hunt's London Journal*, 3 September 1834, p. 182, col. 3; Anon., 'Mesmerism', *The Satirist, or, The Censor of the Times*, 11 September 1842, p. 291.

28 See, for example, Anon., 'Drawing-Room Necromancy', *The Englishwoman's Domestic Magazine*, 1 August 1862, 156–63, at p. 159.

29 Anon., 'Animal Magnetism', *The Penny Satirist*, 9 September 1837, p. 2, cols 1–2 at col. 1.

30 Anon., 'Animal Magnetism', *The Penny Satirist*, 9 September 1837, p. 2, cols 1–2, at col. 1.

31 Mesmer was associated with the French Masonic Lodge Les Philadelphes, where Benjamin Franklin had been initiated into American Freemasonry in Pennsylvania as early as 1831. See John Hamill and Robert Gilbert, *Freemasonry: A Celebration of the Craft* (London: Angus Books, 2004), pp. 238, 232.

32 D'Eslon, for example, states that 'In Magnetism, nature offers an universal means of curing and preserving mankind'. Quoted in Anon., 'Animal Magnetism', *Fraser's Magazine for Town and Country*, 1/6 (July 1830), p. 676, col. 2.

33 Derek Forrest reproduces, as a representative example, the contract between the Marquis de Lafayette and Mesmer, which was signed on 5 April 1784: see Forrest, *Hypnotism*, pp. 37–8.

34 Consider, for example, an advertisement for Monsieur Verbeck, whose performances at London's Piccadilly Hall aspired to produce, twice daily and by stage mesmerism, 'some scientific and extraordinary experiments, such as those done daily at the Salpêtrière Hospital by Dr Charcot of the French Medical Academy in Paris'. Verbeck's performances consisted of 'a series of wonderful illusions' and 'some very funny experiments', the latter being distinguished by such erudite titles as 'The Swimmer', 'The Itching', 'Open Mouthed' and, wondrously, 'Man Transformed to Woman'. See: 'Verbeck, Piccadilly Hall' [advertisement], *The Standard*, 11 April 1887, p. 1, col. 5. Tellingly, advertisements for 'the Egyptian Hall, England's Home of Mystery' and Madame Tussaud's waxworks appear in the same column.

35 Though there are now reputedly fewer than ten exponents of the instrument worldwide, a number of performances on the glass harmonica are available on compact disk. See www.glassarmonica.com/cds.php [accessed 10 February 2014].

36 Published between 1929 and 1991, *The Listener* was envisaged – in the words of its last editor, Peter Fiddick – as 'a way of extending the life and influence of the fledgling BBC's thoughtful broadcast "talks" and of enhancing the BBC's own reputation'. The BBC held control of the publication until 1987. See http://news.bbc.co.uk/hi/english/static/the_listener/story20.stm [accessed 10 February 2014].

37 Jonathan Miller, 'Mesmerism', *The Listener*, 90 (22 November 1973), 685–90, at p. 686, col. 2.

38 Miller, 'Mesmerism', p. 686, col. 1.

39 'G', 'Observations on Animal Magnetism', *Blackwood's Edinburgh Magazine*, 1/6 (September 1817), 563–7, at p. 565, col. 1. Most detailed accounts of Mesmer's séances appear to be derived (with or without attribution) from the report issued by the 1784 Royal Commission. Usually associated with the name of Benjamin Franklin, much of the document was written or phrased

by Jean-Sylvain Bailly. See, for example, Anon., 'Animal Magnetism', *Fraser's Magazine for Town and Country*, 1/6 (July 1830), p. 677, cols 1–2.

40 'G', 'Observations on Animal Magnetism', p. 565, cols. 1–2.

41 'G', 'Observations on Animal Magnetism', pp. 564, col. 2; 565, col. 1.

42 Franz-Anton Mesmer, *Mémoire sur la découverte du magnétisme animal* (1779), translated as 'Dissertation on the Discovery of Animal Magnetism' in George Bloch, trans., *Mesmerism: A Translation of the Original Scientific and Medical Writings of F. A. Mesmer* (Los Altos: William Kaufmann, inc., 1980), 43–78, at p. 72. Accounts of the treatment of Miss Paradis under Mesmer's care are given in Waterfield, *Hidden Depths*, pp. 75–7, and Forrest, *Hypnotism*, pp. 12–16.

43 Anon., 'Galvanism', *Hampshire Telegraph and Portsmouth Gazette*, 4 April 1803, p. 2, col. 4. My italics.

44 Anon., 'Galvanism', *Hampshire Telegraph and Portsmouth Gazette*, 4 April 1803, p. 2, col. 4. The fluid analogy was used in connection with electricity as late as 1882. See 'Electricity' in John M. Ross, ed., *The Illustrated Globe Encyclopædia of Universal Information* (London: Thomas C. Jack, 1882), 12 vols, Vol. 4, p. 512, col. 2.

45 Demonstrations of contemporary electrical technologies such as Leyden jars and Voltaic piles frequently occur in reports of demonstrations conducted in public arenas such as mechanics' institutes, provincial assembly rooms and school lecture theatres. See, for example, Anon., 'Royal Institution: Mr Davy's Lectures on the Elements of Chemical Philosophy', *The Morning Chronicle*, 17 February 1812, p.3, col. 2; Anon., 'Mechanics' Institution', *The Derby Mercury*, 29 October 1828, p. 3, col. 3; Anon., 'The British Association', *The Belfast News-Letter*, 14 August 1835, p. 1, cols 4–5.

46 See, for example, the eighteenth-century example depicted in Thomas B. Greenslade, Jr, 'Nineteenth Century Textbook Illustrations 40: Discovery of the Leiden Jar', *The Physics Teacher*, 32 (1994), 536–7.

47 Henry Christmas, 'Essay on the Origin and Progress of Animal Magnetism', *Analyst: A Quarterly Journal of Science, Literature, Natural History, and the Fine Arts*, 10/30 (June 1840), 464–83, at p. 468.

48 Anon., 'Galvanism', *Hampshire Telegraph and Portsmouth Gazette*, 4 April 1803, p. 2, col. 4; Anon., 'Bury Mechanics' Institution', *The Bury and Norwich Post: Or, Suffolk and Norfolk Telegraph, Essex, Cambridge and Ely Intelligencer*, 18 April 1832, p. 2, col. 3.

49 'Electricity, Animal', in Ross, ed., *The Illustrated Globe Encyclopædia*, Vol. 4, p. 514, col. 1, original italics.

50 The analogy was often made also in lectures where no such demonstration was actually enacted. See Anon., 'Electrical Society', *The Morning Post*, 6 October 1838, p. 3, col. 5.

51 Anon., 'The Todmorden Literary and Scientific Society', *The Manchester Times and Gazette*, 27 May 1837, p. 2, col. 7.

52 'G', 'Observations on Animal Magnetism', p. 565, col. 1.

53 Anon., 'Popular Science: A Word or Two on Mesmerism, Epoch 1', *The Lady's Newspaper*, 30 January 1847, p. 102. The words are attributed to 'A late gifted writer'.

54 Anon., 'Animal Magnetism', *Cleave's London Satirist and Gazette of Variety*, 9 December 1837, p. 2. In this account, *baquet* is not italicised. Cf. also Christmas, 'Essay on the Origin and Progress of Animal Magnetism', p. 471.

55 Anon., 'Popular Science: A Word or Two on Mesmerism, Epoch 1', p. 102, my italics.

56 Anon., 'Animal Magnetism', *Leigh Hunt's London Journal*, 3 September 1834, p. 182, col. 3.

57 'G', 'Observations on Animal Magnetism', p. 565, col. 1.

58 Anon., 'Popular Science: A Word or Two on Mesmerism, Epoch 1', p. 102.

59 For a late affirmation of this belief, see E. B. Foote, *Dr Foote's Home Cyclopedia of Popular Medical, Social and Sexual Science*, Twentieth Century revised and Enlarged Edition (London: L. N. Fowler, 1901), p. 331.

60 See, for example, 'G', 'Observations on Animal Magnetism', p. 566, col. 1; Forrest, *Hypnotism*, p. 21; David A. Gallo and Stanley Finger, 'The Power of a Musical Instrument: Franklin, the Mozarts, Mesmer and the Glass Armonica', *History of Psychology*, 3/4 (2000), 326–43, at pp. 331–3.

61 'G', 'Observations on Animal Magnetism', p. 565, col. 1.

62 Anon., 'Animal Magnetism', *Cleave's London Satirist and Gazette of Variety*, 9 December 1837, p. 2; Cf. also Christmas, 'Essay on the Origin and Progress of Animal Magnetism', p. 471.

63 Anon., 'Popular Science: A Word or Two on Mesmerism, Epoch 1', p. 102.

64 'G', 'Observations on Animal Magnetism', p. 566, col. 2.

65 Anon., 'Popular Science: A Word or Two on Mesmerism, Epoch 1', p. 102.

66 Christmas, 'Essay on the Origin and Progress of Animal Magnetism', p. 467. Original italics. This letter is reproduced, also, in Anon., 'Animal Magnetism', *Fraser's Magazine*, 1/6 (July 1830), p. 675, cols 1–2.

67 For a review of the terms, findings and report of the Royal Academy of Sciences and the Faculty of Medicine, and that produced in parallel by the [French] Royal Society of Medicine, see Forrest, *Hypnotism*, pp. 39–51.

68 See, for example, Waterfield, *Hidden Depths*, pp. 88–92; Stephen Jay Gould, 'The Chain of Reason vs the Chain of Thumbs', *Natural History*, July 1989, 12–21, *passim*.

69 'G', 'Observations on Animal Magnetism', p. 567, col. 1.

70 'G', 'Observations on Animal Magnetism', p. 563, col. 1.

71 'Animal Magnetism' [advertisement], *St James's Chronicle, or The British Evening Post*, 16 December 1784, p. 3, col. 4.

72 'G', 'Observations on Animal Magnetism', p. 567, col. 1.

73 Waterfield, *Hidden Depths*, p. 133.

74 Howard W. Haggard, 'The First Published Attack on Perkinism: An Anonymous Eighteenth Century Poetical Satire', *Yale Journal of Biology and Medicine*, 9/2 (1936), 137–53, at p. 138.

75 A Victorian example is given in Waterfield, *Hidden Depths*, pp. 159–60.

76 'American Metallic Tractors' [advertisement], *The Oracle and Public Advertiser*, 22 May 1797, p. 1, col. 3.

77 'Metallic Tractors' [advertisement], *The Star*, 1 December 1798, p. 1, col. 4. Original capitalisation. A shorter version of this advertisement, referring only to Perkins's book, appears under the title 'Just published, price 2s 6d', in *The Weekly Register*, 18 July 1798, p. 110, col. 3.

78 'Metallic Tractors' [advertisement], *The Star*, 1 December 1798, p. 1, col. 4. This addendum to the advertisement is reproduced also in *The Morning Post and Gazetteer*, 4 January 1799, p. 1, col. 2.

79 Johan Daniel Herholdt and Carl Gottlob Rafn, *Experiments with the Metallic Tractors in Rheumatic and Gouty Affections, Inflammations and Various Topical Diseases*, ed. B. J. Perkins, trans Tode and Kampfmuller (London: J. Johnson, 1799). Perkins is almost certainly the contributor of the 'Reports of about one hundred and fifty cases in England' which concludes the volume.

80 Anon., 'Experiments with the Metallic Tractors' [review], *The Oracle and Daily Advertiser*, 24 October 1799, p. 1, col. 4.

81 Anon., 'Experiments with the Metallic Tractors' [review], *The Oracle and Daily Advertiser*, 24 October 1799, p. 2, col. 1. Original italics and capitalisation.

82 Waterfield, *Hidden Depths*, p. 90.

83 Anon., 'Experiments with the Metallic Tractors' [review], *The Oracle and Daily Advertiser*, 24 October 1799, p. 2, col. 1. Original italics.

84 *Lloyd's Evening Post*, 9 June 1800, p. 554, col. 4.

85 For an account of this work accessible to those not subscribing to the *Philosophical Transactions*, see Anon., 'Article VI. *Philosophical Transactions of the Royal Society of London* for the Year 1800', *Critical Review, or, Annals of Literature*, 32 (July 1801), 297–8.

86 Anon., 'Article VI. *Philosophical Transactions of the Royal Society of London* for the Year 1800', *Critical Review, or, Annals of Literature*, 32 (July 1801), 297–8, at p. 297. For a later account of the communications between Volta and Banks, see Anon., 'Electricity and the Electric Telegraph', *Cornhill Magazine*, 2/7 (July 1860), 61–73, at p. 63.

87 Anon., 'Article VI. *Philosophical Transactions of the Royal Society of London* for the Year 1800', *Critical Review, or, Annals of Literature*, 32 (July 1801), p. 298.

88 'Perkinism' in Richard Hoblyn, *A Dictionary of Terms Used in Medicine and the Collateral Sciences*, Fourth Edition (London: Whittaker and Co., 1849), p. 232, col. 1. First italics mine.

89 The more prestigious Royal Commission, which produced the Franklin Report

remains the best known of these, though the Baron de Breteuil, minister at the Maison du Roi, was involved with a parallel investigation. See also Forrest, *Hypnotism*, p. 39.

90 Anon., 'Odds and Ends', *The Penny Satirist*, 29 August 1840, p. 4, col. 1.

91 Anon., 'Medical Delusions of the Past', *The Penny Satirist*, 20 May 1843, p. 1, col. 3.

92 Anon., 'Odds and Ends', *The Penny Satirist*, 29 August 1840, p. 4, col. 1.

93 Waterfield, *Hidden Depths*, pp. 90–1.

94 A Dr Renwick also apparently demonstrated the fallacy of the tractors, possibly in Liverpool. See Anon., 'Animal Magnetism', Supplement to *The Liverpool Mercury*, 24 November 1837, p. 1, col. 6.

95 Mesmer, intriguingly, would appear to have subsidised the free treatments he offered to indigent Parisians through the high prices charged to his fashionable clients. See Waterfield, *Hidden Depths*, p. 80; Forrest, *Hypnotism*, p. 21.

96 See, for example, Anon., 'Popular Science: A Word or Two on Mesmerism, Epoch 1', p. 102.

97 Quoted in Anon., 'Animal Magnetism', *Fraser's Magazine*, 1/6 (July 1830), p. 676, col. 1.

98 'Letter from M. Mesmer, Doctor of Medicine at Vienna, to A. M. Unzer, Doctor of Medicine, on the Medicinal Usage of the Magnet' (1775), reprinted in George Bloch, trans., *Mesmerism: A Translation of the Original Scientific and Medical Writings of F. A. Mesmer* (Los Altos: William Kaufmann, inc., 1980), pp. 25–9, at pp. 27–8; reprinted in Anon., 'Animal Magnetism', *Fraser's Magazine*, 1/6 (July 1830), p. 675, cols 1–2.

99 Mesmer himself made this point in 1781 (admittedly in a footnote written in French, rather than in English). Such detail was apt to be lost while attention was customarily directed to the spectacular activities that took place around the *baquet*: see Franz Anton Mesmer, 'Catechism on Animal Magnetism', in Bloch, trans., *Mesmerism*, pp. 79–86, at p. 83, n. 1.

100 Anon., 'Animal Magnetism', *The Lady's Newspaper*, 16 July 1853, p. 23, col. 3.

101 Alison Winter, *Mesmerized: Powers of Mind in Victorian Britain* (Chicago: University of Chicago Press, 1998), p. 5.

102 There are several variant spellings of Mainaduc's middle name. 'Bonniot' is used by Forrest, and is the spelling listed in Boyle's *General London Guide*; see Forrest, *Hypnotism*, p. 125; Patrick Boyle, *The General London Guide; or, Tradesman's Directory for the Year 1794* (London: Patrick Boyle, 1794), p. 105. Bonniet is used in a 1785 column advertisement for Mainaduc's *Veritas*: see 'In the Press, and Will Speedily Be Published' [advertisement], *The General Evening Post*, 9–11 June 1785, p. 3, col. 4. A notice of Mainaduc's sudden death from apoplexy in 1797 gives the spelling as Boniot: see 'Died', *London Packet or New Lloyd's Evening Post*, 22–4 March 1797, p. 3, col. 4.

103 Forrest, *Hypnotism*, pp. 125–6.

104 Forrest, *Hypnotism*, p. 126.

105 More's letter, extracted from the *Life of Mrs Hannah More* (1834), was widely syndicated, and appeared in a number of provincial newspapers: see Anon., 'Animal Magnetism', *The Derby Mercury*, 21 February 1844, p. 4, col. 4; Anon., 'Varieties', *Berrow's Worcester Journal*, 15 February 1844, p. 4, col. 1.

106 Forrest, *Hypnotism*, p. 126.

107 Anon., 'Further Particulars of Dr Jemmet Brown, Late Archbishop of Tuam', *European Magazine and London Review*, 34 (September 1798), 164–8, at p.165, original italics. This article was reproduced in *Walker's Hibernian Magazine, or, Compendium of Entertaining Knowledge*, October 1798, 706–11, at p. 706.

108 Forrest, *Hypnotism*, p. 125.

109 Anon., 'Monthly Catalogue: Medical', *Monthly Review*, 74 (June 1786), p. 477.

110 See: 'Mainaduc's Cures (Account of) with Pamphlets and Extracts from News Papers', in *A Catalogue of the Entire and Valuable Library of the Late Rev. Michael Lort, DD, FRS, and AS, which will be Sold by Auction, by Leigh and Sotheby* (London: Leigh and Sotheby, 1791), p. 96; Mainaduc's *On Animal Magnetism* is indexed in *The Monthly Review*, 74 (1797), at p. 477.

111 'Animal Magnetism' [advertisement], *The Morning Herald and Daily Advertiser*, 24 October 1785, p. 1, col. 2. Original punctuation and capitalisation.

112 Indeed, Mainaduc does not appear to have even possessed a *baquet*, at least at the time of his death. The auction of his goods, conducted on 12–13 June 1789, included the customary 'Collection of anatomical preparations, in spirits and dry, and in a high state of preservation, comprising the various parts of the human body, several blood vessel subjects, midwifery figures, &c., and a quantity of surgical instruments, &c.', as well as a 'large barrel organ' and an 'organized piano forte'. Also included were 'a large quantity of benches and stages … calculated for a lecture room'. See 'Anatomical Preparations' and 'Curious Preparations' [advertisements], *The Oracle and Daily Advertiser*, 11 June 1799, p. 4, col. 2.

113 'Dr de Mainaduc' [advertisement], *The World*, 17 June 1788, p. 2, col. 1. Original punctuation and capitalisation.

114 'College for Instructing Pupils in Mesmer's Philosophy' [advertisement], *The Morning Herald*, 7 June 1788, p. 1, col. 2. Original punctuation and capitalisation.

115 'Animal Magnetism' [advertisement], *The Morning Post and Daily Advertiser*, 6 February 1786, p. 1, col. 2.

116 'New System of the World' [advertisement], *The World*, 26 May 1788, p. 1, col. 2.

117 The *Dissertatio Physico-Medica de Planetarum Influxu* was submitted by Mesmer as part of his assessment in medicine in Vienna. For a translation, see Franz Anton Mesmer, 'Physical-Medical Treatise on the Influence of the Planets' in Bloch, trans., *Mesmerism*, pp. 1–22.

118 'College for Instruction in Elementary Philosophy' [advertisement], *The World*, 26 June 1788, p. 1, col. 2.

119 Gabriel-Honoré de Riquetti, Comte de Mirabeau, *The Secret History of the Court of Berlin* (London: S. Bladon, 1789), Vol. 2, p. 200, note r.

120 Forrest lists among these presumably certificated 'disciples' the names of 'Parker, Yedal, Hollway, Cue and Prescott' as well as 'Mr and Mrs de Loutherberg' and 'a Mary Pratt': see Forrest, *Hypnotism*, pp. 126–7.

121 Gregory Gape, 'To the Printers' [letter], *Felix Farley's Bristol Journal*, 20 June 1789, p. 4, cols 4–5, at col. 4.

122 Gape, 'To the Printers', p. 4, cols 4–5.

123 The use of 'Mr', as the distinguishing title of a hospital consultant who might previously have been referred to as 'Dr', is not applicable in this case for Mainaduc – as his publicity betrays – is in private rather than institutional practice.

124 Anon., 'Art. III. On Vaccine Inoculation, by Robert Willan MD, FAS', *Edinburgh Review, or Critical Journal*, 9/17 (October 1806), 32–66, at pp. 55–6.

125 According to a contemporary source, 'Miss Prescott' was 'the friend and executrix of the late Dr Mainaduc, whom she assisted in his lectures and in his attendance on his credulous patients. After his death she published his lectures at the price of five guineas': Anon., *A Biographical Dictionary of the Living Authors of Great Britain and Ireland* (London: Printed for Henry Colburn, 1816), p. 283, col. 1. This may be the same Miss Prescott referenced by Forrest: see note 120, above.

126 Anon., 'Art. III. On Vaccine Inoculation', p. 55. The smiling apothecary, as the article makes clear, is aware that what constitutes a curative dose for one man may be fatal to another. There is no such thing as a universal chemical cure.

127 Anon., 'Art. III. On Vaccine Inoculation', p. 56.

128 Anon., 'Art. III. On Vaccine Inoculation', p. 56.

129 Anon., 'Art. XIII. Hints to the Public and the Legislature, on the Nature and Effect of Evangelical Preaching. By a Barrister', *Quarterly Review*, 4/8 (November 1810), 480–514, at p. 498. The analogy with Roman Catholicism and the Confessional is drawn on p. 497.

130 Forrest, *Hypnotism*, p. 126.

131 'G' [pseud.], 'Revival of Philosophical Quackery', *The Liverpool Mercury*, 17 November 1826, p. 158, col. 1. Dr Albert's article follows this introduction under the discrete title of 'Regeneration of Mesmerism in France'. Both were reprinted in *The Kaleidoscope; or, Literary and Scientific Mirror*, 21 November 1826, p. 158, col. 3.

132 Dr Albert, 'Regeneration of Mesmerism in France', *The Liverpool Mercury*, 17 November 1826, p. 158, col. 1.

133 'G' [pseud.], 'Revival of Philosophical Quackery', p. 158, col. 1.

134 Albert, 'Regeneration of Mesmerism in France', p. 158, col. 1.

135 Forrest, *Hypnotism*, pp. 70, 83.

136 Waterfield, *Hidden Depths*, pp. 105, 107.

137 Anon., 'Animal Magnetism', *The London Saturday Journal*, 1/15 (13 April 1839), 232–3, at p. 232, col. 2.

138 Anon., 'Art. III. On Vaccine Inoculation', p. 56.

139 Anon., 'Animal Magnetism', *The London Saturday Journal*, p. 233, col. 1.

140 Anon., 'Animal Magnetism', *The London Saturday Journal*, p. 233, col. 1.

141 Anon., 'Animal Magnetism', *The Hull Packet*, 18 February 1842, p. 3, col. 4. A later section of this article is attributed to *Mackay's Memoirs of Popular Delusions* (1841), the whole being published within a section of the newspaper entitled 'Our Snap Book; or Extracts from Recently Published Works and Public Journals'.

142 Another French account of Puységur's induction of what might be termed the 'passive' crisis notes the presence of 'an iron rod about fifteen inches in length', though there is no evidence that this information was available to the British public: see Forrest, *Hypnotism*, pp. 75–6

143 See Jessica Riskin, *Science in the Age of Sensibility: The Sentimental Empiricists of the French Enlightenment* (Chicago: University of Chicago Press, 2002), p. 201.

144 Anon., 'Art. V. 1 Histoire Critique de Magnétisme Animal, par T. P. F. Deleuze', *Foreign Review*, 5/9 (January 1830), 96–124, at p. 109.

145 Waterfield, *Hidden Depths*, pp. 105–6; Forrest, *Hypnotism*, p. 75.

146 A rare acknowledgement is found in Anon., 'Art. V. 1 Histoire Critique de Magnétisme Animal, par T. P. F. Deleuze', p. 114.

147 Le Marquis de Puységur, 'The Phenomena of Magnetism', *The Monthly Magazine, or British Register*, 16/96 (December 1833), 681–7, at p. 683.

148 See, for example: Anon., 'Art. V. 1 Histoire Critique de Magnétisme Animal, par T. P. F. Deleuze', pp. 106–9; Puységur, 'The Phenomena of Magnetism', pp. 683–7.

149 Anon., 'Animal Magnetism', *The London Saturday Journal*, p. 233, col. 1.

150 Anon., 'Animal Magnetism', *The London Saturday Journal*, p. 232, col. 1.

151 Anon., 'Animal Magnetism', *The London Saturday Journal*, p. 233, col. 1.

152 Anon., 'Animal Magnetism', *The Hull Packet*, 18 February 1842, p. 3, col. 4, original italics.

153 Anon., 'Animal Magnetism', *The London Saturday Journal*, p. 233, col. 2.

154 Anon., 'Animal Magnetism', *The London Saturday Journal*, p. 233, col. 1.

2

Medical magnetism

The medical profession has obtained considerable credit
for an imputed sagacity in resisting imposition, for an
exemption from the usual liabilities to be humbugged
by appeals to the imagination. Dealing as the physician
does with such positive and tangible matters as chemistry,
anatomy, and materia medica; being habitually conversant
with the sensible properties of a large range of substances,
it is supposed that such a person must be especially guarded
against the delusions of metaphysical abstractions, and
against the substitution of words for things. That this
opinion is well founded we very much doubt.

The Athenæum, 1838[1]

MEDICINE HAS ALWAYS BEEN more than a functional process
of diagnosis and palliative or curative treatment. As *The Athenæum*
makes clear, it is an institution necessarily concerned with the policing of
epistemological boundaries as much as it is a profession engaged in actual
therapeutic practice. This opening statement, penned by an anonymous
reviewer in 1838, initiates a long discussion which explores the relationship
between established medical practice and heterodox innovation. The
article's focus, however, is not the collective power of professionalism but
rather the arguably pivotal role that may be played by the individual practitioner in the accretion of new practices to the existing curative regime. The
reviewer goes on to argue that the individual physician is at times capable of

frustrating the greater profession's reputation for scientific objectivity and
empirical assessment. In such cases, enthusiasm would appear to eclipse
judgement. Hence,

> When, therefore, we hear of Doctor this or Doctor the other being
> decidedly convinced of this startling novelty, a staunch advocate for
> that marvellous discovery, we think the odds are rather against the
> discrimination of the said doctors, than in favour of the miracle.
> The truth is, that a love of the marvellous is a disease which runs in
> the blood; the infirmity is, as we have already hinted [*Athenæum* No.
> 542], obviously constitutional; and Lord Winchelsea was perfectly
> right when he protested the other day against superstition being
> confined to any one class in society.[2]

Such practitioners – being no doubt mindful of both their own local practice
and the personal gains to be had by being associated with progressive or
fashionable therapeutics – are inclined to 'daily and almost hourly put
forth with such eager confidence, announcing striking and multiplied
cures, performed by certain drugs or therapeutic processes'. Such 'eager
confidence' is, as the reviewer tartly notes, usually short lived: characteristically, these 'drugs and processes, after a brief but extensive popularity,
are abandoned as fallacious and consigned to oblivion'.[3]

The reviewer, though, appears perceptibly less concerned by the habitual
faddishness of individual physicians than with the illogical nature of the
profession's sporadic commitment to processes that he likens not merely
to abstract metaphysics but also to simple superstition. He queries, indeed,
why the unprecedented qualities of such innovations do not in themselves
provoke a healthy scepticism. Concerned, somewhat, that the originators
of medical innovations are too readily accepted on the basis of their
public reputations – they being apparently 'men of known probity, and far
removed from the suspicion of voluntary deception' – the reviewer thus
queries the respective place the unprecedented *should* occupy with regard
to existing knowledge:

> every new fact alleged on authority is credible in proportion as it
> harmonizes with previous knowledge. Every anomaly it presents is a
> reason for hesitation; and there is a point beyond which the dictates
> of common sense cannot be forced.[4]

The readiness of the practitioner to give credence to such unprecedented
hypotheses, indeed, renders him inferior in logic not merely to more

cautious or conservative members of his own profession but also to those unqualified persons who, none the less, are possessed of a modicum of judgement and common sense. A cautionary note is thus sounded:

> It is not indeed the circumstance of possessing much learning, of being stocked with an extensive assortment of ideas, that qualifies for the proper estimate of evidence. It is possible to possess a most ample and complete chest of tools, without being able to use any one of them in a workmanlike manner. If the original conception of the mind be not sound, if the natural capacity for cool judgement be superseded by a too fervid imagination, acquirements serve only to overload and embarrass; and we often find a self-educated man of natural shrewdness judging more soundly than very learned professional men, even in respect to their own specialities.

A general reader, it seems, may be more discriminating than one whose enthusiasm has overtaken his or her discretion. The writer of the *Athenaeum* review, implicitly, is just such a reader. He thus proposes a complicity with the piece's recipient – who is likewise a reader of 'natural shrewdness', whatever the formality of his or her education – and encourages him or her to eschew any concurrence with the intellectually disharmonious hypotheses advanced by 'Hot-brained enthusiasts'.[5] Seemingly inevitably, the focus of the reviewer's concern here is one of the many sporadic revivals of interest in animal magnetism which preoccupied the British medical profession up to the close of the nineteenth century.

'The English Pope of animal magnetism': Baron Dupotet, the hospital and the private consulting room

The Athenæum review is nominally concerned with two published works: *An Introduction to the Study of Animal Magnetism* by the French mesmerist Baron Dupotet de Sennevoy; and *Animal Magnetism and Homeopathy* by Edwin Lee, a member of the British Royal College of Surgeons.[6] Its rhetoric, as has been suggested, though, is very much directed towards questioning why magnetism has even been accorded a continued hearing by conventional medical practitioners. Dupotet, though a Frenchman, is denominated 'the English Pope of animal magnetism' in the review, and the writer takes pains to exemplify the 'imputed facts' of mesmerism through reference to his printed words.[7] This is, in itself, a further indictment of the credulity displayed by certain practitioners, for, as the reviewer states of the work we must conscientiously declare that a more unsatisfactory statement, one more replete with self-contradiction, inconsequent reading, daring *petitio principii*, gratuitous assertion and mere nonsense, it has never been our misfortune to encounter. In almost every page is to be found matter tending directly to damage the character of the author, as a cool dispassionate observer, capable of duly estimating the value and consequence of what he sees.[8]

In his analysis of Dupotet's *An Introduction*, the reviewer highlights the inconsistencies of earlier magnetic practice, touching on the author's accounts of both Mesmer and Puységur. His conclusion, though, is that inconsistency – which is incompatible with the standards rightly expected by contemporary science – has been perpetuated into contemporary magnetic practice. Acknowledging Dupotet's own tacit admission of the lack of agreement on the part of magnetic practitioners as to whether the somnambulistic state is induced by the magnetist's manual passes and other gestures, through the exercise of his will or by some other reflex of the fluid logic of mesmerism, the reviewer retorts:

Thus, we see, that not only the will is, by many magnetisers, unceremoniously dismissed, from all share in the process, but the gesticulations themselves are also called in question. What then remains? nothing but imagination. Either these things are necessary or they are not. If they are necessary, whence this disagreement? If they are not, why are they insisted upon at all?[9]

The implicit question behind this statement, of course, may be rhetorically couched in similar terms: if magnetism is credible, why has it not been universally accepted by the medical profession? If it is not, why does medicine continue to discuss it as if it were?

The indignation expressed within this review was no doubt prompted by Dupotet's departure from what was essentially a private practice, such as that adopted by both Mesmer and Puységur, and his apparent acceptance into the privileged inner space customarily reserved for qualified and accredited practitioners of conventional medicine – the teaching hospital. Dupotet had already provided similar clinical treatments, apparently under controlled conditions, within the Hôpital Hôtel-Dieu in Paris.[10] In England, he magnetised at the Middlesex Hospital and was accepted on to the wards of University College Hospital (formerly the North London Hospital) shortly after his arrival in London in June 1837.[11] This latter was a short – and it has to be said – inglorious episode in the history of British clinical hypnotism. Dupotet appears to have taken excessive advantage of the invitation that had been, formally or informally, tendered to him at University College Hospital. He appears to have moved from experimentally magnetising on the hospital's wards to practising in front of an audience in a lecture theatre. This particular activity met with the disapproval of the hospital's trustees, as a report syndicated from *The Patriot* to *The Liverpool Mercury* and other provincial newspapers indicates:

> The experiments of the Baron Dupotet de Sennevoye, in the University College Hospital, (formerly the North London,) have been put a stop to by the intervention of the medical committee. On reading over the various statements of the events that have occurred at this and other institutions, it is impossible to avoid coming to the conclusion that the whole is a system of imposture from beginning to end.[12]

Excluded from the hospital, Dupotet returned to a form of private practice which was as controversial as his brief sojourn within the hospital precincts. He was to leave England in the first quarter of 1839, the point at which English-language accounts of his practice effectively disappear from the British public press.[13] By mid-1839, Dupotet was unfashionable, and well on the road to being forgotten. For just under two years, though, his controversial practice was a prominent subject for the British popular press, though this lay interpretation of his work has for the most part been eschewed by historians of hypnotism in favour of the ostensibly more informed interpretations published in the medical press.[14] None the less, such accounts as were published in daily and weekly newspapers provide a telling index of how the non-professional but literate population of the United Kingdom viewed the practice, ethics and implications of animal magnetism in the late 1830s.

Dupotet's reputation in England was established not through his experimental connection with the Hôtel-Dieu, nor indeed by the time he spent at University College Hospital, but through a private practice whose activities elided the purportedly diagnostic and the imaginatively clairvoyant. As was the case with Mesmer's arrival in Paris, Dupotet's reputation preceded him in England. In an article syndicated from *The Literary Gazette* to several London newspapers in September 1828 an anonymous contributor recalled how he had 'carried from London a lock of hair belonging to a sick friend' with the intention of submitting it for magnetic analysis in

Paris.[15] Clairvoyant diagnosis under somnambulism, where the entranced subject was allegedly capable of viewing the interior of his or her own body, and on occasions the bodies of others also, was a well-known feature of Puységur's work during the first two decades of the nineteenth century. Because the purportedly sick party was invariably present in such instances, it was comparatively easy to dismiss such demonstrations as the mere action of suggestion or credulity. One such account, printed in *The London Saturday Journal* in 1839, is representative. The writer recalls how, upon the supposed malady having been vocally declared by the somnambulist during an act of clairvoyant diagnosis, the putative sufferer became

> so struck with the announcement, and his superstitious imagination so excited by it, that he soon complained of internal pain and took to his bed. Of course, the remedy suggested by the magnetised sleeper was immediately applied, and an immediate cure obtained.

This unnamed and unconvinced columnist, who apparently did not witness either the diagnosis or the cure, was content to conclude, quite simply, that 'Here was nothing but a very ordinary effect of imagination upon the physical organs'.[16] The 'cure', implicitly, is apparently equally imaginative, as the writer's closing stress on immediacy emphasises.

The writer for the *Literary Gazette*, however – who intimates that 'My name, if it can add any weight to the narrative, may be learned by enquiry at your office' – is insistent regarding his actual presence at the clairvoyant evening recalled in his account. His narrative recounts that:

> Twelve days elapsed between the cutting of the lock of hair and my presenting it to Madame Gillaud, a somnambulist, at the apartments of Dr Dupotet, in the Rue des Saints Pères, at Paris. The Doctor, having, by the process of magnetising for a few seconds, produced in this woman the extraordinary kind of walking (or rather, talking) sleep, called somnambulism, she received from him the hair, felt it for a while with attention, then ... she dropped her head upon her breast, and fell into a state of complete torpor, from which her magnetiser had great difficulty in arousing her. At length she recovered, raised her head a little, and said, slowly – 'Je m'en vais, je vais mourier'. She proceeded to tell us that the patient was drawing towards the close of his career, that he had the *maladie noire*, that his blood was corrupted, that there was no use in ordering any thing for him, but that he might be allowed to do what he liked best himself.

In answer to the question, Whether magnetism would be of any service to him, she replied, that it might prolong his life *a little*.[17]

Prior to this recollection, the writer confirms, for the reader's benefit, that the absent friend's life is imperilled by both liver failure and dropsy.[18] The sufferer is, indeed, as the somnambulist's empathy informs those present, *mourir*, going to die. The writer confirms that he 'had carefully abstained from giving any hint, either to M. DUPOTET, the respectable physician, himself, or to his somnambule, which might guide either of them to a previous knowledge of this case'. The writer's conviction is thus apparently rendered all the more certain by the revelation that his friend 'had actually paid the debt of nature on the very day preceding this consultation'.[19] This latter detail, though, is problematic, as the writer himself acknowledges. He notes:

> It may be objected, that if the clear-sightedness of this somnambulist was perfect, she should have known that the person in question was no more at the moment she was consulted about him. But you will recollect, that the hair had been severed from his head *twelve days before*, and the magnetic fluid contained in it could only convey to her perception a sensation of the patient's *then* state, viz. that of a dying man, which she certainly expressed in a very unequivocal manner.[20]

The rhetoric deployed in this eyewitness account subtly evades any suggestion of a merely supernatural explanation. There is no implication whatsoever that the somnambule has somehow penetrated the opacity of the patient's body in order to ascertain the presence of his fatal oedema. Indeed, the somnambule's actions aspire to a form of almost conventional material diagnosis, a logical reading of evidence – some representative component of the patient's body – the condition of which can relate only to the time at which it became severed from the living material body. It is, emphatically, *not* an act of telepathy or mental travelling. A small totem of morbid humanity is here transformed into a synecdoche of the absent patient's illness during a consultation that is both diagnostic and prognostic. On reflection, despite the fantastic nature of the séance, the whole event is represented as being little more remarkable than the customary inspection of a sample of blood or sputum provided by a patient unable or unwilling to attend at the physician's own residence. It is only the lack of an obvious relationship, in conventional or nosological terms, between the hair on the surface of the morbid body and the fluids accumulated within its organs, that disturbs the superficially logical connection that is projected between the pathological evidence and the concluding diagnosis.

Dupotet appears to have aspired towards obtaining a practitioner's respectability as well as an instructor's reputation during his short sojourn in London. His practice in the English capital, if the incidence and frequency of newspaper reportage are to be relied upon, extends from the last quarter of 1837 to the first quarter of 1838: in October 1839, to be sure, he is recorded as again being in practice in Paris.[21] The technique of animal magnetism exhibited by Dupotet in London would appear to be functionally identical to that which he had successfully practised in Paris, and the mode of advertising his services likewise draws on an established mesmeric paradigm. An advertisement, headed 'Animal Magnetism', featured in *The Morning Post* on 27 November 1837, for example, proclaims:

> A permanent series of LECTURES on this science, each followed by the treatment of some patients, by Baron DUPOTET DE SENNEVOY, MD, Professor of Magnetic Medicine at the Athénée Royal of Paris, &c., every day at Half-past Two precisely, at his own residence, 25 Orchard Street, Portman Square.[22]

The Athénée Royal of Paris, located in the present-day rue de Valois, was a *lycée* which was active in providing general education to the public between 1785 and 1848. At first sight it appears odd that the advertisement fails to mention Dupotet's connection with the Hôpital Hôtel-Dieu, the oldest hospital in the French capital – or, indeed, his recent experiments at University College Hospital, London, which had been reported in *The Lancet* and advertised in *The Morning Post* only two months earlier.[23] Medical gentlemen, as these two advertisements testify, *were* readers of *The Morning Post*: no doubt they would be aware that Dupotet's connection with University College Hospital had been terminated, amid some controversy, at least a week before the appearance of the advertisement announcing the Baron's 'permanent series of LECTURES'.[24] The latter advertisement, it would seem, is aimed at an interested – and financially advantaged – educated public, rather than the increasingly hostile metropolitan medical audience.

Fees for private tuition at Orchard Street were high: three guineas would admit a private pupil for a course of instruction, and one guinea could purchase twelve transferable tickets – certainly a more economical investment than a single ticket of admission priced at 2s 6d. For those medical professionals less easily convinced than the moneyed public, however, there was the customary invitation to witness this novel treatment at first hand:

> Baron Dupotet continues to treat gratuitously every day from One till Two all patients recommended to him by respectable parties. Members of the medical profession are especially invited to witness this gratuitous treatment and to bring patients of their own in order to convince themselves of the efficacy and importance of Animal Magnetism. NB None but Medical Gentlemen, or such as bring a Patient for Magnetic Treatment, can be admitted at this gratuitous sitting, except by special permission. From Ten till Twelve Baron Dupotet receives at his residence all persons desirous of consulting him, or of undergoing a private treatment.[25]

An anonymous account of one of Dupotet's séances, published in February 1838, intimates that this invitation was readily taken up by at least some metropolitan medical professionals. The writer of this account advances, moreover, what is possibly the earliest *detailed* description of a magnetic séance conducted on British soil, and written by a participant who, if not truly disinterested, is at least neither magnetist nor patient. After a short but testy preface, the writer recalls that:

> When ushered into the saloon of operations we found ourselves in the midst of a crowd of medical men, amateurs, and patients. The majority of the latter were females of various ages and conditions of life, in the midst of whom an intelligent-looking and very animated little man in black glided incessantly, receiving visitors with one hand, seating patients with the other; at one moment conversing and explaining matters with great earnestness and suavity, in French, to the peripatetic groups; and then turning to the seated portion of his visitors, over whom he appeared to exercise a very singular and unceremonious influence, gently waving and fanning with his right hand, at a little distance from their faces while his left (firmly extended towards their breasts or knees) seemed directed so as if to confine or cut off its action.

Though somewhat frenetic, this scenario is markedly less dramatic than the scenes enacted around Mesmer's *baquet* in pre-Revolutionary Paris. Indeed, the preferred tool of the Baron is the practitioner's hand, albeit with the occasional supplement of a non metallic though still apparently potent medium. The account continues, in laudable detail:

At times he used both [hands] with the motion of gently scraping
or rubbing down with his fingers' ends – now pressing slightly on
the forehead, cheeks, or chest – and, anon, conveying his wonder-
working will through the medium of a drop of water, let fall from
the tip of his finger. It was the Baron, in the midst of his manipulations, spreading a soothing soporific influenza over the sensitive
crowd, whose nervous sufferings had brought them to seek relief
from the healing hands of the professor of natural magic.[26]

Dupotet, for the most part, is depicted here as a sincere figure rather
than a charlatan or an object of ridicule. The account is notably emphatic
regarding the exercise of the magnetist's will, which suggests at least a
passing knowledge of the debate regarding the nature and existence of
magnetic fluid that had troubled mesmerism since the time of Puységur.[27]

The experience of the patients, too, is summarised through accounts
based upon their personal testimonies as well as the writer's direct
observation during the séance: four patients are thus considered, albeit
briefly. The writer, in one such instance, draws upon the rhetorical value
of personal acquaintance:

We discovered a friend among the magnetised who favoured us with
his experience and conviction, both highly favourable to the exercise
of the Baron's art, a rheumatism of some years' standing having half
yielded in five operations although the ordinary sensation of slumber
or semi-consciousness scarcely weighed on his faculties for two
seconds at a time.

Rheumatism, like gout, is one of the painful physiological complaints for
which magnetism (and indeed Perkinism) had historically claimed a notable
success in treatment.[28] The writer's earlier acknowledgement, though, of
the 'nervous sufferings' of Dupotet's subjects teasingly implies also that the
pain experienced by this and other patients at the séance might have their
origins in a sensitivity which might well be termed neurosis in modern
parlance, rather than a neuralgia associated with some lesion or tangible
disorder. Be this as it may, this contributor to *The Morning Post* appears to
have left Dupotet's séance with his scepticism somewhat chastened by the
experience. Having initially entered upon the occasion with 'a very critical
temperament – chilly, captious and cynical', he is liberal enough to admit
that 'As far as we have been able to judge in a first visit, the Baron is the
very reverse of a quack, and his influence over the human frame something

real, however apparently miraculous'. Indeed, the subject of magnetism is, in his opinion, 'well worth the serious and patient investigation of every friend of science and humanity'.[29]

Other writers, however, were less convinced either by the Baron's claims or his personality. Responding to an enquirer identified only through the pseudonym 'Philosophus', an anonymous columnist for *The London Dispatch*, for example, claimed to have been present at a similar event hosted by the Baron. He recalls tersely:

> We have attended one of Dupotet's exhibitions of Animal Magnetism, and saw nothing to induce us to believe that the whole proceeding was not a piece of trickery. The Baron (as he calls himself) is a mean-looking man, with a mutilated finger on the left hand. He is not a classical scholar, as he himself avowed, nor does he speak English. All his explanations are in French.

The crooked finger is a curious, but ridiculous, detail in an account which draws perceptibly on both popular English Francophobia and the suspicion of any aspiring professional who cannot claim a conventional gentleman's education. The subsequent description of the séance, though, is likewise rendered with a vitriol that imbricates this event with Mesmer's Parisian gatherings and theatrical exhibitionism. The account continues:

> Two or three persons were in the room mingled with the strangers, who explained as well as they could the mysteries of the Professor's proceedings. A number of patients were present, who appeared to fall into convulsions or sleep when the finger of the magnetiser was directed towards them. They then spoke a vast quantity of nonsense, which the confederates tried to persuade the audience was the effect of Animal Magnetism. The price of admittance to this show is half-a-crown. Ladies had better remain away.[30]

The allusion to popular accounts of Mesmer's grandiose control over the patients' magnetic crisis is blatant here. The verbal ramblings of Dupotet's entranced subjects, however, allude rather to Puységur's demonstrations of magnetic sleep and that condition's associations with clairvoyance and alternative personality. These latter issues were topical at the time, though not on account of Dupotet's work alone. In their apparent exhibition of a lack of self-control on the part of the entranced subject, they were central also to the equally controversial experiments and exhibitions conducted by

Dr John Elliotson at University College Hospital – activities which were in part shaped by Dupotet's own time within the North-London wards and the English doctor's personal observations of the Baron's technique.

'The theatre of his beastly exhibitions':
The erotic nature of early Victorian magnetism

If the short but detailed account of one of Dupotet's séances appears to be little more than an isolated expression of distaste on the part of the editorial imagination of *The London Dispatch*, the sustained hostility displayed towards the Baron and his practice by a metropolitan Sunday newspaper, *The Satirist*, subtitled *The Censor of the Times*, represents a quite different form of British disdain for the revived science of animal magnetism. The assault upon Dupotet's credibility by *The Satirist*'s columnists was initiated around five months following the Baron's recorded arrival in England in July 1837.[31] It was, without doubt, an intensive campaign: there are no fewer than three separate references to Dupotet's English practice in the issue published on 5 November 1837 alone, for example. In the most specific of these three editorial features, *The Satirist* does not claim a witness's knowledge of the occasion from which the report is derived, but none the less interprets Dupotet's activities as morally questionable. The report – which is headed, simply, 'Animal Magnetism' – opens in a truculent, rather than satirical, tone:

> It appears that a 'Baron Dupotet' (so a correspondent of the *Times* asserts) is practising the above system on a number of young girls, principally at his own residence in Orchard-street. From this veracious correspondent we learn that the first who *under*went the Baron's experiment was a young girl of twenty; he states, 'she was now magnetised – that is, she sat down on a chair whilst the Baron moved his person before her, sometimes drawing towards her, and sometimes the other way.' It appears also that during the operation 'she heaved deep sighs, and breathed laboriously'.

The emphasis on the gender and vulnerability of Dupotet's subjects is maintained throughout. 'The second *patient* was also a *young* woman', the account states, and 'It appears from the writer in the *Times*, that on this lady the Baron ended his business by making "several passes", "rubbing her down", and so forth.' A third female patient was seemingly 'not as susceptible as the former ones', though a fourth exhibited classic mesmeric symptoms. Allegedly quoting the words of *The Times'* correspondent, the columnist notes that 'on beholding the Baron she went into hysterics', and had to be calmed through the implementation of 'a few *anti-hysteric* passes, which had the power of immediately quieting her':

> Thus ended the evening's work. Further on we are told the astounding fact 'that the Baron commenced his *evening operations* on five more women, who were far better *"disciplined"* than the *morning ones*, and who are familiarly called the "Baron's own"'.[32]

The implication of sexual impropriety exercised upon entranced or otherwise susceptible magnetic subjects had long been a context of the French commentary upon mesmerism. It was the subject of a second, confidential, report by the French Royal Commission in 1784 and, as Robin Waterfield notes, had also entered the popular consciousness of late eighteenth-century Paris by way of theatrical satires which 'liberally accused Mesmer of charlatanism, veniality [*sic*] and immorality' and through pamphlets that 'suggested that the bodily magnetic poles that Mesmer worked with on women were in the region of the heart (or breasts) and the vagina'.[33]

Sexual predation, however, was a novel implication for the practice of animal magnetism in Britain, a country where suspicion of the mesmeric practitioner had customarily been associated with charlatanry rather than seduction. As had happened earlier in France, nineteenth-century British fiction was eventually to draw on these same implications.[34] The initial reaction, though, was journalistic. The stress on the youth as well as the gender of the subjects – those under twenty-one were legally minors in the United Kingdom as late as 1969 – is emphasised in *The Satirist*'s account through the columnist's dwelling specifically upon the Baron's back and forth body movements when facing the first patient. There is a suggestion here, if not of the motions of sexual congress, then at least of a predatory hovering over the prone body of a helpless girl. His hand gestures, too, are made to appear somewhat intimate and lingering for a medical practitioner. The suggestively troubled breathing of the first subject anticipates, also, the putative grounds upon which another group of women, whose attributes and behaviour are *not* detailed in *this* account, might be 'familiarly called the "Baron's own"'.

The account reproduced in *The Satirist*, however, departs significantly from its acknowledged and obvious source, a longer column originally published in *The Times* on 1 November 1837. In *The Times'* account, the whole séance appears somewhat less sinister – an exhibition, indeed, but one which is preposterous rather than prurient. The first patient is, specifically, an epileptic and 'was brought by her father, who was not a medical practitioner', it being more usual for patients to be 'brought to the Baron by their medical attendants in order to be magnetised'. If the reassurance conveyed by proper guardianship were not enough here, the magnetising of the patient is itself less luridly rendered in *The Times* by 'a Correspondent whom we requested to attend the exhibition'. Certainly, the conclusion of *The Times*' account of the magnetising of the girl lacks the sexual innuendos contained in that advanced by *The Satirist*:

> She was now magnetised; that is, she sat down in a chair while the Baron moved his hands up and down before her, sometimes drawing them in a direction from her forehead to his person, sometimes in other ways. The patient occasionally breathed deep sighs, or rather breathed laboriously, and this was all.

Apparently, the girl's father confirmed to *The Times*' correspondent that 'her health had improved under the treatment'. No such comforting reassurance is advanced by *The Satirist*. *The Times*' correspondent, though, is notably less convinced by the condition of the hysterical woman, the Baron's second patient. She is a patient 'older than the preceding ones', but the onset of her hysterical state is *not* attributed in *The Times* to Dupotet's presence or agency as it is in *The Satirist*. Indeed, she appears to have actually *entered* the room, according to *The Times*, already

> in a state of hysterical sobbing; on being magnetized she sobbed still more, but was then quieted a little by other passes of an anti-hysteric kind, as we conjecture. She soon relapsed, however, into her original condition.

This second patient was likewise not subjected to any *protracted* physical manipulation by Dupotet, for 'In this case the Baron ended his wavings of hands, or "passes" as they are technically termed, by touching the arms and legs of the patient – rubbing her down, in fact'.[35] A momentary or concluding touch, certainly, would seem less provocative than a more lingering contact.

The treatment of the second patient, though, is at the centre of another imputation of sexual misconduct on the Baron's part, reproduced elsewhere in the same issue of *The Satirist*. This latter, provocatively entitled 'Startling

Experiments', again aids its polemic through a judicious misquoting of the earlier article in *The Times* before concluding that

> We cannot but regard such proceedings in a most disgusting light; and any young woman who can publicly submit to be rubbed down can have but little care as to consequence. If this Baron did but re-establish the celestial bed in conjunction with his animal magnetism, his business would thrive most prosperously.[36]

No doubt the modesty of this young lady had been forever compromised by such indecorous manipulation. The Celestial Bed mentioned by the columnist was an elaborate divan, devised and profitably managed by the failed English doctor James Graham, who marketed it as a cure for infertility in the 1780s. Located in the enticingly named Temple of Health and Hymen on London's Pall Mall, the Celestial Bed was adorned with suggestive illustrations and featured a large mirror which allowed those lovers willing to invest the significant sum of £50 to gaze for a night upon their own erotic endeavours.[37] This facility, in conjunction with the scantily dressed women who were scattered about the Temple, lent an air of sexual licence to the whole institution, and this notoriety is most certainly alluded to by the columnist.[38] More significantly, though, the Celestial Bed was supplied with a form of electric current, this 'fluid' being deemed conducive to both arousal and conception. The analogy being drawn here is one which equates Graham's specifically sexual practice to Dupotet's more general curative regime, and *The Satirist* would appear to implicitly conclude that both institutions are apt to disturb the morals of any woman foolish enough to seek treatment therein.[39] *The Times*, though, is somewhat less insistent upon the sexual implications of the treatment of this particular patient. Even the racing pulse exhibited by the girl – a sign of arousal, to be sure, in the eyes of any other commentator – could, the correspondent concluded 'easily be accounted for by the agitation of a nervous girl on being magnetized in a room full of gazers'.[40]

The penultimate female patient – who receives the least attention in *The Satirist*'s column – is accorded significantly more space in *The Times*. Her admission that being magnetised actually *increased* the abdominal pain she was seeking to anaesthetise is omitted altogether in the derivative account, it presumably having no suggestive or titillating value.[41] Most intriguing, however, of all of the differences between the two accounts are those which detail the composition of the two discrete groups of magnetic patients. If *The Satirist* is to be believed, Dupotet's practice is exclusively

directed at women. *The Times*, however, notes the presence of a *fifth* patient
at the earlier séance, the acknowledgement of whom might well have had
implications for the success of *The Satirist*'s salacious polemic:

> The fifth and last patient was a man, aged 42, a servant out of place,
> labouring under epilepsy, a fit of which occurs, however, only once a
> year or so. This was his first sitting, while all the other patients had
> been at the Baron's before. He became nervous and trembled a little,
> but that was all. The Baron thinks it would be useful to produce an
> epileptic fit in this man by magnetism, in order to cure the disease.[42]

The afternoon séance at Orchard Street, which is recalled in considerably
greater detail by *The Times* than it is in *The Satirist*, is likewise an occasion
during which both sexes were treated by the Baron. Later reports of
the Baron's activities also note how both male and female subjects were
'affected to about an equal degree' during public exhibitions of magnetism
by Dupotet.[43] At the afternoon séance, *The Times* reveals, 'There were
five patients – four women and a lad, besides the hysterical woman of the
morning, who sat on the left of the little battalion like a *corps de réserve*, or
patient of observation'.[44] The military allusion here supplies the context
left wanting in *The Satirist*: this more coherent – or obedient – quorum of
patients is likened to a platoon under the ostensibly absolute command of
an officer:

> We must freely confess that the contrast between the 1 o'clock and
> the 3 o'clock patients was most staggering; the difference between
> an awkward squad and the best-drilled troops could hardly be
> more striking. The morning patients, like so many stupid recruits
> straggling in under the guidance of their enlisting doctors, could
> hardly be got into any state beyond the uncomfortable, while the
> evening regiment, or Baron's Own, were admirably under magnetic
> discipline.

There is no suggestion here of a possibly sinister or sexual possession being
exercised over the bodies of the magnetised. Indeed, *The Times* is explicit
that the male subject is seated in closest proximity to the magnetiser.
The polemical thrust of *The Times*' article is one of scepticism rather than
prurient suspicion. Its report of the morning session concluded that 'it
must be confessed, there was nothing worth going to Orchard Street
for'. The final rendering of the account of Dupotet's séance is perhaps
more temperate, in that it avers that the evidence presented is far from

convincing – and, indeed, in the case of the purportedly magnetised lancet case which Dupotet used in place of a wand or finger, far from durable either.[45]

Salacious allegation, however, remained the predominant tone of the short but intense campaign against Dupotet specifically, and magnetism generally, within the pages of *The Satirist*. This was conducted in part through a series of short, satirical comments in the newspaper's regular 'Chit-Chat' feature, an early example being the following remark, published on Sunday 28 January 1838:

> We often hear of people – females in particular – 'dying of curiosity'. We recommend those suffering under a attack of this fatal disease to visit the ménage of the *animal* du Potet, who professes to cure this and every other malady by a process peculiar to himself. As one part of his system is to lay patients upon their *backs*, we may have a pretty good idea that none but flats visit him a second time.[46]

A fortnight later, on Sunday 11 February 1838, *The Satirist* again made two serious – and rather explicit – allegations regarding the moral propriety of Dupotet's practice. The shorter of these two assertions of sexual impropriety is a mocking poem, structurally unexceptional within the context of the regular 'Chit Chat' column of the paper, but sufficiently barbed as to raise the anxiety of anyone who might consider entrusting his wife or daughter to the curative care of the Baron. The stanza in question is entitled 'The Magnetism Charlatan' and reads, simply:

> Of quack Dupotet's skill, a thousand tales
> Are told. The charlatan asserts (odd whim)
> That his magnetic influence never fails
> When tried on prostrate females under him![47]

It seems surprising that such a blatant allegation of sexual immorality did not result in some form of litigation: the only plausible explanations for the Baron's lack of response must be either that of an ignorance consequent upon his speaking only French or else the likely cost of legal proceedings. If this scurrilous little ditty were not provocative enough, a column on the same page, boldly entitled 'A Magnetising Mountebank', makes further detailed allegations, and these not merely upon the Baron's own behaviour and intentions but also regarding the moral character of some of his subjects.

In this latter account, Dupotet's Wigmore Street chambers are not represented in the grandiose or mystical light customarily associated with eighteenth-century Parisian magnetic practice, but instead partake of the ambience of a contemporary house of ill-repute. Admission to this ostensibly medical salon is granted upon the conveyance of half-a-crown (2*s* 6*d*) 'to a little pragmatical biped who sat at the seat of custom' – an allusion, surely, to the concierge who would customarily admit paying clients to the parlour in which the brothel-keeper would exhibit her human wares. This account is, certainly, as *The Satirist* phrases it, a singularly unflattering and 'round unvarnished report of all we witnessed':

> we mounted to the drawing room. This drawing room is an ill-furnished apartment, having a few dirty Brokers alley looking sofas, and a large assemblage of very seedy easy chairs, poverty-struck curtains and capet [*sic*], a miserable lamp, apology for a chandelier, pendant from the ceiling, and a *'recueil des phrases'* upon the mantelpiece. The little front room through which we passed to gain an entrance where the great man was, contained an assemblage of bloated tawdry looking damsels, who had all the appearance of having just emerged from some of the stews. These we immediately opined were subjects in attendance. The drawing-room itself was filled with about thirty ladies, intermixed with here and there a chaperon with white kid gloves and a silly face.[48]

Broker's Alley, near Drury Lane in Covent Garden, was located in a district notorious not merely for prostitution but also for theft, violence and extortion.[49] This is a most unflattering comparison for Dupotet's accommodation, which was located in the somewhat more salubrious environs of Bond Street, Westminster. The *'recueil des phrases'*, which was probably nothing more than a table of translations provided so as to aid the Anglophone visitors' understanding of Dupotet's French and its application to the behaviour of his patients, is also suggestive of a tariff of prices that might be associated with at least some of the apparently disreputable women on display.[50] Though a sexually ambiguous 'young man with very long hair and a singularly mild and mincing speech' is exhibited amongst 'these objects' – the four subjects to be magnetised at the séance – the majority are female, though hardly attractive: one is 'a very old woman in a very old cloak'; another strongly resembles her; and the third is 'a young woman of bloated face and red staring eyes, about whom their [*sic*] could be no mistake – she was in a maudlin state of drunkenness'. Other subjects are subsequently introduced, including 'a dissipated individual named

Rachel whose disease we did not like to inquire'. The greatest censure, and most explicit exhibition, however is associated with 'a very fair haired girl of eighteen named Lucy'. It is her actions, rather than her appearance, which are manipulated by the columnist so as to cast the Baron if not as a seducer then at least as one who exploits the scarce-contained lusts of the lower classes. Dupotet's actions in initiating Lucy's trance are undoubtedly intimate, even where they are grotesque, for

> The Baron now began to knead Lucy's face about with his hands, to squeeze her cheeks, to press her hands, and generally to bring his body into very active contact with hers. An amiable lady present pricked the girl's finger, but she did not wince: that we do not wonder at – her imagination was doubtless otherwise engaged; the magnetiser's operations were evidently very potent.[51]

The reference to potency here initiates the more salacious interpretation of the Baron's gestures that immediately follows. The account, indeed, might appear astonishingly explicit to modern readers accustomed to the puritan cliché of Foucault's Victorian Prude.[52] Compromising himself somewhat in the process, the columnist continues:

> Even we, albeit the most sceptical of individuals and studiously refraining from all interference in the matter, felt ourselves *rising* into a high state of excitement. Now Lucy began to talk – still being in a magnetic slumber – and rather vehemently too; she seized the Baron's hands, pressed them upon her neck, while she rubbed her cheek somewhat pushingly against that part of his person which is situated immediately beneath the last button of his waistcoat, and she exclaimed, 'O dear, O dear, dear Baron, do open my ears.' 'Vat she say?' inquired the Baron, who appeared now to be full charged with magnetism; and soon after disengaging himself he walked to another part of the room. Lucy, however, whose magnetic fit continued, laid hold of some other gentleman's hand who stood near, and insisted upon retaining it, telling him to *use the other*. What she meant by this he did not seem to comprehend any more than ourselves; but while she continued to hug and palpitate and caress the hand, the Baron returned and released the unhappy gentleman, who was rapidly becoming as highly magnetised as Lucy was herself.[53]

Though the two gentlemen concerned – one the writer, the other he that was 'laid hold of' by the demonstrative Lucy – seem to be ambiguously aroused by the encounter, the prurience of the scenario is ultimately contained by a coda which suggests that such encounters ought not be countenanced by any individual aspiring to gentility.

If effeminacy, drunkenness and suggestive behaviour were not sufficient, it is clear that Wigmore Street is also a place where different social classes are apt to mingle promiscuously. The effeminate young man, it appears, is a humble counter assistant in a linen-draper's shop in Regent Street; Rachel and Lucy may be presumed to be street prostitutes for, under later magnetism

> they talked together very cosily – entirely, however, about their health and the annoyance they suffered in not being able to take their usual evening walks. The bald-headed young gentleman here appeared alarmed lest they go on to talk of the adventures they met with in these recreations, but the Baron assured the company that they had too much *prevoyance* to disclose any secrets.[54]

The reference to '*prevoyance*', or foresight, would seem to disregard the assertion made by other magnetists, such as Puységur, that the entranced subject is both unconscious of the everyday world and forgetful, upon waking, of things said when entranced.[55] As the 'bald-headed young gentleman' (who is no doubt a gentleman in his own estimation) demonstrates by his consternation, the discretion of a prostitute is apparently *not* to be relied upon. The final salvo discharged by *The Satirist*'s columnist, who is now indignant rather than aroused, is unequivocal to say the least:

> It would be foolish for us to enter into a recapitulation of the minute circumstances by which any one who was not an idiot might detect this impudent and beastly piece of charlatanry. But psha! we have no patience to dwell any longer upon the details of their abominable exhibition. It is atrocious, it is almost incredible that a fellow should be allowed to enact such scenes in moral England, that he should be permitted to gain his five or six pounds a day by satiating his filthy appetites before the faces of English women, calling themselves modest women; it is disgraceful to think that any woman one grade removed from the unfortunate creatures who form the subjects of his manipulations, should be borne, even by their curiosity, to such a place.

Clearly, the chaperon's who accompany – one assumes – unmarried women to Wigmore Street provide a less than adequate moral security to their charges. Indeed, the issue of guardianship is raised boldly in this context, in a manner which implicates not merely the irresponsible father who conveyed his daughter to a Wigmore Street séance in *The Times'* account but also any individual who conveys a woman into such company:

> We saw lots of old ladies licking their lips, and the process appeared so palatable to them, that we think the abomination will spread; but we give warning that after this public exposure of the baron's doings, we shall put down any woman of decent character who has been seen at the Baron (!) Dupotet's, as no better than a common strumpet, at least in will and disposition. If we find men taking their female relations to become habituated to the low obscenity and lascivious attitudes of the denizens of the stews, we shall brand them as beasts. Who is this baron? What is he? Where did he come from? Why do not the police abate the nuisance?[56]

Clearly, a moral crusade has been announced. Notably, it is the women who receive censure here, not the paying male clients. Other than Dupotet – who is rhetorically situated in a position analogous to that of the keeper of a disorderly house – only one male present is the subject of direct and unfavourable attention: the effeminate young man. Indeed, a later recollection of the scene by the columnist betrays more than a hint of homophobia, in his admission that 'to see the Baron rubbing down this fellow's thighs and legs inspired us with such a sickness of disgust, at our former visit, that we could scarcely retain our station in the room'.[57] The reporter, who implicitly observes in the public interest, is thus absolved of all complicity in wrongdoing. The historic parallel to the alternately prurient and scandalous reportage reputedly characteristic of some twentieth- and twenty-first-century British Sunday newspapers is surely worthy of acknowledgement here.

The moral crusade first initiated in the pages of *The Satirist* on Sunday 11 February 1848 continued sporadically for another month or so. There was the usual sexual innuendo in the 'Chit-Chat' column. An untitled allusion to a lady who, the rhetoric suggests, had attended one of Dupotet's séances, for example, refers again to the scarce-concealed tumescence of the magnetically potent Baron:

> Speaking of the prevalent humbug of the day, Lady Anne Beckett remarked to Mrs Leicester Stanhope that Dupotet was a man of most extensive and exclusive information. 'Yes', rejoined Mrs Stanhope,

'as far as I can estimate his acquirements, and I have had but few opportunities of judging, I must say he appears to stand perfectly alone.'[58]

Likewise, in the issue dated 11 March 1838, another unnamed poet contributed to *The Satirist* a suggestive stanza entitled 'Animal Magnetism':

> 'Pray tell me', Lady Jersey cried,
> About him and his plan — —
> 'What is he like?' 'Like', Fox replied,
> 'Well, very like a man.'[59]

The same issue also includes a column, boldly labelled 'Mountebank Dupotet Again', which recalls the polemic of the previous month's investigation into the activities at Wigmore Street. Again, the morality of any woman who dares enter the portals of Dupotet's dwelling is emphatically questioned. The column opens:

> We did certainly conceive, after the exposure we made some weeks ago of this impudent vagabond, that the theatre of his beastly exhibitions would have been carefully shunned by all ladies who would think it injurious to their reputation to be seen at the infamous Saloon in Piccadilly. We knew very well that all the demireps, all the *divorcées*, the *entretenues*, and so forth, would be rather attracted by the pungency of the exhibition, and would flock around the impostor, but we certainly were not prepared for the assemblage we witnessed the other day.[60]

Clearly, the columnist has returned to Wigmore Street, though no doubt his masculinity – as much as his valiant commitment to the public interest – insulates him from public censure. He is shocked, indeed, once more by the promiscuous mingling of *women* from different social classes. The account continues:

> Upon entering the drawing-room ... we saw sitting upon a sofa, between that old decrepid wretch, Mother Moore, of Curzon-street, (a procuress of a description we verily believe more horrible than any other about town) and a flauntily-dressed damsel, who is nightly to be seen dispensing her *aillades* in the saloon of Drury Lane Theatre – seated, we say, between these two well known women, we saw a Countess whose youth and beauty are frequent themes of eulogy to the fashionable world. We shall not name her, for we hope that when

she hears from us who her neighbours were it will be a sufficient lesson to her never to venture into this den again.[61]

This is not, however, a commentary upon the vices of the debauched aristocracy or the dubious common sense of fashionable metropolitan elite. Certainly, it is doubtful indeed whether a fashionable countess would be a regular reader of a mass-market demotic newspaper such as *The Satirist*. A more concerned tone, however, pervades the columnist's description of others ranked somewhat closer in the fiscal and social scale to the undesirables whom he troubles to list for the benefit of a scandalised readership drawn, no doubt, from the lower bourgeoisie:

> Huddled together upon the same couches were honest wives and their young daughters and courtezans of the lowest order, component parts of the gangs which make the regions of Lancaster-street and York-square to swelter; procuresses upon the look out, and tradesmen's daughters of hot and curious temperaments; old maids with gold chains and attractive ornaments, and seedy surgeons buzzing about them. The room presented an assemblage into which no modest woman could enter without corruption.[62]

Certainly, the dangers of the transmission of vice between classes are encapsulated – admittedly with a slightly comic effect – when the Baron attempts to magnetise 'an old maid of the most determined juvenility', replete with the prosthetic aid of rouge and false teeth, and drawn spontaneously to his treatment from out of the audience.

> When the Baron began to operate upon her we really trembled for the consequences. As his hand began to roam over her face her eyes began to roll and ogle, her well wadded bosom began to rise with quick and marvellous palpitation, she got gradually more and more excited, seized the Baron's hand, and rubbed it upon her heart – only rather high up – pressed her cheek against him until the rouge came off upon his trowsers, turned, and stretched, and twisted, with an apparent spasmodic affection, in the chair, gasped, and at last uttered something which to us was very incomprehensible, and immediately fell back.

This is again all rather intimate, the attention being directed between the orgasmic writhings of the subject and the unspeakable (or unmissable) protuberance in the Baron's *enrouged* 'trowsers'. Another young girl, accompanied by a misguided parent, when magnetised also 'fell in a most unhappy *abandon* upon the floor in strong convulsions': the columnist notes that the girl's mother 'had received a lesson which we hope she will never forget'.[63] Again, the columnist, having witnessed much in this dubious company, exhorts the yeomen of England to defend their sexual property from the 'gloating debilitated debauchee', the seductive foreigner and the amoral proletarian:

> We shall keep an eye upon this fellow and his den. After what we have heard and what we have seen, we should be surprised at nothing which takes place there. Colonels dragging young ladies to sofas, young ladies clasping, if not kissing the Baron's hands, old fellows kneading and feeling the bodies of young girls, patients – these appear rather extraordinary things for a public exhibition in moral England. The man is making about a hundred pounds a week by this adventure, and we have no doubt that he intends to go quite as far as the public press will let him. If we do not put him down we should not be surprised to find him advertising evening exhibitions, or to find that at a particular moment of a rather exciting operation the gas lights were accidentally turned off. Englishmen, we say, take care of your wives and daughters.[64]

A mere week later, the worst fears of *The Satirist* appear to be approaching the status of a dangerous reality.

> The quack Dupotet seems well to understand the wants and wishes of his patrons. He not only advertises a public exhibition of his magnetic nonsense, but significantly intimates that 'persons desirous of undergoing a private treatment' may be accommodated accordingly. Our previous articles have put individuals in possession of what may expected at the public displays of the science; but it is impossible to tell the lengths to which the baron may go in private.[65]

Somewhat hypocritically, in the same issue *The Satirist* displays an advertisement for 'an amusing collection of Books and Prints' – in reality, a series of identifiably pornographic works. These include the suggestively titled *The Voluptuarian Cabinet*, *Julia, or I Have Saved My Rose*, *The Nun in the Cloister* and *Woman Disrobed*, as well as the more familiar *Life, Poems, &c. of the Earl of Rochester*.[66] One must assume that these illustrated works are intended for private consumption on an individual basis – and that they may indeed form a laudable part of a gentleman's protection against promiscuous sexual congress. A pornography based upon the abuse of hypnotism was, almost inevitably, to join such luminaries of erotic fantasy: *The Power of Mesmerism: A Highly Erotic Narrative of Voluptuous Facts and Fancies*, published in 1891, is perhaps the best known of these, though other, less blatant examples undoubtedly exist.[67]

Though allegations regarding instances of sexual interference effected by mesmerists are comparatively rare in British legal history, they retain some currency in specifically medical writings from the same period. Warnings against the ethics of the uncollegiate and unconventional practitioner, though often rendered in language somewhat less evocative than those of *The Satirist*'s polemic, on occasion temper their rhetoric with a humour that, in context, is every whit as sardonic as the more fulsome prose of the non-professional press. Published around the time of Dupotet's inglorious return to Paris, one account in *The Periscope; or Circumspective Review* (a publication intimate to the *Medico-Chirurgical Review*, and paginated within its volumes)[68] imbricates its medical critique of an unnamed magnetic practitioner and his followers – ludicrously termed 'The MAGNATES MAGNETICI' – with a fictional account of the treatment of a case of dysmenorrhoea, or painful menstruation. The patient, needless to say, is 'A young and hysterical female' who suffers, significantly, pain in the 'hypogastric region', that area of the body below the stomach. The cure, as applied, neatly evades erotic prurience by way of the detached language of medical casework. After proposing the application of magnetic therapy as a cure for the patient's menstrual disturbances, the commentator continues:

> For this purpose magnetized water was injected into the vagina, and a piece of Nickel applied to the loins. The effect was almost magical. The whole of the uterine system fell into profound Mesmeric coma, which lasted twelve hours, after which menstruation went on calmly and free from pain. The same process was employed at the next catamenial period, and with equal success. The third period passed without pain – and without any menstruation at all.[69]

This much appears unremarkable, though the coda to the paragraph's final sentence is the fulcrum upon which the article turns to irony. What follows, of course, is comprehensible to those outside of the medical profession, though the deployment of technical terminology in the remaining portion of the account configures the 'cure' itself as a farcical success. The account continues:

This was considered to be accidental, and that, at the fourth epoch, all would come right. The fourth passed, however, in the same way as the third, and the consequence of this obstruction was, morning sickness, and some qualms and caprices as to certain articles of diet. Soon after this, the mammæ enlarged a little, and the areola round the nipples became of a darker hue. Still later the young female became plumper about the abdomen than she used to be – and, finally, there was no doubt left as to the powers of the magnetized water.[70]

This wonderfully potent fluid is more tangible than that proposed by Mesmer, more intimate to the practitioner, even, than the magnetically charged drops of water that had only recently been observed to fall from Dupotet's manipulative fingers.[71] The humour of the piece rapidly gives way to a fearful warning not that distant from the tenor of *The Satirist*'s desperate plea that those male readers immune to fashionable charlatanry should 'take care of your wives and daughters'.[72] The columnist warns that, if animal magnetism is a credible doctrine, then:

> By a single wave of the hand, we deprive a female of all sense, and throw her into such a profound sleep that the teeth may be pulled out of her head, without the slightest consciousness on her part. Should such a power on the one side, and such susceptibility on the other, be once established, no female in the realm, however high or low her station, would be one day safe from the machinations of the wicked and licentious! In short, the whole foundations of society would be broken up, and every fence of virtue and honour would be levelled in the dust![73]

The collapse of self-control on the part of the female patient, and its corresponding absence on that of a male mesmerist not regulated by any orthodox college, proclaims the impending annihilation of both marital and social property. Though the article later proceeds to proclaim mesmerism 'a fiction – a falsehood', it is wary of those medical professionals who endorse such things and who thus, effectively, permit abuses of this nature to be committed under the guise of therapeutics.[74] The doctrine may be bogus, but the risks to impressionable young women are depicted as being all too real.

Unlike its contemporary, *The Satirist*, *The Periscope* is chary of naming Dupotet as the mesmerist at the centre of this presumably fictional controversy. Even if the Frenchman is not himself being referenced in this imaginative episode, it is clear that the style of writing in this, a journal apparently marketed for the medical professional, has been influenced by the depiction of the salacious mesmerist in the popular press. The manner in which the details of Dupotet's private practice were drawn to public notice in the popular, rather than professional, press is arguably instrumental in shaping how both animal magnetism and the central figure of the magnetist were to be henceforth regarded in the United Kingdom. Even acknowledging the time spent on hospital wards by Dupotet, and the adoption of magnetism into infirmary practice by Elliotson and a number of his contemporaries, the figure of the mesmerist never quite adhered to the respectable paradigm of the professional physician. If the practitioner of animal magnetism was subsequently envisaged, almost invariably, as an individual not formally associated with some credible medical institution, he was also likewise a consistent object of suspicion. The alleged activities of Dupotet, as disseminated in the pages of *The Satirist* and no doubt other popular newspapers, were to firmly associate sexual intrigue with magnetism in the United Kingdom in a way that paralleled (though never quite equalled) the similar infamy associated with mesmerism in France. In France, the popular imagination drew upon *causes célèbres* in which magnetists were formally accused, and often actually prosecuted, in cases of alleged sexual interference.[75] In the United Kingdom, such things appear to have been enacted in the fertile imaginations of columnists and editors rather than across the legal arena of the magistrate's court. The reportage that accompanied Dupotet's private practice is arguably responsible, in part at least, for cementing the connection between magnetism and manipulation in the British consciousness. It is, certainly, instrumental in enforcing the associations that maintained women as both the perfect subject for, and the ideal victims of, the magnetist. Consistently configured as a marginal figure in modern histories of early hypnotism, Dupotet, as the controversy depicted over several newspapers would surely suggest, is worthy of notice in his own right. If he did not shape the future course of British hypnotism by the radical nature of his technique or his explanation for magnetic phenomena, he was at least indirectly responsible for the development of a popular discourse through which the troubling figure of the mesmerist might conveniently be expressed.

'The dupes of impostors':
Dr John Elliotson, Baron Dupotet and Richard Chenevix

The acknowledged place that Dupotet occupies in modern histories of hypnotism limits him to the role of an unknowing catalyst for the development of a distinctively British practice. The Frenchman represents, as it were, the very cusp that separates the distinctive Continental and British applications of magnetic sleep, but also the start of a period during which hypnotism in the United Kingdom became – for a short time – both clinically tolerated and dominated by indigenous medical practitioners. As Alan Gauld suggests, for example, Dupotet's 'most important influence on the development of animal magnetism in Britain was ... indirect: it was he who reawakened John Elliotson's interest in the subject'.[76] Certainly, the latter is demonstrably true.[77] Elliotson, among many doctors, attended séances at Dupotet's chambers, physicians and surgeons invariably formed part of the Frenchman's audience at the two London teaching hospitals and medical researchers at the time considered also the literature published by Dupotet and other contemporary French mesmerists.

Toleration is, perhaps, the most appropriate description of the place attained by mesmerism in the gaze of the British medical profession in the late 1830s and early 1840s. Though the French medical establishment had long since discarded its eighteenth-century interest in animal magnetism, its British equivalent appears to have maintained a healthy though still enquiring scepticism regarding both displays of mesmerism and actual attempts to deploy it in the private and hospital practice of regularly educated physicians. Though some professional periodicals, such as *The Periscope*, were quick to decry magnetism's medical claims as fanciful or untenable, others were at least inclined to dismiss the doctrine following some semblance of empirical enquiry. Such was the tenor, for example, of accounts published in both *The Medical Times* and *The Lancet* in the 1830s and 1840s.[78] Such accommodation, though, was short lived within the professional press. *The Periscope*, though ostensibly critiquing those magnetists who abuse the position of trust customarily associated with the regular medical profession, is critical also of those professionals who have loaned their good names in support of 'such blasphemous mummeries'. The abiding presence of animal magnetism in late-1830s Britain, has in itself

> even already, affixed a stigma on the medical profession, whose members were considered to be too intelligent and too enlightened,

to become the dupes of impostors, and to give credence to absurdities which would scarcely be listened to in the wilds of America or the interior of Australia.[79]

Implicit in such observations is the desire to isolate such sympathisers to quackery, to ostracise them from the intangible collegiate body of professional respect as much as from the more formal associations – colleges, societies and hospitals – which verify their claims to a personal comprehension of medical truth. This is again a point at which lay and professional disdain for magnetism cohere.

The Satirist, whilst characteristically gleeful at the revelation of Dupotet's expulsion from University College Hospital in 1837, was truculently censorious regarding those within the ranks of the medical profession who remained loyal to the faith first preached by Mesmer even following the inglorious departure of the so-called 'English Pope of animal magnetism'.[80] Taking credit on behalf of his publication for the actions of the hospital's management, one columnist in *The Satirist* was quick to turn his basilisk prose towards the Baron's former host in London, Dr John Elliotson. In a short paragraph entitled 'Another Mesmerian Mountebank', he writes:

> We are rejoiced to find that our observations upon the immoral and debasing quackery of Dupotet and his dupes have not been without their effect. We have reason to believe that we have at least expelled this choice specimen from a quarter where it was beginning to embody itself in a serious form, and where it bid fair to taint the medical science of the country at its source. The person, however, who showed himself so destitute of common understanding as to become its dupe, or so destitute of common honesty as to become one of the accomplices – we can hardly tell which – must not escape. Whether he be knave or fool, we must take care that fathers be warned against committing their sons to his tuition, and that the public shall not become his patients without knowing that they are confiding their health to the care of a mountebank.[81]

This is an intriguing evolution of the rhetoric thus far adopted by *The Satirist* in its campaign against metropolitan mesmerism. Elliotson, a fashionable English doctor as well as a respected teaching specialist, clearly could not be pilloried with the impunity hitherto associated with the newspaper's attacks upon Dupotet. Though he apparently enjoyed the reputation of a professional radical – in conventional medicine, he pioneered the use of the stethoscope and the application of quinine; less conventionally, he was an early enthusiast for phrenology – Elliotson's education at Edinburgh University and Jesus College, Cambridge, was thoroughly orthodox.[82] Within the medical profession, though, Elliotson's name was often invoked in the intemperate rejection of innovative techniques or chemical applications by indignant chirurgical conservatives, such novelties being summarily dismissed as 'just the thing for Elliotson to rave about!'[83]

Beyond the often hostile circle of his professional peers, however, Elliotson enjoyed a more positive public reputation which saw him for a short time accelerated into an emblem of the progressive aspirations associated with University College London. Appointed an assistant physician to St Thomas's Hospital as early as 1817, Elliotson was appointed a professor of medicine at University College in 1832, only five years after UCL's foundation. He was instrumental in the campaign to establish a new teaching hospital to be associated with the College, and his personal altruism was signalled by his being one of the professors who – as one non-medical periodical approvingly noted – 'have relinquished their salaries, and declined receiving pupils' fees, until such an establishment should be properly made and provided for'. The same publication, *The Court Magazine and Belle Assemblée*, likewise took pains to report, and to reproduce in part, Elliotson's keynote address to his colleagues and students at the opening of the 1832 academic year. The reporter's summation is, indeed, most indulgent:

> This discourse is characterised by sagacity, liberality, and by a fine manly earnestness, which cannot fail to work out the good cause it advocates. Dr Elliotson appears to be a good general philosopher, and without being such, no man can be a good physician, or a good teacher of the difficult science of medicine.[84]

Elliotson was, likewise, a highly public associate of literary and political celebrities, even before he became medical consultant to the family of Charles Dickens. An advertisement printed in *The Age* in 1833, for example, reveals that the physician acted as a steward at the Literary Fund Anniversary Festival in the company of such stewarding luminaries as Lord Palmerston, Sir Robert Peel and Benjamin Disraeli.[85] In the same year, in the company of the Earl of Leicester, Lord William Bentinck, Viscount Ebrington, Lord Teignmouth and Sir Moses Montefiore, he was steward at the Anniversary Dinner for University College Hospital, held at the Freemason's Tavern in Great Queen Street, London.[86] Enjoying such an established place in metropolitan culture, the urbane, educated and English Elliotson could clearly not be served with those imputations so easily associated with the parvenu Dupotet – to adapt slightly *The Satirist*'s barrage of rhetorical questions, one could not so easily query of Elliotson 'Who is this doctor? What is he? Where did he come from?'[87] Thus, in place of the wilful charlatanry attributed by the newspaper to Dupotet, *The Satirist* proposed a more subtle version of the rhetorical question in which the unnamed Elliotson is invited to clarify whether he be complicit or merely deceived. If he is indeed an 'accomplice' to such an imposture, as the columnist asserts, the implicit question is necessarily raised as to whether he be 'knave or fool'. There is no suggestion of sexual malpractice in the columnist's rhetoric, either. Instead, a warning is tendered to those who would entrust either the professional future of their offspring, or their own delicate health, to a tutor-cum-practitioner whose judgement is alleged to be less than certain or, alternatively, to one whose honesty might be questionable.

Elliotson's interest in animal magnetism, as Gauld suggests, precedes the arrival of Dupotet in London and the Baron's subsequent admission to the wards of University College Hospital. Indeed, Elliotson's enthusiasm for magnetic practice was widely known in metropolitan circles a number of years before the highly favourable notice of his address to the University of London, above, was published in *The Court Magazine and Belle Assemblée* in 1832. It appears to have been hardly controversial at the time, being tolerated possibly as one of the characteristic eccentricities which Robin Waterfield claims were characteristic of his mercurial demeanour. After all: 'he was the first in his circle to wear trousers rather than the knee breeches and black silk stockings which had been the hallmark of the physician, and to affect side whiskers'.[88] Sartorial iconoclasm aside, Elliotson was recording his personal observations of the practice of animal magnetism in professional journals towards the end of the preceding decade, and these were likewise reported in the non-medical press. The doctor's interest appears to have been initially stimulated during a visit to London by the magnetist Richard Chenevix. Like Mainaduc before him, Chenevix's Continental patronymic obscures somewhat his Hibernian origins: uncle to an Irish Member of Parliament, Chenevix was a member of the Royal Irish Academy and a Fellow and Copley Medallist of the Royal Society, and was, as his obituary testifies, associated with 'almost all the literary and scientific institutions in Europe'.[89] A respected chemist by profession – he was heavily involved in the debate regarding the elemental nature of the metal palladium – Chenevix had practised animal magnetism in Ireland in 1828.[90] From 1829, he was treating patients with animal magnetism at several English hospitals – Waterfield specifically names St Thomas's Hospital among them[91] – and was publishing accounts of his work in successive issues of *The London Medical and Physical Journal*.[92]

Chenevix has been granted little more than a few sentences' acknowledgement in recent histories of hypnotism.[93] Though Alan Gauld intimates the existence of Chenevix's professional publications, nothing substantial has to date been published regarding the actual detail of his practice – the practice of a pioneer British magnetist. Elliotson, by way of an article first published in *The Medical Journal* and consequently embedded within a report in *The Morning Post*, provides a rare and widely accessible insight into Chenevix's operations in London.[94] The memorandum, as it is styled, recalls how:

> A fourth patient was now seated in the chair. She exhibited no apprehension of any kind, but was talking very cheerfully to me. Mr CHENEVIX, without saying one word to her, began his manipulations at the distance of half a foot, but did not touch her. In about one minute she said, in a plaintive voice, 'Sir, don't do that', and seemed in great distress. She afterwards told us that Mr C drew weakness into her, and made her feel faint. She complained of pain in the abdomen. Mr C moved his hands transversely before it, and she said the pain was gone ... She then complained of great uneasiness in her chest; and after some transverse movements, made by Mr CHEVENIX [sic] with the intention of removing it, she declared it was gone. The pain in the abdomen returned, and ceased, as before, by the manipulations of Mr C.[95]

Chenevix's treatment of a female patient, as recalled here by Elliotson, lacks any suggestion of the charged erotic atmosphere perceived by *The Satirist* at Dupotet's later séances in Wigmore Street. A decorous distance is kept between the operator's hands and the patient's flesh, and actual physical contact between the two is explicitly eschewed. The abdomen and the chest are here taken as primarily physiological, rather than suggestively erotic, bodily locations. More intriguing though is the odd alternation of pain and relief associated with the deliberate manipulation of magnetism. This whole demonstration appears to be being undertaken for Elliotson's benefit, for the intentions of the operator are communicated to the doctor without reference to the patient herself. Elliotson recalls:

In all these experiments Mr C had most clearly announced to me, in French, what his intentions were, and the effects coincided so accurately with those intentions that I confess I was astonished. Deception was impossible. Mr C looked round at me, and asked in French if I was satisfied? I really felt ashamed to say no, and yet I could scarcely credit my senses enough to say yes. I remained silent. He then asked me, still in a language unintelligible to the patient, 'Shall I bring back a pain, or disable a limb for you once more?' I, of course, requested that he would do so. He complied instantly, giving her a pain in the chest once, and disabling her several times from moving her limbs, and removing those effects at pleasure, according to the intentions which he announced to me; the whole taking place exactly as it had done in every former trial on this woman.

Chenevix, whilst attempting what appears initially to be an unexceptionable palliative relief of the patient's pre-existent abdominal pain, demonstrates his apparent ability, also, of knowingly and specifically *generating* or relocating discomfort through his use of magnetic passes. Earlier demonstrations by the magnetiser, wherein the patient's arms and foot are paralysed, and the pain removed from her chest by the act of *releasing* her from mesmeric trance – 'Mr C demesmerised her, and she said it was gone'[96] – are implicit demonstrations of this power. The colloquy between the two professionals is, however, an explicit acknowledgement of a shift in the relation of power between subject and operator. Mesmer's purported ability to throw an impressionable patient into crisis by a mere glance of the eye, or a wave of his iron wand, seems crude by comparison to this directed imposition of dis-ease or disability. The magnetiser here demonstrates, however it may be interpreted, that he can *control* as well as cure, and that his command over the body and its ailments need not be deployed solely for restorative purposes.[97] Chenevix, as an experimental chemist, is not necessarily bound by the ethical conventions associated with the physician's craft: in theory, he may manipulate a human body with as little regard for its comfort as he might sublimate a lifeless substance from solid to gaseous form. The physician, though, is bound by ethical convention in both its codified and customary forms. With animal magnetism available as an untraceable *pharmakon*, potentially both remedy and poison, the issue of how it may deployed by the physician becomes a matter of balance between professional ethics and the self-interest of an individual.

The position of Elliotson as observer might be seen as ambiguous in this context. The doctor clearly requests further proofs from Chenevix even when he perceives the discomfort of the patient. Moreover, he demands these proofs whilst apparently already convinced – despite his silence when questioned – that the chemist is indeed actively and unequivocally affecting the patient. It is Chenevix, rather than Elliotson, who brings the exhibition to a close for, perceiving that

> she began to feel faint and uncomfortable, Mr C judged it prudent to desist; assuring me that such experiments as these should never be repeated but with moderation, and only by experienced mesmerisers.[98]

There are ethical implications here that are wholly overlooked elsewhere by *The Satirist*'s emphasis upon the alleged sexual abuses attending Dupotet's practice. Clearly, the issue of such abuses – where a doctor knowingly and experimentally manipulates or enhances a human disorder rather than striving to cure it – is not yet so attractive to the popular press as the more blatant sexual interferences customarily undertaken at the unscrupulous practitioner's hands.[99] Chenevix's prudent restraint here is, likewise, not a common feature of the popular representation of the magnetic practitioner.

If Dupotet's presence stimulated once more Elliotson's interest in animal magnetism, the Frenchman's ignominious departure from University College Hospital failed to deter the English physician from continuing the experimental use of mesmerism on the institution's wards. The internally regulated nature of the hospital as an institution, its association with the formal teaching of professionals, and the lack of private space within its wards made implications of sexual impropriety largely redundant. Clearly, however grotesque the practice of magnetism might render both patient and operator, there were few places in a hospital where indelicacies might be conducted without fear of observation or interruption. The relatively public environment of the hospital ward could hardly be so thoroughly manipulated by the desire of the consultant physician, for all his professional power, as the private rooms of a mesmeric mountebank who might extinguish his gas lights, and draw a veil over his salacious actions, at will.

Such a situation motivates, therefore, a change of focus, in the rhetorical decrying of magnetic practice by a hostile press. In the United Kingdom at least, the emphasis shifts in hostile accounts from a mesmerist constructed as wilful seducer and crafty illusionist to the patient as being, alternately, their complicit assistant or else a deliberate fraud whose convincing performance has deceived medical common sense. The rhetoric of the time, most obviously as it concerns Elliotson's practice, thus comes to veer between the suggestions that the patient, if not actually aiding a wilfully fraudulent practitioner, is essentially deceiving him by perpetuating through his or her own behaviour the falsehood that is animal magnetism. In the latter case, the relative roles of skilful predator and naive victim subtly change place, the gentlemanly Elliotson being ridiculed in both the popular and professional media as the dupe of his wily lower-class patients.

'Another Mesmerian mountebank': Dr John Elliotson and the O'Key sisters

Recent histories of hypnotism have presented the relationship between Elliotson and his most celebrated magnetic subjects – Elizabeth and Jane, the O'Key, Okey or Oky sisters – primarily through published accounts of their exhibition at University College Hospital written by medically trained observers.[100] Such accounts, scripted in favourable terms by Elliotson or his close associates, or else with growing impatience by less-convinced contemporaries such as Thomas Wakley, are without doubt an important resource. They provide an index, indeed, of how the *medical* profession reported and dealt with the often disturbing behaviour evoked as the exhibitions at University College Hospital progressed. It would be easy to dismiss this episode in British hypnotism, as many writers have done in recent years, as a simple conflict between heterodoxy, in the form of Elliotson, and medical conservatism, as constituted by Wakley as both contributor to and editor of *The Lancet*.[101] In a more popular context, however, the protracted depictions of both the magnetic consultant and his practice have implications for the very image and authority of the medical practitioner – and for the nature of the intimacy, indeed, that pertains between the presiding doctor and his patient. If, in the pages of *The Lancet* – today, the most commonly utilised source of rhetoric regarding the magnetic treatment of the O'Key sisters – one man's professional hostility to mesmerism was conducted through a directed rhetorical attack on another man's practice, in the popular press such things were given a wider compass, a context indeed which was vastly different to the evidently more personal nature of the disagreement between Wakley and Elliotson.

Modern histories of hypnotism tend to open the narrative of Elliotson's protracted encounter with the O'Key sisters by way of an anonymous account published in the pages of *The Lancet*, subsequently attributed in the same periodical to George Mills.[102] This rendition of events was published shortly after what the article termed 'a remarkable exhibition' of Elizabeth

O'Key (followed by a similar exemplification of an unnamed child and
'O'Key's highly sensitive sister') at University College Hospital on 10 May
1838.[103] The tone of the piece is unusually temperate, when taken in the
context of the hostility which colours later accounts featured in *The Lancet*
and, indeed, when compared to the more fulsome prose that often characterised the commentary advanced at the time by the popular press. The
occasion was, undoubtedly, significant: the lecture theatre appears to have
been unusually full, with many in attendance 'being seated in the area [i.e.,
the floor space or pit] of the theatre after the benches above were filled'.
Those who were more fortunate with regard to their seating included
luminaries whose interests were seemingly not confined to the practical
exercise of medical science. The columnist noted that

> Among the company were the Marquis of Anglesea, Sir Charles
> Paget, the Earl of Burlington, the Duke of Roxburgh, Earl Wilton,
> Lord Dinorben, Dr Faraday, Sir Jos. De Courcy Laffan, Sir J. South,
> and several Members of Parliament.[104]

Of those gentleman named as being present who did not enjoy the title
of nobility, only Sir Joseph de Courcy Laffan was a physician. Sir Charles
Paget, brother of the Marquis of Anglesey, was a Vice Admiral and Sir James
South was a noted astronomer; Michael Faraday's pioneering interest in
the fledgling sciences of electromagnetism and electrochemistry no doubt
piqued his curiosity regarding this display of animal magnetism. Elliotson
was insistent regarding his motivations not merely for experimenting with
mesmerism, but also his deliberate locating of this specific gathering within
the curtilage of University College's medical establishment. Noting that
earlier experiments in a similar vein had been witnessed not merely by
'Teachers from almost every [medical] school in London' but also by 'every
professor, but one, of King's College', Elliotson suggested that 'it was only
courtesy to show them to gentlemen from other schools, who chose to visit
the hospital'.[105] Elliotson's justification of the occasion is, without doubt,
mindful of the still recent criticism levelled against the private nature of
Dupotet's practice and the doubts which were cast upon its scientific probity.
Recalling his recent magnetic experiments at University College Hospital,
Elliotson is reported in the article as specifically expressing a belief that:

> The institution in which they were exhibited was called a *liberal*
> institution, – all institutions should be liberal in the prosecution
> of science, – and he could not perform anything connected with

its inmates with closed doors. Yet he had been asked to take the patients on whom the experiments were tried, away from the hospital, on those occasions, to a private lodging, or an hotel in the neighbourhood. But he knew very well that if he had prosecuted his enquiries with closed doors, suspicion would have arisen that he was afraid of publicity, and of the testing of his assertions. He, therefore carried on his experiments with the greatest openness, and he would still continue to do so, for he was satisfied of the truth of the phenomena produced.[106]

The process of demonstration, as is often the case with those conducted in the earlier days of university science, is far from systematic. As *The Lancet* reports, Elliotson alternates between inducing a state of 'inoffensive delirium or "sleep-waking"' in Elizabeth O'Key, to having her exhibit at different times unconsciousness, garrulousness and imitative behaviour.[107]

In this early account, the columnist establishes Elizabeth O'Key as something of a curiosity, a simpleton, perhaps, rather than a calculated impostor. The earliest summary of her demeanour and appearance is hardly prepossessing:

Dr Elliotson presented on the floor a girl named Okey, eighteen years old, somewhat chlorotic in countenance, and diminutive for her age. She was brought from the wards of the hospital, where she had been placed under treatment for epilepsy of many months duration. The girl had several times before, as we were informed, been made the subject of public experiments in magnetism. Her figure was somewhat womanish, but her face and head were those of a child. No particular character was indicated by her features, or by any expression of feeling that could be observed in them.[108]

The chlorisis – anaemia, an iron deficiency in the blood – adds a nicely ironic edge to her involvement in 'public experiments in magnetism', though at this stage of the evening it is evident that she has not yet been inducted into the sleep-waking stage of mesmerism. Her transition to that state appears to come without prompting from either Elliotson or his assistant, Mr Wood, and this appears to arouse the suspicion of the columnist in his capacity as a witness 'placed close to the girl'. Noting how 'the dull and hippocratic countenance had changed to one of mingled archness and simplicity', the columnist concludes immediately that:

The question of deception was at once met by a conviction, derived from appearances, that the most accomplished actor that ever trod the stage could not have presented the change with a truer show of reality.[109]

Clearly, notions of affectation and performance are invoked in *The Lancet*'s account, and these prefigure the somewhat stagy and grotesque behaviour which O'Key subsequently exhibits, often without prompting from (and occasionally irrespective of the control exercised by) Professor Elliotson. Her focus, indeed, appears to be the grandees gathered closest to the lecturer and his entranced exhibit. For example, one of her earliest actions is to confront two of the noble gentlemen named in the article:

> She then advanced, and said, with innocent familiarity, and a peculiar and agreeable tone of voice, 'Oh! how do ye?' to the Marquis of Anglesea, who sat immediately in front of her. 'White trowsers. Dear! you do look so tidy, you do. What nice things. You *are* a nice man.' The Marquis wore bright buff trowsers. 'Gloves, not white; and what a nice stick.' (Turning to Sir C. Paget.) 'Why do you wear your hat?' She was proceeding to take Sir Charles's hand, when Dr Elliotson approached her, and, waved his hand from the head downwards, behind her, without touching her. She instantly closed her eyes, tottered for a moment on her heels, and fell backwards in a dead sleep.[110]

O'Key's loquacity is certainly less threatening than the intimacies that might have been divulged by the prostitutes Rachel and Lucy, exhibited but three months earlier in the private chambers of Baron Dupotet. It is still indecorous, however, and her grasping of Paget's hand recalls also Lucy's entranced behaviour with another gentleman on the same occasion: he, too, had to be released by the timely intervention of the presiding magnetiser.[111] If O'Key is unacceptably familiar with the Marquis, she is playfully frivolous, and at times actually disrespectful, of Elliotson. Later in his account of her exhibition, the *Lancet* columnist gleefully recalls her behaviour when the physician is alternately revealed to her and concealed from her sight:

> Turning to another point she found the doctor in front of her, and exclaimed with delight, 'Oh, Dr Ellison [*sic*], how do ye?' and on being placed in the chair, with the board before her eyes, she asked dejectedly, 'Ah, where are you gone?' (board removed) 'Oh, Dr Ellison (in raptures) where have you been?'

If this were not enough, O'Key is somewhat arch in her response, even though supposedly mesmerised, when Elliotson attempts to induce her to imitate his own classic mesmeric gestures:

> The Doctor then raised her hand, by passes of his own, in an upward direction, and performed, as it were, ejaculatory motions with his fingers opposite to her own, which for some time she did not imitate, but noticed with laughter and playfulness. 'Don't be silly,' she said, 'you silly man. Oh, but you're a fool, Dr Ellison. Ha! Ha! How do ye? Mine won't go like yours. They ain't so silly. Oh, Dr Ellison, leave off, it's no use.[112]

Clearly, the subject's will has not been abnegated here. Indeed, she is provocative, and actually draws the attention of the audience towards her through her apparently calculated puns and double-entendres. No longer unequivocally in control, the rhetoric suggests, Elliotson is forced to respond to her:

> Relieved from this experiment she placed her hands in her lap, and, leaning forward, said, with archness and good humour, amid abundant laughter, from the company seated around, which she did not at all notice, 'Poor Dr Ellison, would you like some sop, with some milk in it?' – 'No, for then I should be a milksop' –[113]

O'Key's pun is barbed – for all his professional iconoclasm, the physician here appears to be being manipulated by his patient, forced to respond to her, to intervene in her own apparently volitional attempts to engage with an audience of which she is supposedly unconscious.[114] Only her evident exhaustion at the end of the performance, for such it seems, is concluded by the columnist to be truly genuine, it being 'that repose the necessity of which no deception was required to make manifest'.[115] For all its restraint, this is hardly 'a favourable review', as Robin Waterfield interprets it.[116]

If *The Lancet*'s columnist is relatively gentlemanly in expressing his personal lack of conviction at the evidence presented on this occasion by Elliotson, then those commentators who recalled the Professor's activities for the benefit of non-medical readers had fewer qualms regarding their distaste for the physician-magnetist and his subject. Elliotson's own admission – as advanced in *The Lancet* – that O'Key 'had several times before ... been made the subject of public experiments in magnetism' has been somewhat overlooked by recent historians of nineteenth-century mesmerism. Those earlier exhibitions are acknowledged in such works – if

at all – through Elliotson's own account of several case histories within
the pages of *The Lancet* in September 1837.[117] *The Satirist*, though, reported
Elliotson's experiments with Elizabeth O'Key more than a month before
the oft-cited gathering at University College Hospital on 10 May 1838.
The account published in *The Satirist*, for all its mockery and exaggeration,
provides a valuable insight into the events that might characterise an
event arranged for the benefit of medical students at the North London
Hospital (as University College Hospital was then called), rather than for
the approbation of a party of upper-class dilettantes lightly seasoned with
a few surgical grandees.

As might be expected, the satirical portrait of Elliotson's pet subject,
as sketched by the popular newspaper's columnist, is less than flattering:

> Elliotson's chief patient was a Miss Oky, an appropriate cognomen,
> which appears to vouch some close consanguinity with the royal
> family of Oky Poky Wanky Wum, at present the reigning dynasty
> of the Cannibal Islands. This illustrious individual had been kindly
> procured for him by his head mountebank, Dupotet, who it appears
> selected her because she was subject to epileptic fits, and was
> moreover of a remarkably nervous temperament – a class of persons
> who have proved the invaluable tools of impostors of all ages.[118]

The allusion in the first sentence is to A. W. Humphreys's popular song
The King of the Cannibal Islands, published around 1830, though the humour
of this particular ditty has no connection with either mesmerism or
medicine.[119] Its function, beyond its status as a crude pun on the patient's
name, is to establish complicity between the popular paper and its
readership – to flatter the reader that such ridiculous impostures, though
obvious to him or her, apparently pass as credible to those of superior
education and wealth. It is the issue of imposture that complicates this
matter. Dupotet has already been established – to the satisfaction of *The
Satirist*, at least – as an impostor, a mountebank. Elliotson, though, is
depicted earlier in the article as 'a man of shallow and fluctuating mind,
ready to be deceived by any bold absurdity, and quite ready to give all the
little weight of his authority to spread its influence'. Elliotson is implicitly
a more dangerous figure than Dupotet, therefore: his very respectability,
which is considerably more credible than *The Satirist*'s dismissive assessment
of his present worth, adds an authority to the phenomena he espouses far
beyond anything that might be expected from the foreign, linguistically
awkward Dupotet. Tactically, therefore, Elliotson's judgement must be

brought into question by the writer – his professional judgement, to be sure, but also his pretension to any kind of moral probity. He is, in a sense, not merely a dupe of a fraudulent philosophy but one easily misled not just by the questionably ennobled Dupotet but by the proletarian O'Key also. It is not simply O'Key's lowly social origins that are an issue here. She is aligned rapidly in the article with the type of female undesirables that a regular reader of *The Satirist* might well have encountered before within the shabby chambers of Baron Dupotet. Elliotson's contact with O'Key, as recalled in the article, is, to be sure, somewhat less intimate and less dramatic than the Baron's curious manipulations of the prostitute Lucy – he achieves his ends 'without any of the screwing of ears, or mauling of cheeks, or pressing of eyes, such as Dupotet employs to seal up or let loose the senses'.[120] That said, O'Key responds just as Lucy does, in a manner that is 'precisely what was to be expected from a picked specimen from one of Dupotet's well-trained Coventry-court squad'. Coventry Court, near London's Haymarket, was arguably as notorious a centre for prostitution and violent crime as Broker's Alley, Covent Garden, the place where Dupotet (if *The Satirist* is to be believed) apparently obtained both his sofas and his sitters.[121] Elliotson's professional standing has already been compromised through his association with Dupotet: his moral reputation is now imperilled by too close a contact with one of the Baron's characteristic acolytes.

The questionable nature of O'Key's morals is crystallised around the columnist's insistence that she may be 'supposed to have lost her judgement in her trance'. This is ironic, needless to say. If she is an impostor, then her acting is nothing more than that, and the morals of her conscious life are as questionable as the apparently uninhibited behaviour that she exhibits once placed in the trance state by Elliotson. Either she is already of imperfect morals or else Elliotson's own conscious actions are undermining what morality she has. Both the magnetic operator and his subject are in morally questionable positions with respect to each other. As with Dupotet's Lucy, Elliotson's O'Key displays her worst traits through suggestively sexual displays of affection – displays that apparently draw those who witness her behaviour into a compromised position. If O'Key is acting here, the rhetoric advanced by *The Satirist* suggests, then she must surely have had more than a passing acquaintance with the condition she so ably performs for her exclusively male audience:

> Splendidly now she rolled her eyes about; in a fine frenzy certainly, but we think not of poetry. In the course of our professional

career we have once, and once only, seen a well-established case of
nymphomania; and Miss Oky certainly knows at least how to imitate
the symptoms of that malady. We cannot conceive what the future
Mrs Elliotson would have said had she witnessed the scene that
followed. With one jump the chaste Oky cleared all the distance
between the chair and the Doctor, threw her dear magnetised arms
round his neck and kissed him. O, how she did kiss him! 'Oh, oh,
oh! my dear, dear, dear Doctor Elliotson', she cried with an energetic
but soft rapture, her voice growing fainter with every 'oh' and every
'dear'. She hugged the Doctor vehemently; we will not say that he
returned the hug, but he appeared to think it very nice, and 'we
think they both felt it and thought so together'. At last, however,
the Doctor began to look rather foolish, and put an end to the lady's
affectionate embraces, inviting the audience to put questions to her,
in order to ascertain that she had utterly lost her judgement.

This is a rich paragraph. Part of its impact depends upon the contention that
the columnist, who momentarily adopts the magisterial tone of a medical
professional, is capable of recognising O'Key's hypersexuality where
Elliotson is not. In addition to this, the emphasis on the subject's 'magnetised
arms' is a reminder that it is he who has supposedly induced her condition
and thus 'freed' her attraction for him from restraint. Certainly, it would
appear that he is compromised, even aroused somewhat, by her intimacies,
even though these by no means attain the carnal nature associated with
the various attentions hitherto paid by mesmerised subjects to Dupotet's
trousers. The questions that the audience addresses to O'Key, incidentally,
are relatively innocuous, and perpetuate the contention – addressed also in
The Lancet's account of the gathering on 10 May 1838 – that when entranced
the subject is apt to mistake the names of the most common objects.[122]

If Elliotson's closing remarks on having restored O'Key to full
consciousness – that 'she was now quite as much in her senses as he was' –
'drew forth a hearty laugh' from the medical students in attendance, then
the closing paragraph of *The Satirist*'s account plays quietly with the earlier
suggestion that O'Key's immodesty and abandon were, if not actually
generated by Elliotson's actual magnetism, at least encouraged by his
credible position as a physician and a supposed gentleman. The columnist
concludes, with an irony that is yet pointed with a moral barb:

We never before saw a body of students so attentive to any lecture.
They all of them went away with a strong predilection in favour of

Mesmerism, and with a fixed resolve that directly they got down in the country they would imitate the treatment of their professor first upon all their female cousins, and afterwards upon as many of their friends' wives and daughters as they could persuade to let them.[123]

Certainly, however unlikely the efficaciousness of the treatment may seem in this account, its potential for disrupting the moral equilibrium of vulnerable or merely silly women is emphasised. Such a tool, however fraudulent, in the hands of one who owns the conventional title of physician, presumably ought not to be encouraged in the interests of national as well as personal modesty.[124]

Other non-clinical observers of the O'Key experiments – and, indeed, of Elliotson's magnetism of further female patients – were less inclined to dismiss the behaviour of the patient as either imposture of licentiousness. A couple of weeks prior to *The Satirist*'s assault, *The Morning Post*, for example, advanced a tempered review, 'the result of a patient attendance and, we trust, impartial observation on several occasions, within the last three weeks in the wards and lecture-room of the North London Hospital, Gower Street'. On this occasion Elliotson and Wood exhibited Elizabeth O'Key and Hannah Hunter, and the former had been encountered also outside of the lecture room, suffering from the headaches which Elliotson claimed his magnetism was able to ameliorate. On no occasion does *The Morning Post* suggest that O'Key's behaviour is in any way immodest or sexual, its excesses being rather grotesque instead. In consciousness, O'Key is

possessed of an excellent temper and affectionate disposition. Under the operation of magnetism, all her good sense appears lost, but her good feelings remain in full force, and she evinces deep sympathy with some one of the pupils present in whom she takes an interest, and who has unfortunately been eaten up by somebody else standing by!

This latter incident, in which Elliotson suggests to O'Key that he has somehow consumed his assistant, is common also to the accounts rendered in *The Lancet* and *The Satirist*. This, with the frequently referenced perceptual confusions exhibited by the entranced girl – she consistently and incongruously describes brooches as 'oysters' – may suggest a relatively predictable programme for the evening's events. A more protracted acquaintance with O'Key, it would appear, is instrumental in convincing *The Morning Post*'s columnist to take a view opposite to that later taken by

his compatriot at *The Satirist*. Writing of O'Key's entranced condition, the
columnist concludes:

> This state of magnetic semi-existence will continue – we know not
> how long; she has continued in it for twelve days at a time, and when
> awakened to real life forgets all that occurred in the magnetic one!
> Can this be deception? We have conversed with the poor child in her
> ordinary state, as she sat by the fire in her ward, suffering from the
> headache, which persecutes her almost continuously when not under
> the soothing influence of the magnetic operation, and we confess we
> never beheld anyone less likely to prove an impostor.

Indeed, the layman's opinion is verified by that of a more senior scientific
figure even than Elliotson, and one whose name is singularly absent from
the account in *The Satirist*, even though his intervention may be considered
to have predated the publication of its hostile account by a minimum of
two weeks:

> We have seen Professor Faraday exerting his acute and sagacious
> powers for an hour together in the endeavour to protect some
> physical discrepancy in her performance, or elicit some blush of
> mental confusion by his *naive* and startling remarks. But there
> was nothing that could be detected, and the Professor candidly
> acknowledged that the matter was beyond his philosophy to unravel!

Indeed, so convincing is the display that the columnist is emboldened to
assert that

> This treatment is, it appears, no longer looked upon as a matter of
> experiment or curiosity in the hospital, but as apportion of a regular
> (though very peculiar) medical course, which has been found in these
> two cases to be productive of decidedly good results.[125]

A third case, that of the younger O'Key sister, is considered, albeit with
brevity, in *The Morning Post* three days later on 5 March 1838, the two sisters
becoming an object of interest to the paper again around the time of *The
Lancet*'s report on the events of 10 May 1838.[126]

It is *The Morning Post*, indeed, rather than *The Lancet*, which may justly
lay claim to publishing the first report of the more prestigious public
exhibition of the O'Key sisters a mere twenty-four hours after the occasion
in question, on 11 May 1838. While acknowledging the healthy scepticism

of the professional gentlemen present – some of whom the newspaper associates with the interests of the Physiological Committee of the Royal Society – the journalist reiterates once more that

> Our own opinion is already formed, by frequent and attentive observation, that the extraordinary effects produced in Dr Elliotson's lecture-room are real and unsophisticated, however inexplicable they may be on any known theory of disease.

The recollection of the event, though considerably more compressed than the account tendered by *The Lancet*, draws attention to much the same incidents, recalling the nature of Elizabeth O'Key's trance condition, the comparative capability of the self, a child and the doctor in inducing it, and the light-hearted mockery of the Marquis of Anglesey. Her speech as summarised in *The Morning Post*, however, embodies none of the embarrassing gaucherie of *The Lancet*, nor indeed the salaciousness depicted in *The Satirist*. Instead, the columnist concludes that 'During this state of semi-sensation and no-reflection she speaks truth with all the naivete, and non-reservation of a person half seas over'.[127] If apparently intoxicated in her demeanour, Elizabeth O'Key is laudably candid rather than duplicitous in her opinions – at least in the indulgent eyes of *The Morning Post*. She is certainly no victim of a morally questionable practitioner, nor indeed the canny abuser of a naive physician who is himself 'a magnetized idiot'.[128]

'Experiments and facts': Wakley's investigations, the credibility of O'Key and the credulity of Elliotson

When noting the presence of 'the members of the physiological committee of the Royal Society' in its account of the public exhibition conducted by Elliotson on 10 May 1838, *The Morning Post* was careful to remark that 'the rules of that society do not empower them to examine and report as a committee'. Despite this, the columnist confidently suggests, the several opinions of these committee men, 'freely delivered in their individual capacity', are likely to 'have just as much weight with the public'.[129] Whatever the opinion of the broader public, the magnetic enthusiasms of prominent individuals have, however, traditionally attracted the suspicion of journalists and the stigma of delusion when reported in the general as well as professional press.[130] An individual, as it were, may be incautious, excessively trusting, too easily convinced or even susceptible to the glamour (or practical application) of magnetism. A formalised committee of inquiry, however, characteristically resists such frailties, being implicitly composed of several independent minds working in concert, all theoretically motivated by a healthy scepticism and a will to truth. It was such a gathering of scientific and philosophical gentlemen, formally constituted as a royal commission, which proved the downfall of Mesmer's own practice in 1784. In the United Kingdom, some fifty-four years later, it was to be a self-appointed committee of qualified medical professionals that was to finally disrupt Elliotson's own experimental activities, expelling magnetism from the metropolitan hospitals though not, it should be noted, from private practice or institutional surgery in the British colonies.

The initiation of this latter enquiry towards the end of June 1838 may be interpreted as the culmination of an intense journalistic scrutiny of Elliotson's practice conducted across the preceding two months, most notably in the pages of *The Lancet*. A series of anonymous articles by George Mills, styled as numbered reports of 'Experiments and Facts', kept Elliotson and the O'Key sisters firmly within the British medical gaze between the early days of June and the closing days of July in 1838.[131] These accounts considered not merely the public exhibitions but also a number of incidents witnessed upon the private wards of University College Hospital. There were at times, though, perceptible differences between Mills's somewhat liberal tone and Wakley's progressively sceptical attitude towards both the existence of animal magnetism and the current state of Elliotson's professional reputation. In many respects, for all Mills's temperate attitude, the very nature of the matter under study was inherently problematic – and not merely on account of the epistemologically contentious nature of animal magnetism itself. If the ungracious or grotesque behaviour of Elliotson's subjects were not enough to generate concern in Gower Street – one later account was to recall how O'Key was apparently prepared to 'kick [the] a––' of 'a fine young lady' – then accounts of the apparently inadequate facilities of the new university and its appendant hospital were also wont to cast both in an unfavourable light.[132] In the face of such adverse publicity, it is hardly surprising that the hospital's management took prompt and sudden action.

Quoting *The Medical Gazette*, *The Times* quietly intimated on 25 June 1838 that the hospital authorities had suddenly, after more than six months of his private and public experiments with Elizabeth O'Key, terminated Elliotson's public displays of animal magnetism.[133] *The Times'* columnist noted:

We are very glad to find that the public exhibitions at University College Hospital have been discontinued. The objections to the course adopted were so very palpable, that we were astonished they did not sooner lead to this result.

The Professor's magnetic practice upon the wards of the hospital – secluded as those rooms were from the intrusion of the popular press at least – continued without disruption, however. If *direct* access to Elliotson's work was no longer available to the *popular* press from this point, its medical counterpart maintained a continued scrutiny. Subsequent episodes in the life of O'Key and her sister, in effect, were now of necessity to be narrated by way of a far less evocative and dramatic discourse. It is through professional publications such as *The Medical Gazette, The British and Foreign Medical Review* and *The Lancet*, syndicated to or reproduced within non-clinical newspapers such as *The Times*, that the final phase of Elliotson's work at University College Hospital was disseminated to those readers who retained an interest in a story now almost totally stripped of its more salacious implications.[134] This much is made clear by *The Times'* columnist's concluding remarks:

> The subject of Mesmerism meantime is undergoing private investigation by some gentlemen who have voluntarily undertaken the task, and who, we trust, will conduct the inquiry in a manner calculated to satisfy men of science, and without pandering to that passion for the marvellous by which this question has been so lamentably debased. It has been stated in several of the newspapers that a committee, including Dr Roget and Dr Faraday, has been appointed by the Royal Society to investigate the phenomena of animal magnetism. We find, on inquiry, that there is no truth in this report.[135]

The former committee, self-appointed, *ad hoc* and lacking the sanction of any constituted body, apparently wasted no time in launching its programme of investigation. Within seven days of it first breaking the story of the events at University College Hospital, *The Times* reported, again with reference to *The Medical Gazette*, the following development:

> We stated last week that some gentlemen, most of whom are well known as men of science, had formed themselves into a committee to examine the subject of animal magnetism. They began by making some experiments, or rather observations, on O'Key, the chief performer at University College Hospital; and being desirous of

guarding against all sources of fallacy, made it a condition that none
of those more immediately concerned in the recent exhibitions in
Gower-street should be present. On this being made known, Dr
Elliotson prohibited her further attendance, requiring that either Mr
Wood or himself should be present. As this was not agreed to, the
investigation has been for the time interrupted.[136]

History almost seems to repeat itself in this terse notice. Elliotson, like
Mesmer, is attempting here not merely to dictate the terms of the inquiry
to its members but also to retain a level of control over the magnetised
subject that is not conducive to an open investigation. Whatever negoti-
ations broke this impasse remain unchronicled, though the investigation
appears to have begun again in earnest a month later, this time at Thomas
Wakley's house in Bedford Square, Bloomsbury.

The initial three investigations conducted at Wakley's domicile were
reported in a single article published in *The Lancet* on 1 September
1838. This article is the source relied upon most frequently in modern
historical accounts of the final phases of Elliotson's treatment of the O'Key
sisters whilst they still nominally remained patients of University College
Hospital.[137] The emphasis in these latter accounts has been very much upon
the behaviour of the O'Key sisters under what were hardly, by modern
psychological or experimental standards, laboratory conditions. These
modern interpretations stress Elliotson's behaviour at the conclusion of
the experiments rather than his earlier participation, and his involvement
in the trials themselves. He is depicted as a man desperately reacting to,
and attempting to accommodate, the adverse data thrown up as Wakley
deliberately misleads the magnetised subjects into betraying their apparent
duplicity. The embattled Elliotson, consequently, is dismissed as a dogmatist
incapable of admitting that he has been deceived by the two subjects whose
behaviour had up to this point apparently verified his hypothesis to his own
satisfaction.

The article, though, has considerably more to say regarding Elliotson's
place in the public understanding of animal magnetism in the late 1830s.
The rhetoric of the account is subtle in its shift of emphasis from an
apparent 'attempt to prove the influence of mesmerism upon the human
frame' to a rather more pointed investigation into Elliotson's own beliefs
across the three days of experimentation. Elliotson's monopolising of both
the induction of trance and the testing of its veracity were clearly resented
by the committee members present on each occasion, these including

Wakley himself, Mills, Dr Green and Mr Farr – two of the last three (unspecified) preparing the account printed in *The Lancet*.[138] Wakley, in particular, is dismissive of the first two private experiments:

> On this occasion [i.e., the first] the experiments were conducted wholly by Dr Elliotson, and regarded by Mr Wakley not as tests of the reality of the phenomena displayed, but as demonstrations of the supposed discoveries and the real opinions of the Doctor. Accordingly, a fresh appointment was made for Thursday, August 9, when the experiments were again commenced and conducted by Dr Elliotson, and second time rejected by Mr Wakley as evidence of the correctness of the views entertained by the advocates of mesmerism.[139]

The emphasis upon the Professor's 'real opinions' in *The Lancet*'s account, and its later assertion that these are untenable and inconsistent, would appear to suggest the intimacy between Elliotson and animal magnetism in the medical gaze as much as in the broader public eye. Though the behaviour of the O'Key sisters is given due prominence in the account, the reactions of Elliotson, again and again, become a sort of rhetorical commentary upon the veracity of the phenomena supposedly exhibited. Elliotson is forced to accommodate each anomalous reaction as it is witnessed, and must publicly admit, variously, 'that the occurrence was most extraordinary; that he could not at that moment account for it', or else that he 'could not explain how the thing had occurred; it was most extraordinary, but still he had not the slightest doubt that the whole would yet admit of a satisfactory explanation'.[140] The editor of *The Lancet*, on the other hand, is emphatic in his certainty that an imposture was being expressed during these experiments rather than any scientifically credible phenomenon: 'Mr Wakley said that *he* believed that O'Key could herself give a better explanation of the nature of the supposed phenomena, than any other person'.[141] The implication is clear. Should Elliotson, the most prominent domestic advocate of animal magnetism be discredited as a dupe of fraudulent performers, then the whole existence of mesmerism itself might consequently be thrown into doubt. Such discernment *ought* to be true of the readership of *The Lancet*, conditioned as it is by empiricism and experiment, though these evocative, albeit rhetorical, proofs undoubtedly have their application to the non-clinical mind also. Wakley's concluding remarks are damning, and demonstrate as it were the function of the two practitioners as rhetorical antitheses, for 'in his opinion, the effects which were said to arise from what had been denominated "animal magnetism", constituted one of the completest delusions that the human mind ever entertained'.[142]

This polarity, it might be added, was rapidly taken up by the popular press, who eagerly summarised or referenced the recent events in Bedford Square. In a short response to a reader's query, published on 22 September 1838, *The Penny Satirist* – a popular publication at this time more sympathetic to animal magnetism than its contemporary *The Satirist, or, The Censor of the Times*, whilst explicitly admitting that Elliotson 'has suffered himself to be made the dupe of a jade', contends that 'the cause of mesmerism has been injured by its injudicious friend, but not lost for the science'. Wakley, it would seem, though instrumental in undermining his former friend's public credibility, ultimately failed in his attempt to discredit animal magnetism itself.

If *The Lancet* was not widely read outside of the circle of those with an interest in the practice or development of medicine, *The Times* represented a far more extensive medium by which the closing phases of Elliotson's institutionally endorsed deployment of mesmerism might be conveyed to the general public. Six days after *The Lancet* reported the experiments in Bedford Square, *The Times* published an account of the events syndicated from the pages of *The Medical Gazette*. This was, more or less, a paraphrase of the matter printed in *The Lancet*, and concluded, not surprisingly, that 'It is sufficient to remark, that on proper precautions being used, all the experiments totally failed. So much for Mesmerism!'[143]

The Times' article is arguably more significant, though, for its dissemination among a non-clinical audience of the nature of the experiments by which Wakley disproved, to his own satisfaction at least, Elliotson's claims regarding the magnetic susceptibility of the O'Key sisters. This account was almost certainly the most widely available at the time, given the circulation of *The Times* and its function (authorised or otherwise) in informing the coverage of other metropolitan and provincial newspapers. The three days of experiments conducted in August 1838 essentially comprised a number of attempts to induce and modify trance, first in Elizabeth O'Key and later in her sister Jane. These private experiments bear little resemblance to the spectacular displays in Gower Street. In place of the apparently irresistible waving of magnetic hands, the condition of the subject is purportedly modified by her handling of different metallic objects – oval pieces of lead or nickel, or golden sovereigns – some of which had supposedly been magnetically charged by the operator. Wakley intervened in this process not merely by substituting non-charged materials but also by having his associates make remarks as to whether the substances had actually been magnetised within the subject's earshot. Associated experiments included the testing of the subject with drinking water that had – or had not – been purposely magnetised by the operator. The issue of testing revolves upon the subject never knowing for certain which – if any – of the substances or liquids she is being offered has been charged with magnetic energy by her customary operator.

In these derivative encounters, there is no singing or dancing, or any teasing of a celebrity audience on the part of either of the O'Key sisters. Even with the relative paucity of first-hand detail available to them, and the rather muted dramatics exhibited during the Bedford Square experiments, however, the popular press was still able to glean a *frisson* of ridicule from this latest bathetic development in the magnetic saga. If the sisters could not be rendered spectacular, then their dupe, the learned Doctor, might at least still be proclaimed ridiculous and deceived. A slight journalistic event when compared to the excesses of but a few months before, interest in Elliotson and the O'Key sisters reached a final climax in the popular press on 9 September 1838, three days following *The Times*' publication of the extract from *The Medical Gazette*. *The Age*, for one, truculently celebrated the discomfiture of Elliotson by mocking both his longstanding obstinacy and his sudden confusion. 'Last week', the columnist gleefully declares, 'the gaff was blown – in other words, the whole mummery was exploded – and Tom Wakley enjoyed the triumph':

> To effect the prescribed wonders, the manipulator [Wakley] was to employ a metal bearing the ominous title of *Nickel*. The parties operated upon certainly, during the experiment, appeared to be possessed of devils; but under what influence, think you, gentle reader? – That of a piece of leather, and a brass farthing, which Wakley, the magnetizer (cunning dog!), had substituted for the metal; – an exposure which led no less to the confusion of the credulous, than to the consternation of the learned Doctor. – This is not the first time that Wakley has been *leathering* his professional brethren![144]

The ironic rhetoric of demonism here ensheathes another form of witch-hunt, namely Wakley's somewhat aggressive 'leathering' of medical professionals through the editorial of *The Lancet*. The depiction of how Wakley's subterfuge was undertaken, however, is strikingly sparse, suggesting in itself that the readership of this periodical in particular was at least generally aware of what had been done in Bedford Square. In the two short notices it published on the same day, *The Satirist; or, The Censor of the Times* was, characteristically, more salacious on the one hand, and yet more cynical on the other regarding the nature of the relationship between Elliotson and Elizabeth O'Key. The second of these is untitled, and mocks the relative values of metals in both mesmeric and mercenary terms. The columnist writes:

> The experiments practised on the woman O'Key to test animal magnetism, have rather disconcerted the advocates of that doctrine. Wakley found that a lump of lead and an old farthing could produce convulsions as well as the magnetical nickel. But we beg to inform the animal magnetisers that rubbing the palm of the hand with a piece of gold will produce more astonishing effects than rubbing with any other metal. We advise it to be tried; gold has more exciting virtues than anything else in the world.[145]

More characteristic of *The Satirist*, though, is the earlier contribution, an aside published in the regular and characteristically sarcastic 'Chit-Chat' column. The tone is, inevitably, prurient:

> Mr Wakley, it appears, during the repose of political excitement amuses himself by practically testing the Mesmerian theory. We perceive by the *Lancet* that the honourable member has been, in the presence of Dr Elliotson, 'Baron' Dupotet, and 'other gentlemen', performing on *two* females – Jane and Elizabeth O'Key. It is to be hoped Mrs Wakley was present during these performances.[146]

Mesmerism, it is suggested, is suspect even in this experimental form, and the presence of Dupotet at the final gathering in Bedford Square evokes the past spectre of the salacious commercialism already associated with the Frenchman by *The Satirist*'s columnists.[147] Wakley, at this time, was the Member of Parliament for Finsbury, though the deployment here of the term 'member' is unavoidably implicated in the innuendo that punctuates much of *The Satirist*'s writings on mesmerism. The mere reference to Dupotet, whose own 'member' seems to attract both the attention and the rouge of his female subjects, evokes such things, imposing an ironic twist upon the columnist's stress on 'honourable' and 'gentlemen'.[148] Certainly, the implication is, Wakley risks a charge of immorality should he not dissociate himself from the less-than reputable company he has apparently sought for the idle end of amusement. The main victim, though, was inevitably to be Elliotson. Within four months of the report of the *ad hoc* committee on animal magnetism, one medical journal, again quoted in the pages of *The Times*, was to proclaim damningly that 'The public are aware of the thorough, complete and unequivocal exposure of the humbug of mesmerism which was made in Bedford-square, in August last'.[149]

'Bedlam is much too good for such a fool': Elliotson, clairvoyance and mesmerism outside of the hospital

A late assertion of Elliotson's alleged ability to magnetise liquids was to come shortly after the discrediting of his practice by Wakley. Elliotson, no doubt shaken as much by the adverse publicity as by the experience itself, had taken himself more less immediately to France, leaving his two female patients in the care of his colleagues at University College Hospital. Ostensibly in the interest of their health, they were transferred from there to Dover, where they were at liberty to indulge in sea-bathing. *The Times*, in a paragraph that appears to have been widely syndicated in the form of an article, recounts a remarkable occurrence that apparently took place just as the popular press began to dissect the more sober prose of *The Lancet* and other medical journals. The columnist asserts:

> It is well known that about three weeks since Dr Elliotson left London on a journey to France, and shortly afterwards Elizabeth and Jane O'Key went to Dover for the benefit of change of air. On the morning of the 3d inst. the two girls were enjoying the sea breeze on the beach and stooping to drink salt water as the waves rolled upwards. In an instant both were fixed in a mesmeric trance, the cause of which was involved in mystery. A correspondence with Dr Elliotson took place in consequence, when it was found that at the instant of their drinking the saline fluid the Doctor was bathing on the beach at Calais. Need we urge another word in proof of the instantaneous transmission of the Mesmeric power? The Doctor had magnetized the sea, and it produced the usual effect on his susceptible patients.[150]

Mesmer, reputedly, magnetised the sun. The sea, being nothing more than a liquid and the subjects and their magnetiser being effectively connected by its fluid substance across the breadth of the English Channel, would surely represent far less of a challenge to Elliotson. It seems extraordinary that

The Times should publish this account without comment a mere week after implicitly endorsing the opinion of *The Medical Gazette* that the dogma of mesmerism has been effectively exploded.[151] It is, of course, a mordantly ironic aside, and on the following day an editor testily responded to a correspondent known only through the pseudonym 'Justitia' that the latter 'is greatly mistaken if he thinks we will lend ourselves to support that disgusting humbug called "Mesmerism"'.[152]

If the ironic intent of *The Times*' contributor and editor seem to have escaped at least some of that newspaper's readers, a further account of the occasion in *The Penny Satirist* is somewhat tarter in its assertions. The columnist claims to quote directly from Elizabeth O'Key's own written recollection of the incident, her attributed letter being a document which is almost certainly spurious. The diction utilised in this supposed testimony distorts the vocal statements of this simple Irish girl into a barrage of foreign-sounding approximations that bear comparison with earlier newspaper representations of the duplicitous Baron Dupotet, a Frenchman who apparently once uttered the pointed phrase 'Vat she say?'.[153] The quoted and apparently illiterate O'Key likewise substitutes the letter 'v' for 'w' – she was 'vorkin on the beech', when she was 'struck bye the doctors an-i-mauls mag-knits' in such a way that 'the vaves many-pull-ated i'.[154] This, though, is not her only link to mesmeric practice on the eastern shore of the English Channel. The earlier work of French magnetists had included the fostering of those clairvoyant diagnostic capabilities supposedly found in some mesmeric sensitives.[155] Though this aspect of Continental magnetism found little – if any – favour in Britain at the time of Puységur, O'Key was to make it for a short while topical in the English milieu. As was the case with all of O'Key's public performances, the effect was to be spectacular and dramatic rather than sober and scientific. Her activities at this late stage of her magnetic career were almost certainly to prompt O'Key's expulsion from University College Hospital, and added a final notorious footnote to Elliotson's own departure from that institution.

In January 1839, any enthusiastic invocation of the two names associated with Elizabeth O'Key's sudden accession to the medical profession as a diagnostic clairvoyant was apt to generate a response characterised by both amusement and censure in equal measures. Prior to quoting from an unnamed medical journal, *The Times* is somewhat caustic regarding those medical students at University College who are apparently still faithful to the discredited Elliotson. The editorial comment concludes thus:

> If there remain among the students of the hospital any 'sucking
> *sawbones*' who believes in 'Great Jackey' or 'Little Jackey', the sooner
> the young gentleman is sent by the railroad to Hanwell the better.
> Bedlam is much too good for such a fool.[156]

These two mythical projections of O'Key's vivid imagination, Great and
Little Jackey, have received a modicum of acknowledgement in recent
histories of hypnotism, though their full implications have not been
considered.[157] Grotesque and thus ripe for exploitation by the caricaturists
of the popular press, they were Elizabeth O'Key's portentous personifi-
cations of illness and impending death. A temperate view of their evocation
by O'Key, who apparently had a relatively unfettered access to the
private wards of University College Hospital whilst under Elliotson's care,
reveals how these seemingly supernatural harbingers of mortality came
to effectively challenge the conventional diagnostic authority of regularly
qualified medical staff. The account first recalls how Elliotson, by his own
admission, was influenced in his actions not merely by his working-class
patient but also by a junior and female member of the hospital's nursing
staff:

> Dr Elliotson also stated, on this occasion, that having heard the
> nurse of the ward say that Okey had occasionally passed opinions as
> to the issue [i.e., prognosis] of certain cases then under treatment,
> he had taken her into the men's ward, in the twilight, where she had
> prophesied respecting the termination of some of the diseases, and
> these prophecies were written down and given, in a sealed paper, to
> the apothecary.

Elliotson's bold conduct here is strikingly unconventional, and disrupts not
merely the rigid professional hierarchies that separate physician, apothecary,
nurse and patient, but also the boundaries that necessarily pertain between
inmates of different sexes housed within the same institution. Clearly,
Elliotson was aware of the risk he was taking, for the report states unequivocally that 'He had not, however, taken her into the men's ward without
first inquiring of the nurse if that step might be taken with propriety'.
Again, the act of a senior physician apparently submitting his own proposed
actions to the moral arbitration of a nurse represents an enormous breach in
hospital protocol – and one which would test the tolerance of any institutional management. It is the unnamed nurse, intriguingly, who provides the
account of O'Key's clairvoyant practice when Elliotson is summoned before

the House Committee of the hospital in December 1838. Elliotson merely affirms the truth of her report:

> She [the nurse] said, that on approaching the bed of a certain patient, Okey gave a convulsive shudder, and when asked the reason she replied that 'Great Jackey was on the bed', meaning, according to her own subsequent explanation, that 'Great Jackey' was the 'angel of death'. She shuddered slightly only at the bedside of another patient, 'because Little Jackey was seated there!' These prophecies were accredited by the Doctor [Elliotson], as correct indications of the fate of the patients respecting whom they were expressed.

Unsurprisingly, as an unnamed 'gentleman' intimated during the enquiry, 'the ward was in a complete flurry' on the second appearance of O'Key, the former patient having indeed succumbed to death.[158]

Though Elliotson's medical practice might justifiably be said to have reached a new extreme in its disregard for conventional diagnostics and therapeutics, it is clearly the moral issue that perturbs the Professor's peers on the House Committee. However decorous the behaviour of O'Key might have been, her presence as a patient in a private *men's* ward has implications that might be only too readily anticipated by hospital authorities already mindful of her familiar treatment of the Marquis of Anglesey and other dignitaries in public. These fears were subsequently projected in print – fortunately for the institution – *following* the departure of both patient and magnetist from University College Hospital. *The Penny Satirist* gives free rein to the possibilities presented by innuendo in this account of the same occasion, published on 19 January 1839, for example. O'Key, it seems 'goes by the side of a *male* patient's bed, and laying her hand over various parts of it, suddenly cries out with a loud shriek and a swoon, that she has found "Big Jackey", or "Little Jackey"'. Significantly, in view of these manual manipulations on the part of O'Key it is necessary even that 'The good doctor … explains that the man will either die or live', lest any other conclusion be drawn as to what the girl has discovered with her roving hands beneath the institutional sheets of the male ward. This is, admittedly, a derivative account – the columnist refers the reader to *The Medical Gazette* and *The Times* – and it is more of an interpretation and an expansion than a genuine example of reportage. Elliotson is again portrayed as the dupe of 'That arch hypocrite, – the wench [O'Key]', though he is at least properly acquitted by the columnist of knowingly engaging in 'any attempt to gull the public'. The newspaper's rhetoric, though, clearly condemns 'so immoral and indecent an exhibition' before demanding 'Out! Away with it!'[159]

University College Hospital had, indeed, already taken steps to expel Elizabeth O'Key from its care during Elliotson's absence in France. In October 1838 the House Committee met to consider the position of O'Key who, after having apparently being cured of her epilepsy through Elliotson's repeated applications of magnetism, had been readmitted with ischuriua, the inability to urinate. O'Key was ultimately discharged, apparently in conjunction with further measures to prevent the use of mesmerism on the wards, in December 1838. It is impossible to ascertain the relative balance between the need to contain a potentially embarrassing situation regarding the perceived immorality of O'Key's behaviour and a genuine desire on the part of the medical authorities to suppress the practice and teaching of animal magnetism following the investigation by Wakley and his associates. Whatever the case, the decision prompted Elliotson's own departure from the faculty at the close of the year, his formal letter of resignation being circulated amongst the students between 28 December 1838 and 4 January 1839.[160]

A laconic notice in *The Times* announced to the non-medical public the demise of regular and routine mesmerism within University College Hospital:

A correspondent informs us that the authorities of the London University College having intimated that they will no longer tolerate the absurd and indecent mummeries of 'animal magnetism', Dr Elliotson has tendered his resignation.[161]

From this point, modern histories of hypnotism tend to emphasise Elliotson's undoubted zeal for the magnetic cause primarily by way of his editorship of *The Zoist: A Journal of Cerebral Physiology and Mesmerism and Their Applications to Human Welfare* between 1843 and 1856, and his involvement in the establishment of the London Mesmeric Infirmary.

These were, no doubt, significant achievements. *The Zoist*, as its subtitle suggests, was a publication as much concerned with the physicality of the body as with the metaphysics of the trance state: among other studies, it published Elliotson's long account of how he deployed animal magnetism to allegedly dissipate a cancerous tumour.[162] *The Zoist* was also a forum in which mesmerism was speculatively associated with phrenology and, more importantly, with anaesthesia and surgery.[163] Much of the journal's contents, whether acknowledged as such or not, was from the pen of Elliotson himself, and, though Derek Forrest intimates that public figures such as Harriet Martineau – herself a rare female enthusiast for mesmerism – were among the periodical's contributors, their opinions were frequently advanced by way of reprinted letters originally sent to the editor's associates, or else embedded in editorial reports of their mesmeric activities.[164] As a relatively minor quasi-medical periodical, needless to say, *The Zoist* was a somewhat indirect influence upon public opinion outside of those with a specific interest in the deployment of animal magnetism in the medical milieu. *The Zoist* was necessarily founded because *The Lancet* and other mainstream medical periodicals had, by 1843, almost totally ceased to print anything other than dismissive asides regarding the claims of animal magnetism. If anything, its effect was to signal the marginalisation of mesmerism in British medical culture. The same might be said also regarding the establishment in 1849 of the London Mesmeric Infirmary, an institution at which Elliotson fulfilled the role of governor rather than practical physician.[165] Though ostensibly a triumph for the disparate body that constituted mesmerism in mid-century London, the discrete status of that institution surely affirmed the position of animal magnetism as now being beyond the pale of regular medicine. These two activities, both of which were far less evocative than his previous practice in Gower Street, form the core of what may apparently be said regarding Elliotson's public reputation following his resignation. Little more remains for the historian of Victorian hypnotism, it seems, other than to chart Elliotson's slow decline into depression, mental debilitation and death.[166]

Some further light, however, may be thrown upon the later career of possibly the most prominent – and most abused – of British magnetists. Elliotson's almost evangelical zeal, as Forrest considers it, was most certainly encouraged by the controversy that surrounded his departure from University College.[167] Historians of Victorian hypnotism make much of Elliotson's only visit to the University after his resignation date, when he delivered the 1846 Harveian Oration, a formal address customarily delivered in Latin, during which the former Professor actually spoke very little about practical mesmerism.[168] Similar attention has been drawn to the decision, presumably taken by the University authorities, of having a police presence in attendance in anticipation of student unrest.[169] Intriguingly, press reports at the time, while readily acknowledging the controversial nature of Elliotson's presence, characteristically fail to note any unusual security measures.[170] Somewhat less attention has been paid, however, to the astonishing – and well documented – undergraduate disorder which marred his successor's inaugural address, and no doubt enhanced the former Professor's own sense of self-worth and injury. Elliotson was certainly a popular tutor, and his departure from University College Hospital was presented to the undergraduates not merely by way of his circulated letter of resignation but also in person at a dinner which he hosted for a select number of his undergraduate acolytes at his house in Conduit Street.[171] Many students were also present at an institutional gathering on 4 January 1839 at which the letter was formally read and voted upon.[172]

The Scottish physician James Copland was appointed by the University to complete the series of lectures which Elliotson had already begun in 1838. *The Times* judged the first of Copland's lectures sufficiently controversial to send its own correspondent to report upon a collegiate body whose students were now effectively divided into two hostile camps. The columnist reported upon an audience of three to four hundred students who 'amused themselves by hissing and cheering particular individuals as they entered the rooms, as their opinions were known to be favourable or adverse to either party'. Not merely was the lecture delayed by twenty minutes but something approaching 'a general *mêlée*' seemed inevitable, though at the lecture's conclusion 'the results were no worse than one or two torn coats, and peradventure a black eye here and there, caught when some of the most riotous were expelled'. *The Times* concluded that 'the entire blame for the disturbance rests with the Elliotson party, who arranged themselves in parts of the room which were out of view of the professors present, and commenced the uproar'.[173] There is no evidence that Elliotson had the slightest involvement in what was, by all accounts, a disgraceful evening for both sides in the now-bitter debate between animal magnetism and institutional medicine. It may well have been euphemistic for the Chairman of the Proprietors of the University to claim a month later that this particular dismissal had given 'rise to no serious difference between the hospital pupils and the committee and council'.[174]

No longer associated with the teaching hospital, Elliotson continued to practice conventional medicine whilst demonstrating mesmeric phenomena at his house in Conduit Street. He was consulted on neurological illnesses and implicitly advanced his opinions on the moral character of his patients; was curator of the reference collection of the Phrenological Association; and appeared as an expert witness in legal proceedings.[175] He certainly does not appear to have become a 'professional pariah', despite intimations of that nature made by the non-clinical press in later years.[176] If it had apparently passed from the medical field with Elliotson's resignation, mesmerism still held a fashionable cachet in wealthy metropolitan circles: *The Satirist*, for example, reported a séance held by a number of noble individuals in early September 1841, in private rooms, and at which titled ladies were apparently the subjects. Though implications of immodesty were merely hinted in an article otherwise devoid of salacious detail, the columnist was emboldened to suggest – no doubt with irony – that it 'seems not unlikely ... that "mesmerisation" will become extremely fashionable, and soon take its place among the most polite amusements of the day'.[177] It is hard to escape the conclusion that animal magnetism was in danger of becoming simply another parlour amusement, with so-called experiments being conducted with the idle curiosity that often typified domestic forays into table-turning and mediumship.

Elliotson, however, successfully maintained a sedate *cordon sanitaire* from such aristocratic frivolities, as a number of small features in *The Times* was to intimate. One such announcement, published only five days after the column in *The Satirist*, certainly affirms a continued public interest in magnetism that has resisted the disdain of the medical profession. *The Times'* columnist notes, indeed, the existence of what appears to be a thriving mesmeric industry in the metropolis:

> That the mesmeric phenomena are attracting more attention and interest than they have hitherto done in this country there can be no doubt, since, independent of many private magnetizers, there are no less than three public practitioners at present residing in London.[178]

The distinction here is apparently between those who administer therapy, in private, to individual patients and those who maintain the tradition of the public displays only recently discontinued in the Gower Street lecture theatres and on the wards of University College Hospital.

Among the latter was a French magnetist, Monsieur Lafontaine, who practised from rooms in Hanover Square in London's Mayfair, and in the Regency expansiveness of the London Tavern in Bishopsgate. Lafontaine attracted the censure of *The Satirist*, among others, but certainly seems to have capitalised upon the earlier work of Elliotson.[179] Lafontaine's practice, however, seems to have been somewhat more visceral than that of Elliotson, as *The Times* intimates in this account of the Frenchman's activities at the London Tavern:

> The former patient, the young French lad, on whom M. Lafontaine has previously operated, was first placed in the chair, and submitted

to pins being inserted in his head, cheeks, hands, thighs and legs without his evincing the signs of sensibility ... The eyelids were then pulled back, and a lighted candle closely applied to the eyeballs. They presented a wild and spectral appearance, and seemed fixed and immoveable. Lucifer matches were then burned under his nose, and concentrated ammonia applied, but they did not appear to affect him.[180]

Though much of this display appears as gratuitous as it is grotesque, it does signal the increasing importance of anaesthesia in the development of mesmeric practice. A much shorter account in the same column merely intimates that 'On Saturday last, Dr Elliotson exhibited to a select audience in his own house, two very curious cases of the mesmeric or animo-magnetic phenomena'.[181] This latter appears to have involved the imposition of rigidity upon the limbs rather than the more drastic interventive manipulations of Lafontaine. Elliotson's residence was also utilised for displays by other visiting magnetists, most notably a Monsieur Marcellet, who brought his own subject, 'A young gentleman, known as Alexis the Somnambulist', from Paris in 1844 in order to illustrate clairvoyant phenomena. In the somnambulistic condition, Alexis exhibited the bodily rigidity which appears to have characterised much of Elliotson's own practice after his resignation, though it is made clear that the Englishman played no part in the proceedings. If Alexis's reputation of perceiving unknown information at a distance, and his ability to read an enveloped letter whilst thoroughly blindfolded appear uncanny, then his trick of playing *écarté* in the same sightless condition is surely theatrical. This occasion appears to have aroused consternation rather than conviction in the mind of *The Times'* columnist, who concludes, 'We draw no conclusion from the facts: we confess they are mysterious and inexplicable – beyond our comprehension'.[182] Clearly, in 1844 it was still an inadvisable thing to admit publicly to an enthusiasm for animal magnetism. Elliotson's interest in non-diagnostic clairvoyance precedes this occasion, however: he was retained, in some capacity, as a medical adviser in connection with the magnetising of a boy, James Cooke, who whilst entranced at Deptford could apparently describe scenes he had never witnessed at Greenwich, Baker Street and Portman Square.[183]

Elliotson's reputation within the medical profession was undoubtedly undermined by his continued espousal of animal magnetism in the years following Wakley's experiments with the O'Key sisters. A greater degree of sympathy, however, was to be found in the non-clinical press for the man himself though seldom for his cause. Certainly, Elliotson was, it was often suggested, a man of principle, however misplaced that latter may have been. Elliotson's obituary in *The Morning Post* following his death on 29 July 1868 balances the perception of Elliotson as a man wholly convinced by the phenomena he espoused with the rather relentless opposition he faced from his professional colleagues:

> In the course of his practice at University College Hospital certain phenomena developed themselves in the case of two young girls named Okey, and Elliotson was thus led to investigate mesmerism, and with his characteristic boldness and love of truth he published the results fearlessly. He was at this time enjoying as large a practice at the West-end as had ever been the lot of any physician. The result of his bold utterance of the truth was that his learned brethren persecuted him, and his practice fell off to the extent of £5,000 per annum, and in 1838 he was obliged to resign his professorship.[184]

A complex history may well be condensed and simplified in this indulgent appreciation, but the use of the term 'led' here may well stand for how Elliotson was perceived not merely in death but in his lifetime also. In almost all cases, the consensus would appear to be that Elliotson was a well-intentioned professional, duped by his more worldly associates. One of the anonymous writers for *The Penny Satirist*, for example, took pains to distance himself from the more pungent rhetoric deployed by that popular periodical against animal magnetism generally by equivocating regarding Elliotson's role in its development. Replying on 26 January 1839 to a correspondent known only as 'Mr D. Regent's-park', the columnist states:

> No: I assure you I have nothing to do with the article which appeared in this journal against Dr Elliotson. I confess that as soon as I observed the way in which the learned professor endeavoured to establish Mesmerism, I shook my head and said, 'That excellent man has been misled by a French showman. He will do himself harm without promoting his object.' My apprehensions have been realized. I am sorry for it, as I consider the Doctor as one of the greatest physicians of England. I am convinced that he was prompted in his endeavours by the most honourable motives, and I regret that the students of London University have been deprived of such an eminent teacher.[185]

If the columnist will not go so far as to consider animal magnetism as a tenable medical doctrine, he is sufficiently convinced of the credibility of Elliotson's character, even if his judgement is placed in a questionable light. *The Hull Packet*, on the other hand, is less sympathetic in a paraphrase of 'a very amusing' local lecture by a John Richardson, the content of which was hostile to the claims of animal magnetism. Intimating that Dupotet had unsuccessfully attempted to borrow money from Elliotson, and citing this as the cause of the breach between the two, the lecturer depicts the Doctor as one who incautiously submits too quickly to enthusiasm:

> Had not Elliotson taken Dupotet by the hand, it is probable the science [mesmerism] would have slumbered on for many years. It was quite notorious that even the wisest of men might sometimes get most ridiculous crotchets in their heads, and when the public had once got a peculiar theory before their heated imaginations, it generally took a considerable time before they could be brought calmly to reason and consider its true principles.

Elliotson is here aligned with the gullible and fashionable public rather than the wisely sceptical professional. He, like them, can seemingly only be cured of his mistaken faith by careful exposure to credible evidence, and Richardson suggests that the discrediting of the O'Key sisters by Wakley ought rightly to have brought the Doctor to his senses. Such was, however, not to be the case. The columnist continues:

> As a proof [of] how easy the public might be imposed upon, the lecturer mentioned the circumstance of Mr Wakley, fully proving that the two girls named Okey, on whom Dr Elliotson had been operating, were impostors. The Doctor was constrained to believe that the girls had been practising deception, and although he admitted that the experiments had been fairly conducted he still believed in the theory.[186]

Clearly, Elliotson cannot escape censure here, no matter how worthy his motivations for pursuing the potential therapeutic or diagnostic applications of animal magnetism. Elliotson, seemingly, is stubbornly or wilfully committed to the discredited doctrine, even when he is forced to contemplate that he has been deceived. It is a conclusion that is essentially repeated 154 years later in Robin Waterfield's estimation of the alternatives open to Elliotson once Wakley had completed his demolition of the sisters' credibility.[187] Elliotson, as it were, can be memorialised only by his

stubbornness and his unwitting endorsement of the duplicities perpetuated
by ostensibly less talented individuals.

Notes

1 Anon., 'Animal Magnetism' in 'Reviews', *The Athenæum*, 16 June 1838, 417–21
   at p. 417, col. 1.
2 Anon., 'Animal Magnetism', *The Athenæum*, 16 June 1838, p. 417, col. 2.
3 Anon., 'Animal Magnetism', *The Athenæum*, 16 June 1838, p. 417, col. 1.
4 Anon., 'Animal Magnetism', *The Athenæum*, 16 June 1838, p. 417, col. 2.
5 Anon., 'Animal Magnetism', *The Athenæum*, 16 June 1838, p. 417, col. 2.
6 Lee's work is mentioned in only in the two final sentences of the review, and
   is described simply as 'a short, clear, and manly production' which 'should
   be read by anyone desirous of forming a just conception of the value of these
   magnetic mystifications': Anon., 'Animal Magnetism', *The Athenæum*, 16 June
   1838, p. 421, col. 2.
7 Anon., 'Animal Magnetism', *The Athenæum*, 16 June 1838, p. 417, col. 3.
8 Anon., 'Animal Magnetism', *The Athenæum*, 16 June 1838, p. 418, col. 1.
9 Anon., 'Animal Magnetism', *The Athenæum*, 16 June 1838, p. 419, col. 1.
10 Dr Albert, 'Regeneration of Mesmerism in France', *The Liverpool Mercury*, 17
   November 1826, p. 158, col. 1.
11 Anon., 'Animal Magnetism: Experiments of Baron Dupotet', *The Lancet*, 2 (2
   September 1837), 836–40. The same volume contains, on pp. 905–7, 'Animal
   Magnetism: [A] Letter from Baron Dupotet'.
12 Anon., 'Animal Magnetism', Supplement to *The Liverpool Mercury*, 24 November
   1837, p. 1, col. 6.
13 One of the final accounts, and one which gives Dupotet but the most cursory
   of attention, was published in Dublin in February 1839. See Anon., 'Animal
   Magnetism', *The Freeman's Journal and Daily Commercial Advertiser*, 26 February
   1839, p. 3, cols 3–5, at col. 3.
14 Alison Winter's recourse to an account printed in the monthly *Mirror* is a
   rare exception. See *Mesmerized: Powers of Mind in Victorian Britain* (Chicago:
   University of Chicago Press, 1998), p. 44.
15 Anon., 'Animal Magnetism', *The Standard*, 1 September 1828, p. 4, col. 5;
   Anon., 'Animal Magnetism', *The Morning Post*, 2 September 1828, p. 4,
   col. 2.
16 Anon., 'Animal Magnetism', *The London Saturday Journal*, 1/15 (13 April 1839),
   232–3, at p. 233, col. 2.
17 Anon., 'Animal Magnetism', *The Standard*, 1 September 1828, p. 4, col. 5,
   original italics.
18 Dropsy or oedema is the excessive accumulation of fluid in the body tissues.
19 Anon., 'Animal Magnetism', *The Standard*, 1 September 1828, p. 4, col. 5.

20 Anon., 'Animal Magnetism', *The Standard*, 1 September 1828, p. 4, col. 5, original italics.

21 Anon., 'Fashion and Varieties', *The Freeman's Journal and Daily Commercial Advertiser*, 10 October 1839, p. 2, col. 5.

22 'Animal Magnetism' [advertisement], *The Morning Post*, 27 November 1837, p. 1, col. 2. Original capitalisation.

23 '*The Lancet*, Sept. 9' [advertisement], *The Morning Post*, 11 September 1837, p. 1, col. 3.

24 Anon., 'Animal Magnetism', Supplement to *The Liverpool Mercury*, 24 November 1837, p. 1, col. 6.

25 'Animal Magnetism' [advertisement], *The Morning Post*, 27 November 1837, p. 1, col. 2. Original capitalisation.

26 Anon., 'Animal Magnetism', *The Morning Post*, 2 February 1838, p. 5, col. 4. The term 'influenza' is used here not in its modern viral sense, but rather as a euphemism for influence.

27 See Robin Waterfield, *Hidden Depths: The Story of Hypnosis* (London: Pan, 2004), pp. 110–15.

28 Anon., 'Animal Magnetism', *The Morning Post*, 2 February 1838, p. 5, col. 4; Anon., 'Art. III. On Vaccine Inoculation, by Robert Willan MD, FAS', *Edinburgh Review, or Critical Journal*, 9/17 (October 1806), 32–66, at pp. 55–6.

29 Anon., 'Animal Magnetism', *The Morning Post*, 2 February 1838, p. 5, col. 4.

30 'Notice to Correspondents', *The London Dispatch and People's Political and Social Reformer*, 17 June 1838, p. 732, col. 3.

31 Theocritus Brown, 'Animal Magnetism', *The Times*, 28 September 1837, p. 1, cols 4–6, at col. 4.

32 Anon., 'Animal Magnetism', *The Satirist: or, The Censor of the Times*, 5 November 1837, p. 774, col. 3. Original italics throughout.

33 Waterfield, *Hidden Depths*, pp. 91–2, 93.

34 As well as the obvious implications of George du Maurier's *Trilby* (1894), one might consider here also such neglected works as Isabella F. Romer, *Sturmer: A Tale of Mesmerism, to Which Are Added Other Sketches from Life*, 3 vols (London: Bentley, 1841), and Franklyn Wright's 'The Mesmerist's Spell', *The 'Halfpenny Marvel'*, 29 October 1895, 1–13. A humorous response to the serious issue of sexual abuse and hypnotism may be found in du Maurier's unpaginated cartoon 'Hypnotism – A Modern Parisian Romance (In Four Chapters)' in *Punch's Almanack for 1890* (5 December 1889).

35 Anon, 'Animal Magnetism', *The Times*, 1 November 1837, p. 3, col. 6.

36 Anon., 'Startling Experiments', *The Satirist: or, The Censor of the Times*, 5 November 1837, p. 771, col. 2.

37 Lydia Syson, *Doctor of Love: Dr James Graham and His Celestial Bed* (Richmond: Alma Books, 2008); R. S. Porter, 'The Sexual Politics of James Graham', *British Journal for Eighteenth-Century Studies*, 5 (1982), 199–206.

38 As was the case with the entrepreneurial magnetists who succeeded Graham in the popular consciousness, technology and inventor were mocked and parodied, both on the stage and in the metropolitan press of the day. See: Anon., 'Emperor of the Quacks' [song], *Whitehall Evening Post*, 9–12 June 1781, p. 2, col. 4; Anon., 'Poetry: A Song, Introductory to the Celestial Bed', *Morning Herald and Daily Advertiser*, 26 July 1781, p. 4, col. 1.

39 Another account of Dupotet's practice warned that 'Ladies had better stay away': see 'Notice to Correspondents', *The London Dispatch and People's Political and Social Reformer*, 17 June 1838, p. 732, col. 3.

40 Anon., 'Animal Magnetism', *The Times*, 1 November 1837, p. 3, col. 6.

41 Anon., 'Animal Magnetism', *The Times*, 1 November 1837, p. 3, col. 6.

42 Anon., 'Animal Magnetism', *The Times*, 1 November 1837, p. 3, col. 6.

43 Anon., 'Fashion and Varieties', *The Freeman's Journal and Daily Advertiser*, 10 October 1839, p. 2, col. 5.

44 Anon., 'Animal Magnetism', *The Times*, 1 November 1837, p. 3, col. 6, original italics.

45 Anon., 'Animal Magnetism', *The Times*, 1 November 1837, p. 3, col. 6.

46 Anon., 'Chit-Chat', *The Satirist: or, The Censor of the Times*, 28 January 1838, p. 29, col. 3, original italics.

47 Anon., 'The Magnetism Charlatan' in 'Chit-Chat', *The Satirist: or, The Censor of the Times*, 11 February 1848, p. 45, col. 3.

48 Anon., 'A Magnetising Mountebank', *The Satirist: or, The Censor of the Times*, 11 February 1838, p. 45, col. 2.

49 Consider the Covent Garden crimes enumerated in the regular 'Police' column in *The Times*: for example: 18 September 1837, p. 6, col. 6; 11 October 1837, p. 6, cols 5–6, at col. 5; 13 November 1838, p. 7, cols 2–4, at col. 3; 23 January 1839, p. 7, cols 3–4, at col. 4.

50 Such things are a commonplace of those ephemeral guides to the specialities, proclivities and prices of London prostitutes published since at least the eighteenth century. See, for example, *Harris's List of Covent Garden Ladies, or Man of Pleasure's Kalender for the Year 1793*, ed. Hallie Rubenhold (Stroud: Tempus, 2005).

51 Anon., 'A Magnetising Mountebank', p. 45, col. 2.

52 Michel Foucault, *The History of Sexuality: An Introduction*, trans Robert Hurley (London: Penguin, 1984), pp. 1–2.

53 Anon., 'A Magnetising Mountebank', p. 45, col. 2, original italics.

54 Anon., 'A Magnetising Mountebank', p. 45, col. 2, original italics.

55 Waterfield, *Hidden Depths*, p. 109.

56 Anon., 'A Magnetising Mountebank', p. 45, col. 2.

57 Anon., 'Mountebank Dupotet Again', *The Satirist: or, The Censor of the Times*, 11 March 1838, p. 75, col. 3.

58 Anon., 'Chit-Chat', *The Satirist: or, The Censor of the Times*, 25 February 1838, p. 61, col. 3.

59 Anon., 'Animal Magnetism' [poem], *The Satirist: or, The Censor of the Times*, 11 March 1838, p. 77, col. 2. The allusion is to 'Mrs Lane Fox who, it is rumoured, is a great admirer of the Dupotet humbug' (ibid.). The incident is again referred to a week later, this time within the 'Chit-Chat' column: 'Mrs Lane Fox has been but once to the exhibition of Baron Dupotet, but, as she afterwards informed Mrs Leicester Stanhope, she saw enough on that occasion to satisfy her that animal magnetism is a very *"gross* imposition". Mrs Lane Fox has very refined notions of what constitutes vice.' See Anon., 'Chit-Chat', *The Satirist: or, The Censor of the Times*, 18 March 1838, p. 85, col. 3, original italics.

60 Anon., 'Mountebank Dupotet Again', p. 75, col. 3, original italics. An *entretenue* is a kept woman or mistress, and 'the infamous saloon in Piccadilly' is the Royal Saloon, 'a mighty rendezvous, where every variety of character is to be found' according to Bernard Blackmantle [Charles Molloy Westmacott] in *The English Spy* (1824). See Bernard Blackmantle (pseud.) and Isaac Robert Cruikshank (illus.), *The English Spy: An Original Work Characteristic, Satirical, and Humorous, Comprising Scenes and Sketches in Every Rank of Society, Being Portraits Drawn from the Life* (London: Sherwood, Jones and Co., 1825), p. 205. Available online at www.gutenberg.org/files/20001/20001-h/20001-h. htm#link2H_4_0024 [accessed 12 February 2014].

61 Anon., 'Mountebank Dupotet Again', p. 75, col. 3. *Aillades*, in this context, means literally 'sauce' or 'sauciness'.

62 Anon., 'Mountebank Dupotet Again', p. 75, col. 3. Lancaster Street and York Square were also referenced on occasions in the 'Police' column of *The Times* in connection with cases of theft and sexual immorality: see 22 November 1838, p. 7, cols 1–5, at col. 2; 23 November 1838, p. 7, cols 3–5, at col. 4.

63 Anon., 'Mountebank Dupotet Again', p. 75, col. 3, original italics.

64 Anon., 'Mountebank Dupotet Again', p. 75, col. 3.

65 Anon., 'The Quack Dupotet', *The Satirist: or, The Censor of the Times*, 18 March 1838, p. 83, col. 1.

66 'The Voluptuarian Cabinet' [advertisement], *The Satirist: or, The Censor of the Times*, 18 March 1838, p. 82, col. 3.

67 Anon., *The Power of Mesmerism: A Highly Erotic Narrative of Voluptuous Facts and Fancies* (Brussels?: Printed for the Nihilists, Moscow, 1891).

68 *The Medico-Chirurgical Review and Journal of Practical Medicine* was edited by James Johnson and Henry James Johnson, and published by S. Highley of Fleet Street, London. The two titles elide, maintaining a continuous pagination, *The Periscope* being something of a periodical addendum or supplement to *The Medico-Chirurgical Review*. Its extensive capacity to survey not merely current practice but also the contents of British, European and North American medical periodicals militates against it being considered a mere component of the enclosing publication.

69 Anon., 'Animal Magnetism', *The Periscope; or Circumspective Review*, 1 October 1838, pp. 634–6, at p. 634, col. 1.

70 Anon., 'Animal Magnetism', *The Periscope*, 1 October 1838, p. 634, cols 1–2.

71 Anon., 'Animal Magnetism', *The Morning Post*, 2 February 1838, p. 5, col. 4.

72 Anon., 'Mountebank Dupotet Again', p. 75, col. 3.

73 Anon., 'Animal Magnetism', *The Periscope*, 1 October 1838, p. 635, col. 1.

74 Anon., 'Animal Magnetism', *The Periscope*, 1 October 1838, p. 635, cols 1–2.

75 See, for example, the cases enumerated in Jules Liégeois, *De la suggestion hypnotique dans ses rapports avec le droit civil et le droit criminal* (Paris: Picard, 1884).

76 Alan Gauld, *A History of Hypnotism* (Cambridge: Cambridge University Press, 1990), p. 199; cf. Waterfield, *Hidden Depths*, p. 172.

77 Indeed, this was recognised at the time by at least one London periodical. See Anon., 'Animal Magnetism', *The Morning Post*, 16 June 1838, p. 6, cols 4–5, at col. 4.

78 See Anon., 'Mesmerism Unmasked', *The Medical Times*, 9 (9 December 1843), 145–7.

79 Anon., 'Animal Magnetism', *The Periscope*, 1 October 1838, p. 635, col. 2.

80 Anon., 'Animal Magnetism', *The Athenæum*, 16 June 1838, p. 417, col. 3.

81 Anon., 'Another Mesmerian Mountebank', *The Satirist: or, The Censor of the Times*, 18 March 1838, p. 83, col. 3.

82 Anon., 'Dr Elliotson', *The Morning Post*, 3 August 1868, p. 3, col. 5.

83 Irys Herfner, 'Mesmerism', *Dublin University Magazine*, 23 (January 1844), 37–53, at p. 53, col. 2.

84 Anon., 'Address Delivered at the Opening of the Medical Session in the University of London, October 1, 1832. By John Elliotson, MD Cantab., FRS, &c. &c.', *The Court Magazine and Belle Assemblée*, 1 December 1832, p. 309, col. 2. This short report also conveys Elliotson's specific support for the establishment of a teaching hospital to be associated with the University of London, and intimates also that 'the Professors have relinquished their salaries, and declined receiving pupils' fees, until such an establishment should be properly made and provided for'.

85 'Literary Fund – The Anniversary Festival' [advertisement], *The Age*, 12 May 1833, p. 145, col. 3.

86 'University College Hospital' [advertisement], *The Times*, 21 May 1838, p. 1, col. 2.

87 Anon., 'A Magnetising Mountebank', p. 45, col. 2.

88 Waterfield, *Hidden Depths*, p. 173.

89 Anon., 'Dublin, March 24' [obituary], *The Morning Post* [London], 27 March 1830, p. 3, col. 4. Chenevix was no minor figure: his death in Paris was widely acknowledged by the British metropolitan and provincial press. See 'Sunday's Post', *The Bury and Norwich Post: Or, Suffolk and Norfolk Telegraph, Essex,*

Cambridge, & *Ely Intelligencer*, 7 April 1830, p. 1, cols 1–2, at col. 2; 'Died', *The Morning Post*, 29 March 1830, p. 4, col. 1; untitled obituary, *The Caledonian Mercury*, 10 April 1830, p. 3, col. 2; 'Deaths', *La Belle Assemblée; or, Bell's Court and Fashionable Magazine*, 1 May 1830, p. 230, col. 2.

90 Gauld, *A History of Hypnotism*, pp. 198–9.

91 According to Waterfield, Elliotson was in practice at St Thomas's Hospital between 1817 and 1832. See Waterfield, *Hidden Depths*, p. 173.

92 Richard Chenevix, 'On Mesmerism, Improperly Denominated Animal Magnetism', *The London Medical and Physical Journal*, 61 (1829), 219–30 and 491–501; 62 (1829), 114–25, 210–21 and 315–29.

93 See, for example, Derek Forrest, *Hypnotism: A History* (London: Penguin, 2000), pp. 130–2; Gauld, *A History of Hypnotism*, pp. 198–9; Waterfield, *Hidden Depths*, p. 173; Winter, *Mesmerized*, p. 71.

94 The mass-market nature of the *Morning Post* reprint would have made Elliotson's account far more accessible to the general reader than, say, Chenevix's own 'On Mesmerism, Improperly Denominated Animal Magnetism', which was published in the specialist *London Medical and Physical Journal* in 1829.

95 Anon., 'Animal Magnetism', *The Morning Post*, 7 November 1829, p. 4, col. 3. Original capitalisation. Irritatingly, the variant spelling of Chenevix's surname is a persistent inaccuracy in both popular and professional accounts of the chemist's work. See, for example, Anon., 'Early Irish Hypnotists and Mesmerists', *British Medical Journal*, 19 August 1933, p. 348, col. 2.

96 Anon., 'Animal Magnetism', *The Morning Post*, 7 November 1829, p. 4, col. 3.

97 Intriguingly, this form of simultaneously curative and demonstrative practice, punctuated by a colloquy in a language unintelligible to the subject, anticipates the initial mesmeric encounter between Svengali and his neuralgic subject in *Trilby*, George du Maurier's *fin-de-siècle* novel of sexual and financial abuse: see *Trilby: A Novel* (London: Osgood, McIlvaine & Co., 1895), pp. 67–8.

98 Anon., 'Animal Magnetism', *The Morning Post*, 7 November 1829, p. 4, col. 3.

99 Such things become integral to the later debate upon animal vivisection, attaining a sort of fictional apotheosis through the practices of Dr Nathan Benjulia in Wilkie Collins's *Heart and Science*, and the titular protagonist of H. G. Wells's *The Island of Dr Moreau*.

100 See, for example, Forrest, *Hypnotism*, pp. 140–52, *passim*, which quotes extensively from the observations of George Mills, correspondent for *The Lancet*. Mills was sufficiently reputable as to attend the third anniversary meeting of the British Medical Association at the Freemasons' Tavern in Great Queen Street on 7 October 1839, and on that occasion was the subject of, and the respondent to, a toast proposed by Professor Grant at the subsequent dinner. See Anon., 'British Medical Association', *The Lancet*, 12 October 1839, 93–102, at pp. 98–9.

101 Waterfield, for one, subtitles his discussion of the physician's experiments with

the O'Key sisters 'Elliotson Versus the Medical Establishment': Waterfield, *Hidden Depths*, p. 173.

102 Anon., 'Animal Magnetism; or Mesmerism', *The Lancet*, 1 September 1838, 805–11, at p. 805, col. 2. Forrest, *Hypnotism*, p. 143; Waterfield, *Hidden Depths*, p. 175.

103 Anon., 'Animal Magnetism', *The Lancet*, 26 May 1838, 282–8, at p. 287, col. 2.

104 Anon., 'Animal Magnetism', *The Lancet*, 26 May 1838, p. 282, col. 2. The columnist later demarcates between the variant reactions to O'Key's behaviour exhibited by 'the astonished commoners' and 'the carriage company': p. 286, col. 2.

105 Anon., 'Animal Magnetism', *The Lancet*, 26 May 1838, p. 283, col. 1. King's College London was chartered in 1829, and was one of the two initial colleges of the University of London, which was itself chartered in 1836.

106 Anon., 'Animal Magnetism', *The Lancet*, 26 May 1838, p. 283, col. 1, original italics and punctuation. Elliotson's decision to open his experiments 'to every gentleman who feels an interest in the subject' is applauded in one newspaper: see Anon., 'Animal Magnetism', *The Morning Post*, 5 May 1838, p. 3, col. 4.

107 Anon., 'Animal Magnetism', *The Lancet*, 26 May 1838, p. 283, col. 2.

108 Anon., 'Animal Magnetism', *The Lancet*, 26 May 1838, p. 282, col. 2.

109 Anon., 'Animal Magnetism', *The Lancet*, 26 May 1838, p. 284, col. 1.

110 Anon., 'Animal Magnetism', *The Lancet*, 26 May 1838, p. 284, col. 1, original italics.

111 Anon., 'A Magnetising Mountebank', p. 45, col. 2.

112 Anon., 'Animal Magnetism', *The Lancet*, 26 May 1838, p. 285, col. 1.

113 Anon., 'Animal Magnetism', *The Lancet*, 26 May 1838, p. 285, col. 2.

114 Anon., 'Animal Magnetism', *The Lancet*, 26 May 1838, p. 284, col. 1. O'Key's trance-induced state of ignorance is quietly challenged in the account when the columnist recalls how she observes 'Look here, what lots of feet!' whilst 'pointing with her hand to the feet of the sitters all around the area': p. 284, col. 2.

115 Anon., 'Animal Magnetism', *The Lancet*, 26 May 1838, p. 288, col. 1.

116 Waterfield, *Hidden Depths*, p. 175.

117 See, for example, Waterfield, *Hidden Depths*, p. 174.

118 Anon., 'Another Mesmerian Mountebank', p. 83, col. 3.

119 A. W. Humphreys, *The King of the Cannibal Islands* (London: A. Hughes, [1830]). The song is reproduced in Anthony Bennett, 'Rivals Unravelled: A Broadside Song and Dance', *Folk Music Journal*, 6/4 (1993), 420–45, at pp. 422–3.

120 Anon., 'Another Mesmerian Mountebank', p. 83, col. 3.

121 For a near contemporary account of sexual activities in Coventry Court, see: 'Police', *The Morning Chronicle*, 5 February 1825, p. 4, col. 3. See also: Anon., 'A Magnetising Mountebank', p. 45, col. 2.

122 Anon., 'Another Mesmerian Mountebank', p. 83, col. 3; Anon., 'Animal Magnetism', *The Lancet*, 2 (1838), p. 284, col. 2.

123 Anon., 'Another Mesmerian Mountebank', p. 83, col. 3.

124 Accounts of Elliotson's practice with the O'Key sisters in *The Satirist* seldom attain the intensity of salaciousness associated with Dupotet's practice by that periodical's columnist. One untitled exception is to be found in *The Satirist*, 15 April 1838, p. 117, col. 2.

125 Anon., 'Animal Magnetism', *The Morning Post*, 2 March 1838, p. 6, col. 5.

126 Anon., 'Animal Magnetism', *The Morning Post*, 5 March 1838, p. 3, col. 1.

127 Anon., 'Animal Magnetism', *The Morning Post*, 11 May 1838, p. 6, col. 5.

128 Anon., 'Another Mesmerian Mountebank', p. 83, col. 3.

129 Anon., 'Animal Magnetism', *The Morning Post*, 11 May 1838, p. 6, col. 5.

130 Anon., 'Animal Magnetism', *The London Saturday Journal*, 1/15 (13 April 1839), 232–3, at p. 232, col. 2.

131 See, for example, Anon., 'Animal Magnetism: Second Report of Facts and Experiments', *The Lancet*, 9 June 1838, 377–83; 'Animal Magnetism: Conclusion of Second Report of Facts and Experiments', *The Lancet*, 16 June 1838, 400–3. Reports from University College Hospital were published on an almost weekly basis by Wakley following the cessation of public demonstrations. See Anon., 'Animal Magnetism: Fourth Report – Remarks and Experiments', *The Lancet*, 7 July 1838, 516–19; 'Animal Magnetism: Fifth Report of Experiments and Facts', *The Lancet*, 14 July 1838, 546–9; 'Animal Magnetism: Sixth Report of Experiments and Facts', *The Lancet*, 21 July 1838, 585–90; 'Animal Magnetism: Seventh Report of Experiments and Facts', *The Lancet*, 28 July 1838, 615–20. These reports were all drawn up by Mills.

132 Anon., 'The Lancet', *The Lancet*, 15 September 1838, 873–7, at p. 873, col. 2; Anon., 'Animal Magnetism: Second Report of Facts and Experiments', p. 377, col. 1.

133 Derek Forrest notes that Elliotson's case register indicates that Elizabeth O'Key had been privately exhibited to Charles Dickens and George Cruikshank as early as 4 January 1838: see Forrest, *Hypnotism*, p. 143.

134 Other popular non-clinical periodicals both quoted freely from, and summarised extensively, the accounts rendered in *The Lancet* and the *British and Foreign Medical Review*. See, for example, Anon., 'Literature', *John Bull*, 12 May 1839, p. 224, cols 1–3.

135 Anon., 'Animal Magnetism', *The Times*, 25 June 1838, p. 7, col. 2. The existence of a investigation of the O'Key sisters by members of the Physiological Committee of the Royal Society is asserted in a footnote to Anon., 'Animal Magnetism: Fifth Report of Experiments and Facts', p. 549, col. 2.

136 Anon., 'Animal Magnetism', *The Times*, 2 July 1838, p. 3, col. 3.

137 Forrest, *Hypnotism*, pp. 154–7; Waterfield, *Hidden Depths*, p. 177.

138 Anon., 'Animal Magnetism; or, Mesmerism', p. 811, col. 1.

139 Anon., 'Animal Magnetism; or, Mesmerism', p. 805, cols 1, 2.

140 Anon., 'Animal Magnetism; or, Mesmerism', p. 807, col. 2.

141 Anon., 'Animal Magnetism; or, Mesmerism', p. 808, col. 1, original italics and punctuation. Cf. pp. 809, col. 1; 811, col. 1.

142 Anon., 'Animal Magnetism; or, Mesmerism', p. 811, col. 1.

143 Anon., 'Animal Magnetism', *The Times*, 6 September 1838, p. 2, col. 5.

144 Anon., 'Mesmeric Humbug', *The Age*, 9 September 1838, p. 285, col. 2. Original italics.

145 Anon., Untitled Paragraph, *The Satirist; or, The Censor of the Times*, 9 September 1838, p. 286, col. 3

146 Anon., 'Chit-Chat', *The Satirist; or, The Censor of the Times*, 9 September 1838, p. 285, col. 3, original italics.

147 Dupotet was Elliotson's invited guest at the final gathering in Bedford Square. See: Anon, 'Animal Magnetism; or, Mesmerism', p. 805, col. 2.

148 Anon., 'Mountebank Dupotet Again', p. 75, col. 3.

149 Anon., 'The Humbug Called Mesmerism', *The Times*, 7 January 1838, p. 6, col. 6.

150 Joseph Miller, 'Remarkable Proof of the Truth of Animal Magnetism', *The Times*, 11 September 1838, p. 4, col. 5. Reprinted in *The Bradford Observer*, 20 September 1838, p. 1, col. 6; *Cleave's Penny Gazette*, 29 September 1838, p. 1, col. 3.

151 Anon., 'Animal Magnetism', *The Times*, 6 September 1838, p. 2, col. 5.

152 Anon., 'To Correspondents', *The Times*, 12 September 1838, p. 4 col. 1.

153 Anon., 'A Magnetising Mountebank', p. 45, col. 2.

154 Christopher South, 'The Humbug Mesmerism', *The Penny Satirist; A Cheap Substitute for a Weekly Newspaper*, 19 January 1839, p. 1, col. 1.

155 Waterfield, *Hidden Depths*, p. 109; Forrest, *Hypnotism*, pp. 77–8.

156 Anon., 'The Humbug Called Mesmerism', *The Times*, 7 January 1838, p. 6, col. 6. Hanwell was the site of the first Middlesex County insane asylum. This embedded article was reprinted verbatim in several other London and provincial newspapers: see Anon., 'Mesmerism', *John Bull*, 13 January 1839, pp. 19–20, at p. 19, col. 3; Anon., 'The Humbug Called Mesmerism', *Hampshire Telegraph and Sussex Chronicle*, 14 January 1839, p. 2, cols 5–6.

157 Forrest, *Hypnotism*, pp. 163–4; Waterfield, *Hidden Depths*, p. 179.

158 Anon., 'The Humbug Called Mesmerism', *The Times*, 7 January 1838, p. 6, col. 6.

159 South, 'The Humbug Mesmerism', p. 1, col. 1.

160 Anon., 'The Humbug Called Mesmerism', *The Times*, 7 January 1838, p. 6, col. 6.

161 Anon., Untitled Notice, *The Times*, 31 December 1838, p. 5, col. 1. Versions and variations of this notice appeared in several London and provincial newspapers. See: Anon., 'London, January 1', *Jackson's Oxford Journal*, 5 January

1839, p. 4, col. 1; Anon., 'Personal News', *The Examiner*, 6 January 1839, p. 8, col. 3.

162 The former was sufficiently celebrated to be reprinted on more than one occasion as a pamphlet: John Elliotson, *Cure of a True Cancer of the Female Breast*, reprinted from the Last Number (XXII) of *The Zoist*, with Introductory Remarks by Dr Engeldue, Fourth Edition (London: Walton and Mitchell, 1848).

163 Anon., 'Phrenological Society', *The Zoist*, 1 (1843–4), 134–7; John Elliotson, 'Surgical Operations Without Pain in the Mesmeric State', *The Zoist*, 3 (1845–6), 380–9.

164 Forrest, *Hypnotism*, pp. 169–71; Anon., 'Health of the Hon. Mrs Hare and Miss Martineau', *The Zoist*, 3 (1845–6), 535–7; John Elliotson, 'Mesmeric Cure of a Cow by Miss Harriet Martineau', *The Zoist*, 8 (1850–1), 300–3.

165 Forrest, *Hypnotism*, p. 189.

166 Waterfield, *Hidden Depths*, pp. 183–9; Forrest, *Hypnotism*, 169–92, *passim*.

167 Forrest, *Hypnotism*, p. 169.

168 Forrest, *Hypnotism*, pp. 166–8. Elliotson's oration was widely reported, as was customary for this important event in the medical calendar: see Anon., 'Royal College of Physicians', *The Times*, 29 June 1846, p. 8, col. 4. The Oration was subsequently printed by a medical publisher, an appended English translation facilitating its circulation beyond the chirurgical profession. See John Elliotson, *The Harveian Oration, Delivered Before the Royal College of Physicians, London, June 27th, 1846* (London: H. Baillière, 1846).

169 Forrest, *Hypnotism*, p. 166; Waterfield, *Hidden Depths*, p. 188.

170 Anon., 'College of Physicians: The Annual Celebration', *The Examiner*, 4 July 1846, p. 426, col. 3; cf. Anon., 'The College of Physicians and the Forthcoming Celebration', *The Morning Post*, 22 June, 1846, p. 5, col. 2; Anon., 'Royal College of Physicians', *Trewman's Exeter Flying Post, or Plymouth and Cornish Advertiser*, 16 July 1846, p. 2, col. 1.

171 Anon., 'Mesmerism', *John Bull*, 13 January 1839, p. 20, col. 1.

172 Anon., Untitled Column, *The Morning Chronicle*, 7 January 1839, p. 3, col. 3.

173 Anon., 'Fracas at University College', *The Times*, 15 January 1839, p. 5, col. 5.

174 Anon., 'University College London', *The Morning Chronicle*, 28 February 1839, p. 3, col. 7.

175 Anon., 'Miss Helen Faucit', *The Era*, 15 March 1840, p. 297, col. 4; Anon., 'Judicial Committee of the Privy Council', *The Morning Post*, 18 April 1840, p. 3, col. 4; *The Standard*, 19 December 1840, p. 3, col. 5.

176 Anon., 'Hypnotism and Healing by Suggestion', *The Times*, 2 January 1914, p. 3, col. 1.

177 Anon., 'Fashionable Mesmerism', *The Satirist; or, The Censor of the Times*, 5 September 1841, p. 287, col. 3.

178 Anon., 'Mesmeric Phenomena', *The Times*, 10 September 1841, p. 3, col. 5.

179 Anon., 'Fashionable Mesmerism', p. 287, col. 3.

180 Anon., 'Mesmeric Phenomena', p. 3, col. 5. A later lecturer hostile to the claims of mesmerism claimed that Lafontaine's ammonia bottle was so contrived as to have a double-stopper, by which means its pungent odour might be made available to the witnesses but not to the subject: see Anon., 'Lecture on Quackery', *The Hull Packet and East Riding Times*, 15 December 1848, p. 5, col. 3.

181 Anon., 'Mesmeric Phenomena', p. 3, col. 5.

182 Anon., 'Somnambulism', *The Times*, 25 June 1844, p. 6, col. 6.

183 Anon., 'Mesmerism at Deptford', *The Times*, 20 December 1843, p. 3, col. 3.

184 Anon., 'Dr Elliotson', *The Morning Post*, 3 August 1868, p. 3, col. 5.

185 Anon., 'Town Correspondents', *The Penny Satirist*, 26 January 1839, p. 4, col. 2.

186 Anon., 'Lecture on Quackery', p. 5, col. 3.

187 Waterfield, *Hidden Depths*, p. 177.

3

Surgical hypnotism

In 1841 James Braid was in practice as a physician at Manchester. Thither came La Fontaine [sic] lecturing on mesmerism and performing experiments of the familiar type, illustrating the theory of the stronger will and the dominant idea. Braid was interested in the lectures, suspected the experiments to be impostures, and declared the theory to be false. He worked at the subject himself, and in the years following issued several books containing most remarkable experiences regarding what he called neuro-hypnotism, but which after him was a for a long time known as Braidism, and is now described in all the dictionaries and text-books as hypnotism.

The Leisure Hour, 1887[1]

CONTEMPORARY REPORTS of John Elliotson's interaction with the O'Key sisters were inclined to remind the reader of the doctor's apparent naivety through the reiterated citation of his name. Indeed, Elliotson's name seemed, when deployed in contemporary accounts, to serve only as an index of personal culpability if not of intellectual and professional failure. Later surveys of the intellectual developments which progressively transformed mesmerism and magnetism into Braidism and hypnotism seem inclined, indeed, to excise Elliotson's very presence from the history of induced sleep. Its owner being tainted, as it were, by too willing an association with a proven imposture that brought him into intimate contact with charlatans who were, variously, foreign and questionably noble or else British and unequivocally working-class, Elliotson's name became evocative in both medical and popular culture only in a personally derisory sense. There was never a dogma or a movement termed Elliotsonism.

If Elliotson was too ready to accept both the theoretical claims advanced by Dupotet and the supposed candour of the O'Key sisters, his successor as the pre-eminent practitioner of induced sleep in Victorian popular consciousness enjoyed a perceptibly more favourable status on account of his scepticism and the relative accessibility of the theory which lay behind his public and clinical demonstrations. James Braid was a Scot, educated at the University of Edinburgh, with experience in surgery and – significantly – ophthalmology. Having worked initially as a surgeon in the Scottish mining industry and in private medicine in Dumfries, he established a practice in Manchester in 1828, and published papers on, among other things, the surgical treatment of club foot and the ocular disorder strabismus.

Braidism – a term which enjoyed currency long before Elliotson's death in 1868[2] – was initially applied as a derogatory label, coined with some sarcasm in a rhetorical attempt to equate Braid's practice with the mesmerism he so publicly derided.[3] Braid himself was more modest regarding his personal association with the phenomenon which he was to rename hypnotism in 1841,[4] referring only to 'Animal Magnetism, Hypnotism and Electro-biology' in the title of one of his books, advertised for the popular market some ten years later.[5] The central significance of Braid's practice, which he developed primarily in Manchester in the 1840s and further modified in the 1850s, is in its assertion that hypnotism has a physiological rather than mystical basis. The induction of trance, Braid asserted, was a consequence of predictable conditions prevailing (or made to prevail) within the patient's body rather than the result of some occult or innate force deriving from the person of the operator. Hypnotism was, in short, a technique to be learned rather than an occult or innate quality to be released, and a practice which seemingly any intelligent individual could emulate.

The philosophical implications of this are clear. As a practical technique rather than a mystic dogma, Braidism *could* be philosophically deployed in medical practice with much the same justification as might be associated with a new drug or an innovative method in surgery. Even though early demonstrations of Braidism shared the same culture of public exhibitions and newspaper reportage as the discredited practice of Braid's frequently non-clinical forebears, its tendency was ultimately to draw itself away from the lecture theatre and into the operating theatre, where it was to enjoy a short but popularly recognised functionality in the years before the availability of reliable chemical anaesthesia. If Braidism were still available to the layperson as a curiosity or party trick – for its philosophy and methodology were widely disseminated in the popular as well as medical press – its results were notably less spectacular than those characteristically achieved in drawing-room mesmerism. With the advent of Braid's practice, artificial sleep was to become increasingly distanced from clairvoyance and clairaudience, and the subject body – though still implicitly vulnerable in its suggestible unconsciousness – was to pass progressively into the protective custody of the surgeon. Under Braid and his immediate successors, hypnotism thus gained a specific functional purpose, and a place within the collective specialisms which underwrite the progress of a patient from diagnosis through treatment and recovery.

'Anyone may mesmerise himself in accordance with the rules I lay down': James Braid, self-hypnotism and the British Association

Braid is distinguished in his contribution to the popular consciousness of hypnotism by a consistent scepticism that suggests more the professional tenor of Wakley than that of Elliotson. Like his mesmeric predecessors, Braid disseminated his own interpretation of induced sleep to the intelligent laity by way of public lectures, these being widely quoted and summarised in both provincial and metropolitan newspapers. These events tended to follow the structure of earlier mesmeric exhibitions, where an initial exposition of the doctrine was followed by exemplification – the so-called 'experiments', where a subject was made to display characteristic phenomena – and a conclusion which again reiterated the practitioner's own position with regard to the theory and its practical deployment. The phenomena illustrated in Braid's earlier experiments are, in most respects, essentially the same as those associated with mesmerism. At one such gathering, held in the lecture theatre of the Mechanics' Institute in Cooper Street, Manchester, on 8 December 1841, Braid is reported as having

> undertook to shew the effects of his important discovery, by exhibiting its power of producing sleep, insensibility to pain, the *cataleptiform* state, somnambulism, and *clairvoyance* upon a number of patients who would walk, hold conversation, act as required,

and even name what was held before them whilst their eyelids were closed.[6]

This apparently surprising degree of congruity can be explained through Braid's acceptance of the historical phenomena of mesmerism but *not* of those associated explanations which prioritise the central – indeed, controlling – role of the magnetic operator.

Attending a Manchester *Conversazione* hosted by Lafontaine, Braid was at first inclined to dismiss the same phenomena he was later to himself exhibit as nothing more than 'the results of delusion or illusion, or the effects of excited imagination, sympathy, or imitation'.[7] Subsequent visits, though, convinced Braid of the recurrent nature of certain mesmeric phenomena, and to these he applied what he termed '*rigid* but *candid* investigations after truth' – in short, a more scientific and less emotive consideration of the possible cause behind the observed effect.[8] Though others had already rejected the original fluid model of mesmeric phenomena, proffering in its place theories which retained the analogies of relative force and polar attraction associated with magnetism, Braid pioneered an innovative explanation based upon what he termed a 'physiological solution'. This latter was predicated upon the physical effort associated with maintaining a fixed stare, and the effect such an artificially and strenuously maintained gaze – termed 'a double internal squint, or a double internal downward or upward squint' in which 'the pupils are powerfully contracted' – would have upon both the patient's ocular muscles and their state of mind.[9] To first initiate and then maintain this artificial squint necessitates a quite surprising degree of self-control in the entranced patient. This act of will, though, has implications for those involuntary and responsive functions of the body not normally modified by simple exertions of the conscious will. Braid notes specifically that the contracted pupils of the patient's closed eyes may become dilated 'irrespective of the amount of light passing to the retina' should he or she vary their position within the ocular orbit. Hence, as Braid concludes, 'in this manner we can contract or dilate the pupil at will', the 'we' here being as applicable to the patient as it is to the operator.[10] If Braid acknowledges the suggestibility of the patient immediately following this observation, he is unequivocal in his opinion that the animal magnetists' traditional claims to exercise control over the mesmerised body constitutes nothing more than an act of 'imagination' on the part of the operator.[11]

Demonstrated in his lectures, and disseminated far beyond their limited attendance through the popular press, Braid's theory was refreshingly clear in its association of induced trance with quite unexceptional physical conditions. Speaking in Manchester in 1841, Braid states:

> My theory is this, – that by an individual keeping up a steady gaze or fixed stare at an object placed in such a position as to put the greatest number of muscles connected with that organ and its appendages into action, and which of course requires an abstraction of mind from other subjects to enable the individual to maintain this fixed stare without winking or moving the eyeballs, congestion takes place in the eye, and a rapid exhaustion of the natural sensibility of the retina and motor nerves of the eye and eyelids.[12]

The eye, in this interpretation, is nothing more than a physiological organ, subject to muscular exhaustion and part of a delicate bodily economy associated with, and regulated by, the conventional circulation of the blood. If a patient is fascinated by some object or some person, their precipitation into trance is associated by Braid not with that which the eye actually *sees* but rather with the *effort* necessary to maintain the association of the gaze with its focus. Mesmer's wand, his eyes, a bright light, a cork projecting from the neck of a wine bottle, or any supposedly significant object upon which the subject is compelled – by suggestion, fear or any other form of guidance – to concentrate may form the catalyst for a gaze which, because it is maintained beyond the point of comfort, exhausts the eye, tires the brain and disturbs the even flow of blood.[13] As Braid says regarding the exhausted condition of the eye which is compelled to gaze,

> This is reflected on the brain, and from that to the heart and lungs, producing enervation, and consequent sinking in the force and frequency of the heart's action. The enervation of the brain is still further increased by the enfeebled action of the heart, and from the same cause the blood is sent to the extremities in diminished quantity, and is therefore accumulated in the large blood vessels in the region of the heart. The heart is now stimulated to greater efforts, and in order to overcome its increased labour is compelled to increase in velocity to compensate for its diminished power. The pulse now rises, and is followed by determination to the brain, as evinced by the flushing of the face, &c., and now succeed all the phenomena of mesmerism, arising from congestion and irregular circulation through that important organ, the brain, and its appendage the spinal cord. Such is my theory.[14]

Braid's theory replaces Mesmer's intangible fluid with a familiar and conventionally corporeal liquid, but more significantly undermines the centrality hitherto accorded to the magnetiser. The eye of the subject, rather than the directing gestures of the magnetist, is the prime mover in the induction of trance. This was essentially the Victorian understanding of Braid's methodology, as an 1889 account in the *Pall Mall Gazette* confirms:

> His plan of inducing artificial sleep, which is still employed, was to weary out the optic nerve of his patients by making them fix their eyes upon some spot for a time, the spot being generally situated where it was a little wearisome for the eyes to find it. The fatigue thus induced spread, according to his explanations, from the ocular muscles to the system, and deep sleep ensued. That is practically the whole of Braidism, and if it is not much it is as any rate sound as far as it goes.[15]

To take this new contention to its logical conclusion, it is the subject, essentially, who induces the trance through the deployment of his or her own body, the magnetist or hypnotist being merely a facilitator, one who directs that gaze and through words or actions compels it to be maintained to the point of physiological exhaustion and consequent mental enervation. Effectively, as Braid states,

> the phenomena hitherto attributable to *animal* magnetism can be produced *independently of human agency*, beyond that of the individual operated upon. In short … any one may mesmerise himself who will comply with the rules that I lay down for insuring the enervation of the brain, and the irregularity of the circulation through that important organ of the animal economy.[16]

With this much acknowledged, what should become clear is that very little, other than the easily obtained knowledge of how to direct the gaze, separates the two parties in any inductive relationship. The publicity accorded to Braid's interpretation was central to the final demise of mesmeric practice in its guise as a secret art, licensed only to adepts.

Braid's own inductive technique, as reported by a reporter present at his Manchester lecture, makes use of equipment the utility of which contrasts strongly with Mesmer's elaborate paraphernalia of gowns, wands and baquets. It is clear from a representative account published in *The Manchester Times and Gazette* that, in hypnotism, the operator – here, Braid himself – merely initiates a process which is *progressed* by the subject.[17] A request by the doctor for experimental volunteers from the audience precipitated what the reporter described as 'an instantaneous rush of candidates' to the stage, from whom fourteen – apparently a mixture of working men and gentlemen – were selected:

> To nine of these Mr Braid affixed a cork, which projected from the centre of the forehead; the remainder he directed to look up at a point of the ceiling of the theatre. They were directed to preserve a steady gaze, and as far as possible to abstract their minds from everything going on around them. These persons were, we believe, all strangers to Mr Braid and none of them had submitted to the operation before.[18]

As *The Manchester Times and Gazette* reported, the subjects displayed various degrees of somnambulism, rigid catalepsy and clairvoyance, one exhibiting also an acute enhancement of his hearing.

These particular consequences are, of course, the familiar attributes of mesmerism. Braid, though, whose own theoretical rationale for the evening is embedded within the reporter's observations, ultimately intimates the narrower purposefulness which was, in the 1840s, to distinguish the application of hypnotism not as a curative technique but, for a short time at least, as an ancillary to conventional interventive surgery.[19] The temporary insensibility which might be introduced into a subject's limbs as an aspect of his greater catalepsy had long been recognised in the application of mesmerism, and this had customarily been tested by the application of sharpened pins to, and through, the epidermis.[20] The gentlemanly Mr Cope, one of Braid's volunteer subjects at the Mechanics' Institute, indeed, had requested, whilst within his trance, that before he was restored he should be 'tested ... with the pin'. This request was duly acceded to, and pins were applied to his hands and forehead. On being awakened he reported that 'When the gentleman tested me with pins I did not feel pain; the sensation was as though some thick, blunt instrument had been thrust against my hands and forehead'.[21]

Cope's sensory experience, again, is not unusual in context. Braid, though, has clearly considered its implications, as his reported response to a question tendered at the time betrays. One hypnotised subject – 'a mechanic dressed in his corduroys, with a somewhat dirty face', who was apparently pacing the stage with his arms held rigidly in front of him – was selected by the doctor as an illustration of how hypnotism might be selectively applied.

> A gentleman asked if Mr Braid could render one part of the body
> sensible, while the other was cataleptic? He replied in the affirmative;
> and the mechanic we had before alluded to had one arm rendered
> quite supple, by means apparently of a gentle tap on the elbow, to
> rouse the circulation of the blood. When afterwards released from
> this state altogether ... he described his sensations, and said he was
> sensible of everything going on around him. He said that one of the
> sensations was a tingling or pricking similar to that produced in the
> hands or feet after remaining in one position, or 'going to sleep' as
> it was called.[22]

At the conclusion of his lecture, the doctor is reported as having responded
to a question from the audience as to whether 'any good may be produced
by the experiments Mr Braid had exhibited' with the equivocal suggestion
that 'all the advantages of the discovery had not yet been ascertained',
these further discoveries being hindered by the pressing demands of the
doctor's professional practice.[23] A similar reason was given for Braid's
reluctance to deliver further lectures or demonstrations of hypnotism in
Manchester.

Despite his apparent reluctance to demonstrate hypnotic phenomena
at length, and apparently in direct response to published assertions by
Lafontaine regarding the falseness of the phenomena exhibited at the
Mechanics' Institute on 8 December 1841, Braid was to return to the
podium before the end of that month. At this latter exhibition, held at the
Manchester Athenaeum in Princess Street on 28 December 1841, Braid was
first minded to talk in somewhat Biblical terms of hypnotism as a seemingly
miraculous treatment for chronic or incurable illness, one by which 'he
had speedily enabled the lame to walk, the deaf to hear, and the dumb to
speak'.[24] His focus, though, is recorded in the account as passing rapidly
again to the apparent insensibility of the hypnotised subject with regard
to acute pain. One subject alone was exhibited for this purpose, because
the physical methods by which the proposed 'proofs' were to be exhibited
'partook in some degree of cruelty'. Braid is not exaggerating for effect,
here: the exhibition from this point took an unusually visceral turn, as the
reporter for *The Manchester Times and Gazette* made very clear. The subject, a
female servant of Dr Braid, was placed in what he termed 'the deeper stages
of catalepsy':

> The head, face, and hands were then punctured with pins, and there
> was no evidence of sensibility to pain.

Mr Dancer (of the firm of Messrs Abraham and Dancer, Opticians) was then directed to give the patient a shock by means of an electro-magnetic current passed along wire grasped by the hand of the patient, and this was done without apparent sensibility, amidst loud cheers. Mr Braid then demesmerised the head of the patient, or partially restored sensibility, when the shock was repeated, and she now gave evident symptoms of feeling, by movements of the head and contortions of the face. To prove that there was no deception, the shock was tried by a gentleman in the audience, who expressed his satisfaction that it was a fair test.

Subsequent applications, to the subject's presumably anaesthetised nose, of the irritants snuff and ammonia were also to produce no effect.[25] The whole performance seemed to satisfy, at least, the newspaper's reporter, if not its proprietors.

If Braid's physiological explanations of what had hitherto been called mesmeric phenomena were predictably dismissed by Lafontaine and his associates, he was to receive a corresponding lack of sympathy from his own professional associates. Conscious, no doubt, of the ridicule heaped upon Elliotson in London, the Medical Section of the British Association – a learned body founded in York in 1831 – rejected a paper on hypnotism submitted to them by James Braid for publication.[26] In a column inserted in the second edition of *The Manchester Times and Gazette* on 25 June 1842, an anonymous commentator proclaimed with a mordantly regional truculence:

> We have learned with some astonishment that a paper communicated by our townsman, Mr Braid, has been returned to him under peculiar circumstances, and in a manner which, appearing to us as requiring some explanation, induced us to apply to Mr Braid to ascertain the facts of the case. It is desirable that the members of the Association, generally, should be made acquainted with this unprecedented act of discourtesy before they separate, and it may be worth their while to inquire why the Committee took it upon themselves to declare why a subject which had occupied the attention of many of the highest intellects in Manchester, was 'unsuitable' for the deliberations of a body met for 'the advancement of science'.[27]

This was followed by a letter from the hand of Braid himself, describing how his paper had been returned in an open envelope without any other advice save the pencilled inscription '*Rejected by the Committee as* UNSUITABLE'.[28]

The anonymous reporter concluded that the rejection was not institutional but rather the consequence of *'professional jealousy'*, the Committee in question consisting '(with the exception of three names) of local men in Mr Braid's profession'.[29] Public interest in the rejection of Braid's work was apparently sufficient to motivate the same newspaper to reprint the whole exchange verbatim on 2 July 1842 under the strident headline 'Extraordinary Conduct of the Medical Section Towards Mr Braid'.[30] Appended to this was an account of further experiments upon strangers at Braid's hands and the exhibition (but, apparently, not *demonstration*) of some of the doctor's own patients, whose disorders included problems of sight and paralysis.[31] It is significant, though, that 'Mr Spencer, a stranger, and Mr Clay, surgeon, Piccadilly [Manchester]' were prepared to confirm specifically that the body of one of Braid's experimental subjects – the doctor's manservant – was comatose and 'expressed their satisfaction that a kind of sleep, followed by a high degree of insensibility, had been produced'.[32] This is, perhaps, the least spectacular of all symptoms – and, yet, arguably the most useful in an interventive surgical situation.

'I never knew anything more; and never felt any pain at all':[33] Surgery under mesmeric trance

Braid, however, was not the first practitioner to seriously and specifically consider the anaesthetic possibilities of hypnotism. Elliotson, in the ponderously titled *Numerous Cases of Surgical Operations Without Pain in the Mesmeric State, with Remarks Upon the Opposition of Many Members of the Royal Medical and Chirurgical Society and Others to the Inestimable Blessings of Mesmerism* (1843), opened his customary anti-institutional polemic with an account of an amputation above the knee, undertaken at the district hospital at Wellow, near Ollerton, Nottinghamshire, on 1 October 1841. Elliotson's account (to which he at times added emphasis and interpolation) was derived from a paper read to the Royal Medical and Chirurgical Society in London on 22 November 1842, this being a source which the doctor freely acknowledged.[34] That paper, which detailed the patient's mesmeric regime before, during and following the amputation, had enjoyed a degree of currency beyond the medical fraternity some twelve months before the publication of Elliotson's *Numerous Cases* following significant exposure in the popular press. The *Standard*, published in London, appears to have been the first newspaper to report the presentation of what was styled as an 'account of a case of successful amputation of the thigh during the mesmeric state, without the knowledge of the patient'.[35] Syndicated or derivative reports were rapidly disseminated through the provincial press, the same account being reproduced almost verbatim in periodicals as diverse as the *Derby Mercury*, *Ipswich Journal* and the *Belfast News Letter*.[36]

The mesmeric technique administered upon James Wombell, a labourer, by 'W. Topham, Esq., Barrister of the Middle Temple' on behalf of 'W. Squire Ward, Esq., Surgeon, of Wellow Hall' is that of Mesmer via Elliotson rather than Braid.[37] It is the words of the lay practitioner, Topham, rather than those of the surgeon, Ward, which initiate the newspaper account, and which are heavily drawn upon in Elliotson's deployment of the paper read in London in November 1842. The inductive apparatus of passes and gestures feature prominently in the patient's descent into insensibility, as Elliotson makes clear, quoting Topham:

> Mr Topham continued to mesmerize him for fifteen minutes, and then informed Mr Ward that the operation might be begun, and '*brought two fingers of each hand gently in contact with the patient's closed eyelids; and there kept them, still further to deepen the sleep*'.[38]

It is noteworthy here that the lay operator, another professional gentleman but emphatically *not* a physician or surgeon, advises his medically trained colleague as to when it is safe to operate. In an adjoining room, Elliotson notes, another patient has been subjected by Ward to 'a tedious and painful operation' without anaesthetic, and his cries were sufficient to distress the semi-entranced Wombell.[39] Elliotson digresses at this point, noting the importance of the patient's eyes as physiological organs, though in a manner which is, with its assumption of an *exterior* mesmeric influence, still strikingly distant from Braid's practical model of ocular exhaustion.

> Of all parts of the body, the eyes are the most ready receivers and transmitters of mesmerism ... The moist mucous membranes are more susceptible than the skin; and of membranes, the surface of the eye and the inner surface of the eyelid, to say nothing of the nervous interior of the eye to which there is admission through the pupil to projected mesmeric influence are the most susceptible. Intervening bodies impede mesmerism, and, *cæteris paribus*, in proportion to their substance; the eyelids therefore prevent so strong an effect as would result if the mesmerizing [sic] body were applied to the eye itself. Still the points of the fingers placed upon the eyelids would have a great effect.[40]

The different (and dissonant) explanations of how the patient's eye functions in Elliotson's mesmerism and Braid's hypnotism do not disguise, however, the rise of a more physiologically orientated model of artificial (or artificially induced) sleep. This change from the mystical to the medical is what eases the incorporation – short as it was – of hypnotic practice into practical (as opposed to speculative) medicine, and its deployment in routine operations rather than in more experimental situations.

The remainder of Topham's account does not spare the details of surgery practised under the medical regime which prevailed before reliable chemical anaesthesia, though the initiation of the operation is remarkable for what *does not* happen rather than what does:

> Mr Ward, after one earnest look at the man [Wombell], slowly plunged his knife into the centre of the outer side of the thigh, directly to the bone, and then made a clear incision around the bone, to the opposite point on the inside of the thigh. The stillness at this moment was something awful. The calm respiration of the sleeping man alone was heard, for all other seemed suspended.[41]

The conventional expectation that the patient *should* cry out in pain, if not actually convulse, is fully acknowledged here through both the stress upon 'calm' – which Elliotson emphasises in his account through italics – and in the bated breath of those in attendance.[42] The remarkable atmosphere of surgical calm, though, is maintained even when the complexity of Wombell's case necessitates some 'tedious and painful' manipulation of the diseased limb in order to facilitate its final amputation. Despite all this, as Elliotson indicates, with added emphasis:

> the patient's 'sleep continued as profound as ever. *The* PLACID *look of his countenance never changed for* AN INSTANT; his whole frame rested, *uncontrolled*, in *perfect stillness* and repose; *not a muscle was seen to twitch.* To the end of the operation, including the sawing of the bone, securing the arteries, and applying the bandages, occupying a period of upwards of twenty minutes, he *lay like a statue.*'[43]

The patient was roused with *sal volatile*, and on recovering consciousness proclaimed a total ignorance of any sensation connected with the amputation: '*I never knew anything more, and never felt any pain at all: I, once, felt as if I heard a kind of crunching*'.[44]

Newspaper accounts of the treatment of Wombell almost invariably reproduce or append the testimony of the surgeon, Ward, in addition to that of the lay mesmerist, Topham. This account, appropriately, is imbricated with a conventional and specific physiological insight that far exceeds Topham's rather superficial symptomatological observations of the patient's bodily movements and occasional utterances whilst unconscious. Ward notes,

> Beyond what has already been so well described by Mr Topham, I need only add that the extreme quivering or rapid action of the divided muscular fibres was less than usual; nor was there so much contraction of the muscles themselves; I must also notice that, two or three times, I touched the divided end of the sciatic nerve, without any increase of the low moaning described by Mr Topham; and which, to all present, gave the impression of a disturbed dream.[45]

A more or less identical version of the story reproduced in a Colchester newspaper, *The Essex Standard*, adds to this a coda, derived from another provincial news sheet, the content of which echoes the physiologically informed opinions of Dr Ward as expressed in the London *Standard*:

> *The Hampshire Telegraph* adds a *pendant* to the above extraordinary case, stating that an operation took place at Portsmouth, on the 19th August, when a medical gentleman, to cure a contraction in the knee joint, put a female in a mesmeric trance and while she was in that state divided the ham-string muscles, without her being conscious of the circumstance; and the individual now walks with facility.[46]

The significant difference between the two accounts, lay and professional, is simply one of their specific awareness and perception of the function of anaesthesia. For Topham, the successful negation of pain through the imposition of an artificially induced sedation is confirmed by the patient's behaving as if he were in a deep sleep, where any form of interference with the prone body – such as touching or tickling – might result in nothing more than a change of position, a slight movement or a murmured, incoherent protest. Wombell is subject to a far more severe manipulation of his body whilst unconscious, but behaves as a conventional sleeper would: Topham, indeed, refers throughout to the induction of 'mesmeric sleep'.[47] For Ward, though, the success of the anaesthetic is vouchsafed not by the behaviour of the patient's body as a whole but by the lack of spontaneous response associated with severed nerves and tissue. That the neural connection between the traumatised limb and the perceptive mind appears to have been temporarily suspended is significant. More significant for Ward, though, is the topical behaviour of the exposed neural or muscular tissue, given that these betray a notably lessened sensitivity as manifested by their contraction or oscillation when divided or touched. Nerves and muscle tissue, because they respond involuntarily to probing and manipulation, are a true test of the depth of anaesthesia. The operation may be judged a success from a surgical perspective not because the patient's mind fails to perceive the cutting of tissue and the dividing of nerve fibre but because those elements of the body themselves behave in a manner which suggest that they have become less sensitive as a consequence of the patient's mesmerised state. If this might seem less than totally efficient – Wombell does betray some awareness of the intervention into his body – then it is none the less a significant improvement upon surgery conducted, as it was at that time, without any anaesthetic.

'The apostle of mesmerism in India': James Esdaile and experimental Indian surgery

In the period during which Braid, Ward and others were experimenting in England with the anaesthetic possibilities of mesmeric or hypnotic sleep, James Esdaile, a practical surgeon born and educated in Scotland, was pursuing a parallel – though ultimately a considerably more protracted – course of experiments in India. Appointed an East India Company surgeon in 1830, Esdaile arrived in Bengal in 1831, and practiced at the Hooghly Hospital in Calcutta between 1839 and 1846. His initial response to mesmerism appears to have been one of scepticism, as a British review of Esdaile's influential 1846 study, *Mesmerism in India*, betrays. According to the reviewer, Esdaile's book

> is remarkable not only for the facts it contains but for its freedom from anything like passion or advocacy. Dr Esdaile does not seem to have had any natural love of the marvellous, and has become a believer in the wonders of mesmerism in opposition to a strong tendency to doubt whatever cannot be accounted for upon known principles. Indeed it is with reluctance he admits there is any thing unaccountable in the matter; and he tries again and again to persuade himself and his readers that it may all be resolved into a modification of ordinary phenomena.[48]

Indeed, James Esdaile's interest in mesmeric practice appears to have been first approached casually and somewhat in the manner of a distraction from colonial life for, as David Esdaile – the author's brother, and editor of

Mesmerism in India – confides, the surgeon 'surprised me by announcing that he had now found something to dispel the *ennui* of Indian life, and that his mission was to become "the Apostle of Mesmerism in India"'.[49]

As Esdaile's book reveals, however, the author did not himself seek an apostolic succession which would proclaim him a revivalist devotee of Mesmer, or indeed of any other hypnotic savant. *Mesmerism in India* is a considerably more coherent and, withal, less polemical work than Elliotson's *Numerous Cases*. If it is a rhetorical as well as an evidential study – as all speculative medical works must surely be – it is one which lays an early emphasis upon the valid and detached judgement which may be exercised by non-medical professionals when contemplating the subject as they would any other matter of contemporary interest. The importance of the subject here is such as to force a balance between professional prejudice and self-interest as opposed to the general good which might be associated with the disputed therapy. As Esdaile suggests,

> The public are too apt to consider the subject of Mesmerism as a professional one, and not to take the necessary means to become acquainted with it till the doctors shall have decided what is to be believed about it. This is an error on the part of the public, for, I am sorry to say, medical men in general as yet know nothing about it; and there is nothing in their previous knowledge, however great and varied, that bears upon the subject, or can entitle them to decide, *ex cathedrâ*, on the truth or falsehood of the new discoveries.[50]

Hence, as Esdaile later intimates,

> I would therefore recommend the public to exercise their common sense, and sober judgement, in determining for the doctors the matter of fact; and if the community decides that it is really a remedy of great efficacy, that there is no resisting the proofs in support of it, that to know nothing about it is no recommendation to a medical man; then Mesmerism will assume its proper rank as a remedial agent, and be lodged in the hands of those who should alone practise it.[51]

Esdaile is, in a sense, here anticipating a progressive development of the medical profession *beyond* the longstanding demarcation that customarily separated surgeons from physicians. The mesmerist here is envisaged as a sort of proto-anaesthetist, and, if this lay practice seems to be associated with non-clinically trained men elsewhere (as it is in Ward's association with Topham), there is no suggestion in *Mesmerism in India* that a surgeon or a physician might not *himself* become an anaesthetic specialist if he earnestly embraces the philosophy of trance achieved not by mystical means but through what Esdaile describes as 'an influence ... of a purely physical description'.[52] This is not the physiological self-hypnotism espoused by Braid, therefore. Esdaile's explanation of mesmeric phenomena, rather, is something of a late (and, in places, explicit) revival of Mesmer's fluid philosophy, one which involves 'a transmission of some vital product from one person to another'.[53]

Esdaile's practice, as he recalls it in his account of the first experiment he conducted at the Imbarah Hospital, is somewhat conventional, recalling the traditional physical gestures of mesmerism rather than the ocular strain associated with Braid. The patient is Mádhab Kaurá, a felon being treated for a double hydrocele, a type of testicular dropsy in which the scrotum is distended by fluid. The accepted surgical treatment of the time, in which the fluid was necessarily drawn from the scrotal sac is, as might be imagined, extremely painful, and Esdaile's intervention was provoked by the evident distress of the patient following the drawing off of the fluid and the administration of a subcutaneous injection. With the patient seated, Esdaile recalls,

> I placed his knees between mine, and began to pass my hands slowly over his face, at the distance of an inch, and carried them down to the pit of his stomach. This was continued for half an hour before he was spoken to, and when questioned at the end of this time his answers were quite sensible and coherent.[54]

The patient is perceptibly calmed through this process, though Esdaile appears unconvinced that any deeper state of nervous change has been achieved. Further passes were administered, and the account records the progressive lassitude of Kaurá over a period of around an hour and 45 minutes. At the end of this time

> He opened his eyes when ordered, but said he saw only smoke, and could distinguish no one: his eyes were quite lustreless, and the lids were opened heavily. All appearance of pain now disappeared; his hands were crossed on his breast, instead of being pressed on the groins, and his countenance showed the most perfect repose. He now took no notice of our questions, and I called loudly on him by name without attracting any notice.[55]

Kaurá's state of repose, of course, might well be a consequence of an opiate, if this were the substance of the two drachms of 'the usual cor. sub. injection' administered after the operation. Esdaile, though, clearly believes this not to be the case, and administers the customary tests associated with experimentally induced mesmeric trance. The account continues:

> I now pinched him, without disturbing him, and then asking for a pin in English, I desired my assistant to watch him narrowly, and drove it into the small of his [Kaurá's] back; it produced no effect whatever; and my assistant repeated it at intervals in different places as uselessly. [56]

Kaurá, presumably, did not speak English. [57] With the benumbed patient now reclining 'in a state of "opisthotonos"' (that is, in a rigid and arched posture), Esdaile was sufficiently convinced that 'we had got something extraordinary' and sought 'intelligent witnesses' among the colonist community of Calcutta to supplement his evidently bilingual Indian assistant, a young doctor in training. With the arrival of 'Mr Russell, the judge, and Mr Money, the collector', the testing of the unfortunate Kaurá's insensibility was to take a further and rather more visceral turn. [58] Esdaile continues:

> We found him in the position I had left him in, and no hallooing in his ear could attract his attention. Fire was then applied to his knee, without his shrinking in the least; and liquor ammoniæ, that brought tears into our eyes for a moment, was inhaled for some minutes without causing an eyelid to quiver. This seemed to have revived him a little, as he moved his head shortly afterwards, and I asked him if he wanted to drink; he only gaped in reply, and I took the opportunity to give, slowly, a mixture of ammonia so strong that I could not bear to taste it; this he drank like milk, and gaped for more. As the 'experimentum crucis', I lifted his head, and placed his face, which was directed to the ceiling all this time, in front of a full light; opened his eyes, one after the other, but without producing any effect upon the iris. [59]

The 'experimentum crucis', under which the involuntary behaviour of delicate ocular tissue is observed, caps Esdaile's argument as much as it does that of Ward. As Esdaile concludes, at this juncture 'We were all now convinced that total insensibility of all the senses existed', and the account advises the reader that the condition was endured for some two hours, Kaurá being eventually awakened (and not on Esdaile's orders) by Kurreem Ali Khan, 'The native doctor of the jail', who threw water in the patient's face.[60] On being questioned, Kaurá expressed no recollection of being pricked, burned, or administered ammonia, and did not recall the later presence of F. W. Russell and D. J. Money, the witnesses who, with Budden Chunder Chowdaree the Sub-Assistant Surgeon, signed Esdaile's deposition in affirmation.[61]

Kaurá was to act as Esdaile's subject during further impositions of what was apparently known locally as '"Belatee Muntur" (the Europe charm)', and the technique was varied at times to feature the use of significantly directed fingers 'with the idea of concentrating the mesmeric influence of the whole body into one conductor'.[62] Under such conditions, and with several European witnesses present, Esdaile removed a further liquid secretion from Kaurá's scrotum, apparently without pain.[63] The third chapter of *Mesmerism in India* details further incidences of trances induced, scrota drained and other operations performed apparently without pain upon native Indian patients.

If Esdaile appears reluctant to identify exactly *what* he feels lies behind the ability to induce, and the susceptibility to be inducted in, trance, he is more certain regarding what it is not. If it may be directed, as he sporadically asserts, by way of the finger tips or through more generous passes of the hands, it does not appear to be an intangible fluid as envisaged by Mesmer. Rather, as Esdaile envisages it, mesmeric trance is something akin to conventional sleep, its successful induction being associated broadly with the type of physiological phenomena being popularised in Britain in the same decade by James Braid. Esdaile intimates:

> By a comparison of the effects of natural and mesmeric sleep on the human system, it will be seen, I think, that they only differ in degree, and in the greater command we have over the artificial than the natural state of sleep; and I feel disposed to think that extreme conditions of the nervous system, its exhaustion or repletion, and the irregular distribution of the nervous secretions, produce the same effects on the bodily and mental organs in normal and abnormal sleep.[64]

If the closing stress on secretions seems something of a throwback to Mesmer's fluid rhetoric, Esdaile's attempts to demonstrate mesmeric phenomena as intensified versions of more conventional conditions – sleepwalking, sleep-waking, unconscious cerebration, dreaming and catalepsy – are more successful.[65] In essence, nothing mystic or magical is taking place, and it is the artificial nature of the practice which intensifies a process already organically part of the physiology and psychology of the patient.

In this respect, Esdaile emphatically distances his own practice from that of earlier mesmerists who sought to maintain trance and its implications as essentially human sciences, artificially crafted and quite distinct from any homeopathic implication. Esdaile considers medicine, to a greater or lesser extent, to have 'so far deserted nature, that, in return, she has renounced us as unnatural children, and left us to our self sufficiency and artificial resources'. Hence, 'the routine practitioner will rarely condescend to divide with nature the merit of the cure. He and his pills, powders and potions, must have all the credit.' Correspondingly, 'The whole art of the true physician is exerted to induce nature to interfere and take up the case of his patient'.[66] Mesmerism, implicitly, is but one aspect of that homeopathic nature which may be deployed by the open-minded physician, and 'So far from Mesmerism being a new and unnatural art, there is every reason to believe that it is the oldest and most natural mode of curing many of the severe, uncomplicated diseases of the human race'.[67] Its efficacy in India, implicitly, is dependent upon that nation's perceived isolation from European cynicism, and the open-minded attitude of the native population to the restorative claims of indigenous charmers and magicians who, Esdaile contends, relieve the pain of their patients through a variety of mesmerism.[68]

If *Mesmerism in India* was widely reviewed by publications outside of the medical press in Britain so, likewise, was its author's practice on the Subcontinent considered with evident interest by non-clinical commentators. Despite the wealth of accessible information which may be derived from popular sources, Elliotson's somewhat partisan and unashamedly specialist periodical *The Zoist: A Journal of Cerebral Physiology and Mesmerism*, which was published between 1843 and 1856, has been the traditional route through which Esdaile's career as a colonial mesmerist has been considered in histories of hypnotism.[69] *The Zoist* is a primary conduit for Elliotson's laudatory commentary upon Esdaile's Indian practice. In Volume 6 (1848–9), for example, Elliotson reports extensively (and, it must be said, by way of derivative sources) upon Esdaile's surgical treatment of primarily scrotal disorders at the Calcutta Mesmeric Hospital.[70] The tone of Elliotson's account is consistently technical, being laced with phrases in medical Latin.[71] However, the author's observations regarding Esdaile's treatment and prognoses are sporadically punctuated with reminders of the cures apparently effected by Elliotson in England, with polemic directed against British practitioners and publications, and also occasionally with Horatian satire, quoted in the original Latin.[72] This and similar narratives by the editor of *The Zoist*, it might be concluded, represent neither Esdaile in his own words nor even Esdaile in a relatively neutral context of reportage. It is Esdaile *by* Elliotson, and Esdaile *through* Elliotson.[73] As such, Elliotson's accounts of Esdaile's practice embody an element of deliberate – and at times desperate – self-justificatory deployment that undermines their value as an index of how the Scottish doctor's practice was perceived in Britain and appreciated in less polemical circles.

Popular newspaper reports of Esdaile's work are for the most part contemporaneous with the publication of *Mesmerism in India*. In this respect, they mark a turning point in the surgeon's mesmeric career, for his volume publication was in part prompted by his departure from the Calcutta hospital and his short period of participation in British military medicine on the Subcontinent. Prior to this point in Esdaile's mesmeric career, his surgical subjects had been taken from the indigenous rather than the colonist community, and this facilitated what were essentially racist generalisations with regard to the susceptibility of Indians to mesmeric influence. In the first chapter of *Mesmerism in India*, for example, Esdaile notes that though he had successfully submitted a 'small number of Europeans' to mesmeric influence, the 'artificial' nature of western life has somewhat inhibited the likely benefits to be derived from a treatment which he associates with 'the steady and enduring curative powers of nature' rather than the sophistication (or sophistry) of human medicine.[74] Regarding his Bengali subjects, Esdaile concludes:

> The people of this part of the world seem to be peculiarly sensitive to the mesmeric power; and as it has been observed that a depressed state of the nervous system favours its reception, we can understand why they, as a body, should be more easily affected than Europeans. Taking the population of Bengal generally, they are a feeble, ill-nourished race, remarkably deficient in nervous energy; and natural debility of constitution being still further lowered by disease, will probably account for their being so readily subdued by the Mesmerist.

If the physicality of the underfed Bengali temptingly resembles that of another ready victim of the mesmerist's craft, the woman – who is also, as Victorian medical consensus suggests, 'unwell' at least once every twenty-eight days – then his perceived nature as a being less civilised than his colonial master further underlines his readiness to be controlled as much as cured.[75] Esdaile continues:

> Their mental constitution also favours us: we have none of the morbid irritability of nerves, and the mental impatience of the civilised man, to contend against; both of which resist and neutralise the efforts of nature. The success I have met with is mainly to be attributed, I believe, to my patients being the simple, unsophisticated children of nature; neither thinking, questioning, nor remonstrating, but passively submitting to my pleasure, without in the smallest degree understanding my object or intentions.[76]

The true test of the *general* efficacy of mesmerism, therefore, is its capability – or otherwise – when applied to less 'primitive' races and more 'sophisticated' or thoughtful individuals. The experiment – for Esdaile's curative surgical procedures were both styled and reported as experimental – ultimately demands an application to the adult, white, British male – a subject, if the hypothesis is to be tested with rigour, who ought to be in good physical health and not of a simple or deficient cast of mind.

'I shall soon ascertain to what extent other varieties of mankind are capable of benefiting by this natural curative power': Military surgery and the European subject

The greater efficacy of mesmerism as a surgical tool is thus the context for the author's dedication of *Mesmerism in India*, this small component of the work being in fact the announcement of the new field in which the surgeon aspires to test his theory. The dedication to the author's father, the Rev. James Esdaile, DD, dated 1 February 1846, reads:

> My Dear Father,
>
> However new and strange the subject of this work may be to you, I am sure that it will afford you pleasure to know that I have introduced, and I hope I may say established, a new and powerful means of alleviating human suffering among the natives of Bengal.
>
> I shall soon ascertain to what extent other varieties of mankind are capable of benefiting by this natural curative power, as I am ordered to join the army in the field, and depart tomorrow, by dâk, a journey of eleven hundred miles.[77]

The broad details of Esdaile's work amongst the native Bengalis, and his effective conscription into the army as a surgeon, appear to have been well known in Britain from some point in 1846, as an account in the *Newcastle Courant*, for example, testifies.[78] This news item (which is derived, as the editorial acknowledges, from an earlier article in *The Scotsman*) references what is almost certainly a review of *Mesmerism in India*, before outlining an unexpected hiatus in Esdaile's progress. The anonymous commentator notes:

> In a recent critique on Dr Esdaile's work on mesmerism, the reviewer inferred that we should soon hear of the doctor's mesmeric doings with the army of the Punjaub. We learn, however, that Dr Esdaile's services not being needed, he was ordered back to Hooghly the day after joining the army. He thus lost the opportunity of trying, on a grand scale, the effects of mesmerism on the wounded. Chance, however, threw him in the way of a detachment of wounded soldiers proceeding to Ferozepore; and being unprovided with medicine, he had nothing for it but to resort to mesmerism.

An opportunity lost is one gained, it would seem, and Esdaile took full advantage of a range of injuries and recent amputations inflicted upon explicitly British bodies in order to lessen pain and facilitate mobility. The results, conveyed in Esdaile's own words, are colourful, if not grotesquely flippant, in places: one paraplegic private soldier, Esdaile remarks, 'kept crying "How strange!" "How wonderful!" "How delightful!" "It's a miracle!", much to the doctor's amusement'.[79]

At this juncture, though, Esdaile makes a small but significant distinction between the Indian patients he has hitherto worked with and their British counterparts. Prior to his short military adventure, Esdaile had necessarily been forced to train non-Europeans – 'young Hindoos and Mahomedans' – as mesmeric anaesthetists, so as to leave himself free to perform practical surgery at the Calcutta hospital.[80] This strategy should not be thought of as remarkable, however. Esdaile is consistent regarding the universality of both the mesmeric quality and the ability to satisfactorily deploy it.[81] What *is* telling, though, is the apparently deliberate choice made by Esdaile that native mesmerists should not anaesthetise or influence their European employers. The *Newcastle Courant* recalls, in Esdaile's own words: 'Other aching stumps were soothed by local mesmerising, and I encouraged the men to learn the process that they might be able to instruct their comrades how to relieve them'.[82] Mesmerism is here deployed as a post-traumatic analgesic rather than an anaesthetic in interventive surgery, but it might be contended that Esdaile's decision avoids any suggestion that a European might be subjected to the will, even temporarily, of a native Indian. If the traditional balance of power between mesmerist and patient had been eroded in the practice of Braid and Esdaile, both of whom freely disseminated their methodology for inducting trance, the customary racism which imposed discipline and segregation in civil as well as military life in British India was not negotiable.

The *Newcastle Courant* passes no comment upon the racial politics of Esdaile's practice, but concludes its article with the announcement of what was almost certainly the first systematic consideration of the claims of mesmerism sponsored by a governmental agency since the eighteenth century. The correspondent notes:

> Dr Esdaile's return to Hooghly has been followed by a result which must be gratifying to all lovers of truth. Having there performed his hundredth painless operation, his repeated demands for investigation have induced the Government of Bengal to appoint a commission of inquiry, under whose inspection Dr Esdaile is to conduct a lengthened series of experiments. For this purpose he has been relieved from duty at Hooghly, and directed to take up his residence in Calcutta. – *Correspondent of the Scotsman*[83]

If the *Newcastle Courant* appears almost invariably inclined to give a favourable report of Esdaile's aspirations, other popular papers were rhetorically a little more cautious. The London *Daily News* reported, on 9 January 1847, for example, how:

> Dr Esdaile, having professed to perform surgical operations without pain to patients (provided they be natives) by means of mesmerism, a committee of medical officers was appointed by the Deputy-Governor of Bengal to investigate the subject and to superintend Dr Esdaile's experiments. The result is that the Deputy-Governor has determined, with the sanction of the supreme Government, to place Dr Esdaile for one year in charge of a small experimental hospital in some favourable situation in Calcutta, in order that he may extend his investigations to the applicability of this alleged agency to all descriptions of cases, medical as well as surgical, and to all classes of patients, European as well as native. On reports to be furnished by certain 'medical visitors', to be nominated by the authorities,

will mainly depend what further steps the Government may deem it
expedient to take in the matter.[84]

The Commission's Committee – which was exclusively European in consti-
tution – met formally on no fewer than fourteen occasions during the
course of its twelve-month investigation, each meeting being of two hours'
duration.[85] The Committee was to receive statements from both participants and witnesses: the *Essex Standard* for example, citing a correspondent
to the *Bengal Times*, reported that 'the Deputy Governor and two ...
Government secretaries' were present at later surgical operations.[86] The
'experimental hospital' certainly *was* 'small': indeed, it was nothing more
than 'a house lately erected in the grounds of the native hospital, having on
the ground floor three apartments', two of these being 'Small rooms, each
provided with three beds', the other a 'Committee and Operating Room'.[87]
There could never be more, therefore, than six experimental subjects in
residence, and the whole experiment may well have been far more modest
in compass than it appeared in British press reportage.

Oddly, given the formal nature of the Commission and the great public
interest aroused in both the United Kingdom and India, there remains some
confusion with regard to the exact dates of the investigation's initiation
and conclusion. Esdaile's entry in the current *Oxford Dictionary of National
Biography* dates the Commission to November 1846.[88] However, the *Essex
Standard* reports the actual *submission* of the report in its 'Foreign News'
column on 4 December 1846, with the authority of information derived
from 'the Calcutta papers' and the confident conclusion that 'There is
reason to believe that it [the report] will prove most interesting, and highly
satisfactory to mesmerists'.[89]

The *Essex Standard*, apparently aware of a domestic interest in the subject
of Esdaile's experiments, but still explicitly dependent upon the reportage
of other publications (in this case a correspondent of the *Morning Herald*, by
way of the offices of *The Times*), returned to the topic at the start of 1847.
Under 'Foreign News', an anonymous writer noted that:

> Dr Esdaile's reports on his proceedings at the Mesmeric Hospital,
> at Calcutta, have lately been published under the authority of
> Government, and are highly satisfactory as regards both the
> medical and surgical cases of science. Ere the report had appeared,
> Government showed its sense of the value of the new agent, and of
> the success of its experiment in establishing the hospital, by issuing
> an order that all passed students of the Medical College should

study practical mesmerism for two months under Dr Esdaile before receiving any appointment in the public service.[90]

The decisive – and, it would appear, prompt – action of the British administration in Bengal represents an unprecedented consideration of the claims of mesmerism. In effect, a non-medical body – an arm of colonial civil administration, utilising the evidential processes of public enquiry and professional observation – has institutionalised a practice which had but recently been dismissed as a pseudoscience in London.

The implicit endorsement of Esdaile's procedure contained in such a gesture may, of course, have had little practical impact upon professional medical and surgical practice on British – rather than Indian – soil. The strikingly different attitude displayed towards mesmerism in India cannot be dismissed lightly, however.[91] No doubt, the ostensibly receptive and liberal attitude which from the outset underpinned the Bengal Commission's investigation into the contemporary claims of mesmerism was assisted by Indian medicine's physical and philosophical distance from the polemic and partisan self-interest which characterised *The Lancet*'s consideration of John Elliotson and his associates. Again, if mesmerism was but an unproven adjunct to British medical, surgical and diagnostic practice, the prospective uses of which were in the 1840s both vague and uncertain, its practice in India could be said to have a very specific deployment in the treatment of testicular hydrocele, which was apparently endemic amongst all castes of the native population. India, in other words, provided a unique environment for both the testing and the habitual deployment of mesmerism as a reliever of pain and a provider of relatively reliable temporary insensibility. The Indian Subcontinent provided, also, a ready supply of compliant patients, charitable surgery being the only hope of a cure for many of the physiological ailments suffered by the indigenous population. In India, as it were, medicine could take a quite different course than it might within the United Kingdom.

Curiously, the specific contents of the Bengal Commission's report appear not to have been reproduced at length in the British popular press. Indeed, the only substantial reproduction of the report is to be found in an Australian newspaper, the *Geelong Advertiser and Squatter's Advocate*, which extracted the report – which it considered 'free from suspicion' – on 23 April 1847.[92] This latter provides the small details omitted from British summaries, details which thus remain essentially unknown to modern historians of hypnotism. The article included such information as the nature of the experimental environment (for which a diagram was provided); the origins of the subjects (ten surgical cases, named individually, 'all native males from ten to forty years old, Hindoos and Mahomedans in all conditions of general health, from extreme emaciation to ordinary strength', the majority suffering hydrocele or other genital disorders); and the composition of the attendant mesmerisers ('young men, Hindoos and Mahomedans, from 14 to 30 years of age, most of them compounders and dressers from the Hooghly hospital').[93] Three of the subjects were later dismissed, one for drinking spirits, the others for being apparently immune to the passes and breathings administered by their individually assigned mesmeric operators.[94] The usual physical tests for insensibility were applied to those subjects who were apparently susceptible, namely 'loud noises', 'burning, pinching, and cutting the skin and other sensitive organs'.[95] In seven cases, surgical operations were performed in the mesmerised state, and the report pointed out that during three of these the anaesthetic power of the trance appeared to be limited:

> While the patients did not open their eyes, or utter articulate sounds, or require to be held, there were vague or convulsive movements of the upper limbs, writhing of the body, distortion of the features, giving the face a hideous expression of suppressed agony, the respiration became heaving, with deep sighs. There were, in short, all the signs of intense pain, which a dumb person undergoing operation might be expected to exhibit, except resistance to the operator.[96]

The report, as quoted in the *Geelong Advertiser and Squatter's Advocate*, concludes that in four cases of surgical intervention there was no evidence of the sensation of pain, and 'in the three other cases the manifestations of pain during the operation are opposed by the positive statement of the patient that no pain was experienced'.[97]

One might consider again, bearing this concluding remark in mind, the possible reasons why the report was never quoted as extensively in a British popular periodical as it was in this Australian newspaper. The later testimony of the conscious subjects does not sit easily against the involuntary spasms of their supposedly anaesthetised bodies. There is something here, therefore, that draws upon the same evidential logic as is associated with the ocular iris when held under a strong light, the contractions of which, according to Esdaile's rationale, apparently cannot be faked.[98] Notably, the report utilises this very test of anaesthesia, remarking of one subject – who when entranced displayed an 'apparently perfect insensibility to pain' – that his 'pupils were insensible to light'.[99] The report, read with this equivocation in mind, thus appears somewhat less favourable to Esdaile's claims than British readers might otherwise have believed it to be.

In its British context, therefore, the report appears to have been manoeuvred into a position where it might function rhetorically without ever needing to be quoted or criticised. It is a document which seemingly valorises and verifies its contentious subject matter primarily through the authority of its mere existence rather than by way of evidence derived or quoted from its contents.

In essence, therefore, the report does not exist in the British popular consciousness, other than as a distant document to be evoked as an affirmation of truth in general terms. This, certainly, would seem to be the sole function of the report in British reportage. Consider, for example, a column in the *Bristol Mercury* for 25 September 1847, which reported an exhibition of mesmerism conducted in the city some eight days earlier by a Dr Storer in the city's fashionable Park Street.[100] Little space is given in this account to the mesmeric phenomena exemplified. Much of the piece, rather, enforces Storer's opinion that Britain has excluded itself from a favourable consensus with regard to mesmerism which embraces 'France, Germany, Prussia, Berlin, Stockholm, Russia, Moscow and Petersburg, Denmark and Holland', as well as the United States. The eclectic geography of Storer's list is however offset by his recourse to a familiar and topical example from the British Empire. Storer states:

> In India, the Government, impressed with its great importance, had caused two hospitals to be erected, one at Calcutta, the other at Madras, and a third was about being established in Bengal. At home they had also the example of a mesmeric infirmary in London, supported by some of the most enlightened men in the kingdom. With these examples before us (the doctor observed) he hoped shortly in this city and elsewhere to see the science of mesmerism placed on its legitimate basis, and applied extensively among the poorer classes to diseases which have hitherto been pronounced as incurables.[101]

In associating the native population of India with the domestic proletariat, Storer is in one respect extending the boundaries of the racism imbricated in Esdaile's *Mesmerism in India*. The working classes, as it were, become fit subjects for charity medicine, but are also a population to be governed, controlled, and treated to imperial discipline by intelligent and patrician governance. One should not forget that Elliotson's experimental subjects were working-class also, and that mesmerism has thus tacitly been allocated a specific role in the maintenance of economically or racially subaltern peoples in the 1840s.

If the report itself was less favourable regarding Esdaile's claims and practice than it might first appear, news of other developments on the Subcontinent helped to maintain the impression of mesmerism's apparent rise to respectability. In June 1848, for example, the *Dundee Courier* was to report a significant advancement in the career of James Esdaile who, unlike Elliotson, is not perceived to have suffered unduly as a consequence of his advocacy of the mesmeric cause:

> Lord Dalhousie is understood to be favourable to the re-establishment of a mesmeric hospital at Calcutta. He has appointed Dr Esdaile Presidency Surgeon, though youngest on the list, in evidence of his estimation of the services performed by him.[102]

A note of caution with regard to Dalhousie's purported enthusiasm ought to be sounded here, though. Dalhousie was appointed Governor General on 12 January 1848, and thus had no involvement in the original adminis-trative support for the experimental hospital. No further investment by the British government in Bengal appears to have been advanced. A columnist for *The Times*, writing some sixty-five years after Esdaile's experiments, noted pithily that 'As, however, the Governor General closed this hospital, a private institution was founded'.[103] *The Times'* correspondent's rhetoric here hints at an interventive termination initiated by the Governor General, though this implication is not substantiated. Whether the experiment ran its full course or not, it is clear that Dalhousie's enthusiasm – if it *were* anything more than a rumour – was at most nominal. It might well be contended that reportage in some quarters of the British press appears to have been on occasions manipulated in order to maintain the positive reputation of Esdaile and his experimental venture.

Contemporary enthusiasm for Esdaile's cause was not confined to anonymous columnists, such as those who provided topical copy for the *Dundee Courier*, however. A month later, in July 1848, the writer and journalist Harriet Martineau, a lay enthusiast for mesmerism, was sufficiently confident to urge a programme of investigation with regard to the phenomena of Egyptian clairvoyance on the model of the experimental paradigm 'so triumphantly pursued by Dr Esdaile in India'.[104] It has to be said, though, that Esdaile's reputation in the United Kingdom would seem to be founded in part upon public ignorance as much as personal achievement, and the facts of the Bengal Inquiry appear to have been lost in the enthusiastic rhetoric which saw an institutional recognition in India as the first step in the corresponding rise of the mesmeric infirmary as a force – albeit a short-lived one – in British medical culture.

'Established for the alleviation and cure of diseases': The Mesmeric Infirmary in London

The founding of a mesmeric infirmary in London in the 1840s was almost inevitable. Elliotson's expulsion from the wards and lecture theatres of University College Hospital in 1838 effectively institutionalised hostility towards the claims of mesmerism in the established metropolitan hospitals. In consequence, the new and purposeful application of hypnotic sleep as a surgical anaesthetic became a practice associated with individual practitioners and smaller institutions in both London and the provinces.[105] There was no longer a high-profile forum, under this new regime, for the public exhibition of charitable subjects in the tradition of Elliotson's experiments with the O'Key sisters. Though Elliotson's private practice and mesmeric experimentation appear to have continued without significant interruption into the 1840s, it would seem almost certain that Esdaile's successes in India were the significant catalyst that finally advanced mesmerism as a perceptible alternative to – rather than an aspiring component of – the monopoly of London professional medicine. This much, certainly, was recognised at the time. At the first annual general meeting of the Society behind the Mesmeric Infirmary, the Reverend George Sandby claimed:

> It was a most remarkable fact, and one of which they ought to be ashamed, that the first Mesmeric Hospital had not been established in civilised Europe – had not been established in the centre of this great metropolis – had not been fostered in scientific society, but had been established in what Shakspere called 'the furthest steppes of India'.[106]

Elliotson, as consultant and figurehead, was heavily implicated in the development of a dedicated mesmeric infirmary for the capital – though the whole project, it would appear, was saturated with a surgical purposefulness that distanced it greatly from earlier dilettante exhibitions of insensibility, clairvoyance and submission of the will. In many respects, when the project was finally realised, the London Mesmeric Infirmary was to be an institution cast in the mould of Esdaile's Calcutta hospital, and one which applied the principles of mesmeric anaesthesia to the European bodies which were apparently never included in his formal Indian experiments.

Short statements regarding the prospective establishment of a mesmeric infirmary in the capital began appearing in the provincial press in the summer of 1846. A more substantial announcement, though – and, unusually, one not attributed to any earlier published source – was made in the *Sheffield and Rotherham Independent* on 25 July 1846. The paragraph read:

> MESMERIC INFIRMARY: – At a meeting held at the Earl of Ducie's, Belgrave Square, on the 9th instant, it was unanimously resolved that a mesmeric infirmary should be established, for the application of mesmerism to the cure of diseases, and the prevention of pain in surgical operations. The Earl of Ducie was elected president; and, a committee having been appointed, a subscription to a considerable amount was entered into.[107]

Henry George Francis Reynolds-Moreton, the Second Earl of Ducie, is an interesting figure, and one whose involvement with the mesmeric cause appears to be a consequence of personal curative experience rather than mere enthusiasm or financial self-interest. A politician with Free Trade sympathies, active both in the House of Commons and the Lords until his resignation from active work in the latter in 1847, Ducie served as President of the Royal Agricultural Society between 1851 and 1852. He was, it appears, if not a natural leader then at least a desirable figurehead for such bodies, as a later announcement of his involvement with another mesmeric infirmary makes clear:

> Earl Ducie has consented to become President of a 'Mesmeric Institute' just formed in Bristol. His Lordship stated, 'He felt bound to tell them the history of his conversion, for he used to laugh as much at mesmerism as any person in that room could do. Some years ago he had suffered much from gout and other affections. One day, a clergyman, a friend of his, came to him in great glee, and told him that he had it in his power to be cured. His informant went on to tell him that he had been cured by clairvoyance of a nervous attack he had suffered from for many years. If he was not afraid, he was recommended to go to a curative clairvoyante. Being piqued on his being afraid of going, he sent for the lady, laughing, he must confess,

at the whole affair. He was, however, cured after being mesmerised regularly for some time.'[108]

Certainly, with the prestige of Ducie harnessed, and his personal testimony conjoined, the proposed London Mesmeric Infirmary promised to be no insignificant project. One can only speculate as to whether Ducie's unnamed clerical friend, and the similarly anonymous surgeon-mesmerist he was later to associate himself with in London, were listed in the table of supporters that was published in several provincial newspapers at the time:

> Earl Ducie is president; and the vice-presidents are – Baron de Goldsmid, Viscount Morpeth, MP, R. Monckton Milnes, MP, J. H. Langston, MP, Rev. G. Sandby, jun., Rev. T. Robertson. In the committee are Drs Ashburner, Buxton, Elliotson, and eight surgeons. In the list of subscriptions stands Earl Ducie, for £100.[109]

Elliotson, ultimately, was to become Treasurer of the Infirmary. Of the others mentioned, Isaac Lyon Goldsmid, a prominent member of a banking family, was the first Jew to be created a baronet (in 1841): there is a suggestion of divided loyalties in *his* association with the project, however, for he served as Treasurer of the North London Hospital between 1834 and 1850, this being the institution which, as University College Hospital, forbade Elliotson to practice mesmerism upon its wards. Viscount Morpeth was a Liberal politician with an interest in public health reform; Richard Monckton Milnes was likewise a Liberal, who became a peer in 1863. Langston was a Gloucestershire neighbour of Ducie who, like him, enjoyed agricultural interests.[110] George Sandby was at the time researching *Mesmerism and Its Opponents*, which he published in 1848. It is uncertain whether Robertson was the same clergyman who had been 'Chaplain of the East India Company on the Bengal Establishment' as early as 1832.[111] If so, he would have been an appropriate choice: Esdaile's work was undertaken in west Bengal. The lay membership of the body could thus hardly have been more prestigious, and it is notable that these supporters of the Infirmary are given greater prominence in reportage than the anonymous 'eight surgeons'.

With such a prestigious group of backers, the project did not struggle to realise the finance necessary to acquire and fit a suitable building for medical purposes. Movement towards the physical actualisation of the project, however, came more slowly. Recalling the initial gathering in 1846 at the first annual general meeting of the Mesmeric Infirmary on 6

May 1850, the ubiquitous Sandby – no doubt in ponderous tones, and with suitable pauses – 'read the report of the committee of management':

> A few friends of mesmerism, considering the establishment of an infirmary for the treatment of disease by its means, a very desirable object, met at the Earl of Ducie's, in the year 1846, and passed some preliminary resolutions to that effect. Among the steps taken at that meeting was the appointment of a committee, to whom was entrusted the power of carrying the plan into operation. Sundry circumstances, however, delayed the immediate execution. But in the course of last year it was felt that the time was at length arrived when any further delay would be undesirable. The progress that mesmerism had made in public opinion, the increasing number of its advocates, and the growing demands on the part of the sick and suffering for assistance and advice, all lead to the conviction that the infirmary could at once be opened with every prospect of success. (Hear, hear.)[112]

As the report confides, finances were indeed healthy at the start of the project. The 'liberal donations and subscriptions of many friends and patrons' had already realised the significant sum of £903 17s, with a further £200 promised to the project, plus interest on investments of £23. A freehold estate at Edmonton had also been donated to the cause, as had the commercial accommodation provided by 'five railway arches at Stepney', these realising £40 and £5 annually in rents, respectively.[113] With the rent for the Infirmary's initial accommodation at 9 Bedford Street, Bloomsbury, and the salary of the Secretary totalling a mere £12 11s 6d each quarter, the Mesmeric Infirmary was in as strong a position as any conventional hospital at the time.[114]

Indeed, the Committee's first report states explicitly that the Infirmary's practice 'already shows a promise of growth', and this much is confirmed by another correspondent, writing for the East Anglian press a few days later.[115] Noting that 'W. Fisher, who had been recommended by Mr Tubbs, of Upwell, was permanently engaged as "mesmeriser", at a salary of 1/- a week' at the Infirmary, the anonymous correspondent then intimated:

> The applications at the Infirmary for relief from one malady or other are so augmented that Mr Tubbs has been solicited to train up and send Fisher an assistant, and four young men are daily attending his instructions, in order to acquire the practice, one of whom is expected to become proficient in about a fortnight.[116]

This may well have been a consequence of the Infirmary's charitable mission. Sandby was explicit that the function of the Mesmeric Infirmary was not merely 'to prove their science' but also 'to extend the advantages of mesmerism to the very poorest of their fellow subjects', the restoration to health of these beneficiaries being presumably be the most suitable evidence for the supporters of the Infirmary 'to show to the world the truth of their principles'.[117] In a sense, the poor of London might be seen to function as evidence for the veracity of the theory and the success of the treatment, duly referenced in newspaper accounts and topical conversation, in much the same manner as the Indians exemplified by Esdaile.

Those principles would necessarily need to be demonstrated by a disciplined control over the activities and dignity of the Mesmeric Infirmary. This much is conveyed by the first sentence of the preface to the institution's formal laws: 'This infirmary is established for the alleviation and cure of diseases, and for the relief and prevention of pain, by means of mesmerism'.[118] Monckton Milnes, indeed, specifically urged upon the meeting 'the necessity of the institution strictly confining themselves to the use of mesmerism as a curative operation and eschewing experiments'.[119] This, surely, was an anticipatory gesture, calculated to discourage any attempt by Elliotson to transfer his own experimental practice from his private chambers to the wards of the Mesmeric Infirmary. Implicitly, Monckton Milnes's words bracketed the doctor's practice with the 'idle curiosity' of the less-qualified observers who had once flocked to exhibitions in public wards: 'any imputation of quackery', the trustee suggested, might be fatal to the good name of the Mesmeric Infirmary.[120] This was not to be, in other words, a continuation of Elliotson's work at University College Hospital, and, if the doctor's name was necessary to the project as a medical consultant, his presence is notably muted in this recollection of a significant event in the history of London's first dedicated mesmeric hospital. His name is not mentioned in this account of the meeting, though it is associated with his position as Treasurer in an advertisement published in the *Morning Post* later the same month, which also prominently foregrounds the names of the President, Vice-Presidents and Committee before quietly soliciting subscriptions.[121]

Monckton Milnes's desire that the Infirmary might carry out its business 'under the eye of the public, under the notice of the press' was realised.[122] Press coverage of British mesmeric surgery (as opposed to the broader coverage of public experimentation) across the 1840s and 1850s was consistent, if at times rather laconic. Birth announcements, such as

those sporadically published in *The Times* and other newspapers, pointed
out the ubiquity of mesmerism as an analgesic during parturition in the
years immediately before the regular administration of chemicals such
as chloroform. The following announcement is typical, though a reader
might question why the mode of delivery should be so explicitly specified
other than as a public affirmation of a personal commitment to mesmeric
anaesthesia: 'On the 19th ult., at Rotherhithe (in the unconsciousness of
mesmeric sleep, induced by Mr Chandler), the wife of Mr Thomas Moss,
of a son'.[123] More extensive coverage, though, was afforded to descriptions
of mesmeric surgery where disease or injury was an issue, whether the
operation was effected in private premises in London or in a doctor's
chambers in the provinces.[124]

The establishing of the Mesmeric Infirmary provided an opportunity
for newspapers to consider regular hospital practice in a way that had not
been previously possible. In such reports, the tone is customarily respectful
and contained, and what spectacle there is lacks the visceral detail of
descriptions of the tests previously applied to those apparently placed
under mesmeric sedation. The ambience conveyed is less one of experimentation than of confident practice, in other words. One such account,
which describes an operation undertaken at the Infirmary's later premises
in Marylebone, is representative, its muted tone no doubt being further
conditioned by the nature of the operation and the respectable status of
the patient.

> On Wednesday last, at a quarter past 2 o'clock, Mr Tubbs, surgeon,
> of Upwell, Cambridgeshire, in the presence of above a dozen
> gentlemen, at the Mesmeric Infirmary, No.36, Weymouth-street,
> Portland-place, cut away the right breast of a most respectable
> married woman, of Upwell, named Flowerday. He first threw her
> into the state of sleep-waking by holding her hands in his, and
> staring at her eyes. After a time her eye-lids quivered, and her eyes
> converged and turned upwards; and, in nine minutes from the first,
> her eyes closed, and her head drooped as she sat in her chair. Mr
> Tubbs then ceased to hold first one hand and then the other, and
> each dropped powerless into her lap. The left hand was allowed to
> lie where it fell; the right hand was held up and aside by Mr Burman,
> surgeon, of Wisbeach, in order to be out of the operator's way.

Tubbs's technique here, with its emphasis upon the patient's ocular concentration, resembles that of Braid, rather than recalling the more frenetic

hand gestures that Elliotson appears to have deployed when urging a state of lucid 'sleep waking' upon the O'Key sisters. Here, the atmosphere is calm and contained, the patient eased into passivity, so that the extraordinary phenomena associated with painless surgery – something which Esdaile does not seem always to have achieved – can be the better advanced to the reader. The report continues:

> During the whole of the operation, which was performed with unusual slowness, not a sound escaped the patient. She sat perfectly still, silent, and relaxed, like any one in the sweetest sleep – not a part quivered or twitched; her lips were relaxed and motionless; and, in order further to show that she exerted no effort to restrain herself, Dr Elliotson, while the gashes were making, moved the ends of her fingers backwards and forwards in complete relaxation, with the tip of one of his fingers. There was no holding or catching of her breath; all was the relaxation and placidity of complete repose. In fact, her countenance, which is extremely good, expressed the height of composure; and she was not subjected to restraint of any kind.[125]

Elliotson here seems to be something of a junior partner. He is neither surgeon nor anaesthetist, and his presence seems merely to be that of an observer, or else a facilitator of the evidence of the patient's unconsciousness – by way of his manipulation of her fingers – for those present.

It seems curious, however, that the surgery was performed in London, despite the patient, the surgeon and the mesmerist all being resident in Cambridgeshire, where the basic surgical facilities appropriate to a mastectomy were undoubtedly available. The justification for performing the operation in London was not connected with the patient's benefit but was, rather, intimate to the mission of the Infirmary. Elliotson's report on Mrs Flowerday's mastectomy, publicly presented to the Infirmary's supporters later that year, makes this much clear:

> Mr Tubbs, a surgeon in Cambridgeshire, one of our earliest and very liberal subscribers, who for many years has practised mesmerism … wrote up to say that he was about to remove a female breast in the mesmeric state of insensibility to pain, and would perform the operation in the infirmary. The committee agreed to it – as so public a proof of the power and utility of mesmerism in the metropolis, when no hospital surgeon had ever operated under mesmerism or employed it, seemed likely to produce a decided conviction in the

minds of society at large, and through this conviction to improve the
conduct of the medical profession.[126]

Hitherto the mesmeric administrations undertaken at Weymouth Street
appear to have been confined, for the most part, to palliative or analgesic
treatment. A significant surgical operation of this nature would, inevitably,
garner a far greater degree of both public and professional interest. Needless
to say, the operation was performed in the presence of suitable witnesses
drawn from the committee, the medical profession and the laity. Interest in
the operation was gratifyingly significant in the capital and the provinces.
The *Standard* printed a report of the operation on the same day, and, though
most of the report seems to be derived from the witness statement utilised
by *The Times*, the former article is considerably more detailed with regard
to the actions of the surgeon in both excising the tumour and regulating
the patient's bleeding.[127] Several provincial publications also recorded the
operation, albeit in less detail.[128] It was, as it were, a successful publicity
coup for the Infirmary.

Other surgical operations were also recorded in the provincial press,
as well as within the more specialist pages of journals such as the *Zoist*. In
the *Examiner*, for example, the rather technical record of the removal of a
tooth under mesmeric sedation by Thomas Bell, Professor of Zoology at
King's College, is quoted from its original appearance in the *Zoist* as a sort
of authorising preface to the recollection of 'a similar operation performed
last week upon the same patient in the Mesmeric Infirmary at which the
writer of this notice was present'. The columnist, having quoted the report
of the initial extraction of a molar and the near-painless probing of other
decayed teeth in the patient's mouth, notes:

> In the operation at the Mesmeric Infirmary last week Mr Chandler
> extracted two teeth. One was too much decayed to admit of being at
> once removed, and the operation must have been extremely painful.
> Both were double teeth, and singularly firm and deep in the jaw.
> The man – whose simple manner and honest expression of face were
> sufficient guarantee for his perfect good faith, even if the nature of
> the operation had not forbade the possibility of trick – remained
> entirely unconscious of anything having been done to him until
> roused from the Mesmeric trance.[129]

Certainly, sufferers of mundane as well as exceptional disorders appear to
have patronised the Mesmeric Infirmary as subscribing as well as charity
patients. Reportage from this period is emphatic that the institution was

run in the manner of a regular hospital; that its procedures were open to those who were genuinely seeking knowledge or evidence rather than sensation; and that no immodest displays were contemplated, let alone permitted, in its wards and theatres. The rhetoric, though, still betrays the characteristic fear of being associated with imposture. The names of credible witnesses are listed to bolster the reputations of the practitioners; the evidence of the entranced body's insensibility to pain is stressed; the difficulty of the operation – which may be complicated by the state of the teeth or the comparative size of the tumour or depth of incision – is marshalled as another evidential element when asserting the efficacy of mesmeric anaesthesia. Detailed descriptions of significant operations are, however, rare in the annals of the Mesmeric Infirmary. It is clear that mesmeric surgery was never practised in London to the extent it was under Esdaile's supervision in India.

Such reports – based as they are on physiologically conventional surgery and the two accepted modes of inducing trance (by way of manual passes or the strained gaze of the patient) – can convey only the strictly *practical* aspect of the Infirmary's day-to-day existence. The annual meetings of its governing body (which was styled variously as a Committee or a Council), which were consistently reported in the metropolitan press, provide a considerably richer guide to the contemporary culture of mesmerism and its practitioners. The Infirmary's second annual general meeting was, of course, an opportunity to report on the first year of the institution's existence, and detail was not spared in the eulogising of its success. Sandby, as Chairman, was quietly confident in his words to the gathered supporters of the hospital:

> he could not but congratulate them at the very favourable progress their institution had made during the past year. They would see by the report that there had been a great variety of cases treated most successfully. He had been in the habit of frequently attending the hospital, and had invariably found the committee sedulously attentive to their duties, and the mesmerisers performing their various offices in the most efficient manner. He was happy to say that their funds were also improving, and several donations had been sent them.

These donations were a source of prestige as well as of essential finance. The Archbishop of Dublin – who was to be elected President upon the death of Ducie – and the Earl of Stanhope (who had been three times elected as a Whig MP between 1806 and 1816) were both acknowledged publicly for their generosity.[130] Elliotson, in his report as Treasurer, was slow in coming to the state of the Infirmary's finances, however. His report, for the most part, tabulates some of the successful cases handled by the hospital before noting rather briefly that

> Donors have presented to the infirmary 998*l*. 8 s. We have 118 annual subscribers who, with one lately deceased, have contributed from the commencement 325*l*. 10 s., and the 118 contribute annually 197*l*. 19 s. 6d. We receive 23*l*. 0 s. 2 d. as the interest of five Exchequer bills. We have 844*l*. 4 s. 3½ d. in hand.

This represents a slight, though probably not a serious decrease on the figures associated with the Infirmary's opening balance sheet, though one which may readily be associated with the expenses of equipping the building and training up the requisite staff. Elliotson concluded his report – characteristically, perhaps – with a dismissive tirade against Wakley.[131]

All this, perhaps, is rather conventional, with nothing in substance that might not be found in the record of the annual meeting of any other hospital or charitable concern. Buried in the account, though, is a somewhat radical development in mesmerism and one which does not have a parallel in mainstream medical practice at the time. In an age in which women were debarred from practising medicine other than in its unregulated aspect, the Mesmeric Infirmary was proactive in promoting female professionalism amongst its cohort of paid mesmerisers.[132] The motivations behind this strategy were as much moral as they were a matter of acknowledging the equal facility of both sexes in inducing trance. Recalling Sandby's address to the gathering, the anonymous columnist notes:

> There was one part of the report to which he felt particularly anxious to direct their attention. A proposition had been made that the committee should have the power of adding lady mesmerisers to their number. That might seem rather a novel proceeding, but he hoped that it would be received favourably, for there were many reasons of a peculiar nature, which it was unnecessary for him to mention, why such a suggestion was exceedingly necessary. The presence of ladies would, in a great measure, silence all the suspicions of low and vulgar minds, who, conscious of their own iniquity, judged others by themselves. (Cheers.) To the ladies they were already greatly indebted, for, through their instrumentality, mesmerism had been introduced to families with the greatest success.[133]

This proposition appears to have been carried into practice at some time before the meeting, for Elliotson notes that a third mesmeriser had already been engaged by the Infirmary, she being 'a married woman'.[134] This individual may have been the 'Miss Cooper, Medical Mesmeriser (late Operative member of the Mesmeric Infirmary)' who was later soliciting out-patients for treatment 'on liberal terms' in an advertisement placed in the *Morning Post* on 11 September 1858.[135] Presumably, her specific focus was upon women or else children, as Sandby suggests. It must be stressed that she was not practising diagnosis or surgery, though her accession to a salaried professional status resembling that of a modern anaesthetist would have no equivalent in the patriarchal domain of institutional medicine until the last decade of the nineteenth century.[136] If the engagement of female mesmerisers was not a sufficiently radical step in itself, Elliotson was equally enthusiastic regarding the participation of women in the Infirmary's governing body. A proposal was again offered to the floor by one of the Infirmary's male supporters.

> The committee are anxious to propose to the meeting what they believe will be a great improvement. A lady, the wife of distinguished mathematician and philosopher, proposed to Dr Elliotson that ladies should be upon the committee, and offered to join if other ladies would do the same. He at once highly approved of the plan, and mentioned it to the committee, who equally approve of it. Such a measure must be advantageous in many respects, as, in addition to our having female patients, we now employ a female mesmeriser.

The proposal, the newspaper reports, 'was unanimously agreed to'.[137] Despite this, ladies did not become full members of the Committee at all, but were sidelined to a 'ladies committee', which met weekly, visited the infirmary and provided 'suggestions and general assistance'. A radical promise, entered into in the presence of gentlemen of politically liberal sympathies, was thus never properly effected.

If the Infirmary's third annual meeting was graced by a 'large attendance of ladies and gentlemen', sufficient to necessitate the gathering's transfer to a more capacious chamber at Willis's Rooms in London's St James's, it was somewhat less sanguine with regard to the reality of the institution's financial position, for all Elliotson's bullishness. The Treasurer's report, as with the previous year, was in part a tabulation of curative success and in part a polemical dismissal of professional opposition towards mesmerism, though on this occasion it was tempered by copious allusions to Elliotson's own journal, the *Zoist*. The Infirmary, Elliotson reported, still had funds in excess of £844 in hand, though its receipts of £437 9s 6d. had been slightly exceeded by outgoings of £437 10s 1d. If finance was becoming a potential problem for the Infirmary – particularly as the lease to the Bedford Street house was due to expire at Christmas – Elliotson maintained an assertive front, claiming in the face of the figures that 'We may therefore consider ourselves very prosperous' and soliciting further financial support through the intimation that

> we are anxious to extend the benefits of mesmerism – we are anxious to be able to mesmerise a much larger number of patients, and to have an hospital in which patients may reside, as the sick cannot obtain the advantages of mesmerism in the ordinary hospitals.[138]

For all Elliotson's confidence, this meeting was to mark a perceptible shift in the fortunes and nature of the Mesmeric Infirmary.

The 1853 meeting was somewhat sombre in tone, with the death of Ducie on 2 June 1853 necessitating the installation of the Archbishop of Dublin as President of the Infirmary. The structure of Elliotson's address resembled his delivery in previous years, though his proposal of the institution's accounts is both ingenious and possibly slightly deceptive in its presentation of the real state of the Infirmary's finances and reserves. Elliotson advanced a balance sheet which claimed that

> The total income for the past year, including a balance of 394*l*. 2 s. 10 d. from the previous one, amounts to 815*l*. 13 s. 5 d., and the expenditure to 467*l*. 5 s. 8 d., showing a balance of 347*l*. 7 s. 9 d. in favour of the institution.[139]

Even a casual glance at these figures suggests something is wrong. Where, for example, are the funds of £844, formerly denominated as a reserve? How could the institution's income suddenly leap from £437 to £815, other than through some sort of creative accounting which does not seem to have acknowledged the nominal loss posted in 1852? One possible explanation for the loss of reserves might be found in the anticipated termination of the lease of 9 Bedford Street. A lease of £110 per annum had – apparently hastily – been taken out on 'a spacious house situated on the corner of Fitzroy-square and Grafton-street', though the residents of the former appear to have objected to the presence of a hospital in a select residential area. Elliotson's discussion of the situation intimates that the Infirmary was still unable to accommodate in-patients. Little is said, beyond this, of financial affairs. The Treasurer appears to have been unable to reaffirm his statement regarding prosperity, moral or fiscal, made only thirteen months previously.

The 'friends and subscribers', as they were termed, next met formally a year later, on 7 June 1854. It may be an indication of further financial pressure that the advertisement of this meeting in the *Morning Post* was a small fraction of the size of earlier announcements made by the Infirmary.[140] Elliotson announced further changes in the accommodation and management of the Infirmary: it was now occupying a house at 36 Weymouth Street, Portland Place, and a new secretary – a Mr Gardiner – had been appointed, at an unspecified salary. For the first time in four years of reporting by the *Morning Post*, no figures regarding the cash in hand, income and expenditure associated with the Infirmary were presented to the reading public. Instead, the Treasurer simply announced that there had been '27 donations, and 25 new annual subscribers'.[141]

If the tone of the 1852 meeting had been set by Elliotson's ongoing antagonism to both *The Lancet* and institutional medicine, the 1854 gathering appears to have adopted a far more defensive tone in its assessment of the Infirmary's work over the preceding twelve months. Monckton Milnes, as Chairman, initiated this defensive theme in his opening remarks, by noting how mesmerism appeared to have become a last resort for cases which saw no improvement under the treatments specified by conventional chemical or surgical practice. This, he intimated, rather distorted the public record of the Infirmary's (and, indeed, of mesmerism's) achievement in the field of curative medicine. Hence,

> If persons only applied to mesmerism for cure, when their consti-
> tutions were exhausted from trying all other descriptions of remedy,
> it was not to be wondered at if, in some cases, it refused to perform
> its work. But if, on the other hand, it were regarded as a natural
> agent, a patient would no more think of applying to it as a last
> resource, than he would think of applying to any other of the healing
> agencies.[142]

This sounds rather desperate, even in the context of the ongoing hostility towards mesmerism which Monckton Milnes acknowledges elsewhere in his statement. The rather despondent tone, though, is maintained by Elliotson in *his* subsequent report, a statement in which the doctor's rhetoric is forced to work hard in the context of the discouraging statistics he is compelled to present. Elliotson notes that the Infirmary has 'treated 237 patients during the last twelvemonth':

> There were 39 on hand at the beginning of it, 43 were on hand at present, and there had been 198 fresh patients; 42 cases had been cured; 9 were all but cured; 64 improved to a greater or less extent; 43 were still under treatment. Nearly all the rest of the patients attended but a short time, far too short for improvement to have been possible; some attended only two or three times; some even only once.

Even eliding those patients who were *almost* cured with those whose treatment had been satisfactorily concluded, these statistics suggest a relatively meagre curative success rate. Assuming that the total number of patients treated across the year was 237 – namely the 39 already 'on hand' supplemented by the 'fresh' 198 – the 51 individuals whom Elliotson considers substantially relieved represent fewer than one in four of the Infirmary's total admissions for the year. Even when the 64 improved patients are added to this total, it is still evident that just under 50 per cent of those treated by the Infirmary were formally recorded as having seen some improvement in their condition.

Clearly, some contextualisation is necessarily demanded in order to explain what otherwise might seem to be an abysmal performance by a highly public institution, and Elliotson is quick to provide this by deflecting blame away from the science and towards those patients – often unlettered charity cases, no doubt – who availed themselves of it. Elliotson continues:

> Mesmerism was conceived of by a large number of people as a magical remedy, curing at once if it does cure, and not worth being continued beyond a day or two, nor capable of doing good unless sleep or some peculiar effect was produced; whereas it often required long perseverance, and often simply cures without any other effect. It is to be remembered that the greater number of patients came after other treatments had failed, and when other is not likely to succeed. A large number had been under several medical men, been in more medical institutions than one, and gone through long and not unfrequently severe treatment in the way of strong and disgusting drugs and severe external applications, to which some of the medical profession had rather that their patients be subjected,

even with little or no chance of benefit, than be treated by a mild
and easy, nay, agreeable method, with great probability of cure or
alleviation.[143]

It is hard to read this as a confident statement, the more so as it simply
reiterates the earlier remarks advanced by Monckton Milnes. It is more
an act of defiance, possibly one conscious of a worsening situation that
embraces both the financial health and the public image of the Infirmary.
The meeting was no doubt gratified to receive specific notice of the
mastectomy performed upon Mrs Flowerday by Tubbs and Burman, but
the evident success of this operation must be taken in the context of an
aside associated with it in Elliotson's report. This was – surprisingly,
given the four years of its existence – 'almost the first surgical operation
that had been performed in the infirmary'.[144] Clearly, the successful cures
briefly enumerated in Elliotson's earlier summaries had been incidents
of minor surgery or else concerned with the alleviation of pain. It was
small wonder, therefore, that this highly invasive and excisive procedure
captured the imagination of the metropolitan and provincial press, and was
desperately seized upon by the Treasurer as evidence of the Institution's
progress and reliability. Be that as it may, the closing remarks contained
in the management committee's annual report, delivered by Elliotson,
hint of difficult financial times, for it was to be hoped 'that the friends
of mesmeric science would come forward in support of an institution
which had alleviated so large an amount of human suffering'.[145] Notably,
later advertisements, which intimated that 'Patients can admitted by the
recommendation of subscribers', were to stress the charitable nature of
the Mesmeric Infirmary.[146]

The *Morning Post* was to continue to report the annual gatherings of
the subscribers and supporters of the Mesmeric Infirmary in its columns,
albeit with some curious variations in terms of emphasis and detail, until
1858. Fewer items of specific information tend to be advanced by the
newspaper's columnist in the years following 1854 regarding cases treated
or cured, for example.[147] The columnist, though, *is* consistent when
recording the various speeches delivered by the illustrious chairmen, who
vary from year to year, and by Elliotson in his role as Treasurer and orator
of the Committee's formal report. The two speakers, invariably, adopt a
consistent polemical defensiveness, which decries, on the one hand, the
intellectual reluctance of the established medical profession while still
claiming the progressive advance of mesmerism into public acceptance.

The numerical tabulation of cases treated and cured remains a prominent component of Elliotson's discourse, however, and is always reported in the newspaper's yearly column. At the 1855 meeting, Elliotson claimed that 'The cures last year exceeded by 27 the number of those achieved in the previous year', though from a total of 247 patients treated, only 69 had been regarded as cured and '9 nearly cured'.[148] In 1856, the figures were less encouraging: of 237 patients treated, '49 had been perfectly cured, 5 nearly cured', and, if 55 had been 'greatly relieved', one had died.[149] They were worse in 1857, where the total of 266 patients treated yielded only 63 who had been either 'cured, or [who had] benefited to a greater or less extent'.[150] In 1858, a tiny column – less than a quarter of the size of any earlier report on the Infirmary's annual meeting by the *Morning Post* – conveyed a more encouraging range of statistics, with 251 patients recorded as being treated, and just over half of these – 126 – 'cured or relieved'.[151] The elision of figures usually kept discrete here is, perhaps, significant. *The Morning Post* continued to advertise the annual meetings of the Mesmeric Infirmary into the 1860s, though it did not summarise the proceedings thereat following that final, short account in 1858.[152] Possibly the public interest was waning, and this annual formulaic recital of defiant confidence and disappointing statistics was necessarily dropped to make way for more compelling stories in the capital's constant *charivari* of news. Subscribers, after all, could purchase the full *Annual Report* of the Committee, should they be unable to attend the annual gathering at Willis's Rooms.[153]

The last balance sheet which appears to have been widely circulated amongst the reading public (rather than distributed only amongst those subscribers who received the Infirmary's *Annual Report*) shows a serious depletion of the institution's once impressive finances. Printed in the *Morning Post* on 13 June 1856, the figures are tempered by a reliance on the sure continuation of monies promised but recently:

> With regard to the financial condition of the institution, it was gratifying to find that there were 28 new subscribers, and 58 new donors, added to the list of its supporters, and that the amount of subscriptions showed an increase of £8 10/10½ on the year. The Council had 5 Exchequer bills on which they did not intend to encroach, and had lodged at 4 per cent interest in the Union Bank £384, which they had received for the sale of Archways under the Blackwall Railway, and had, after paying all expenses, a balance of £56 9/8 d in hand.[154]

With its assets being liquidated, and a start-up capital of around £1000 being reduced to little more than a twentieth of its initial value in just six years, every source of income became crucial to the continuation of the Infirmary's mission. A report in the *Morning Chronicle* on 19 June 1861 – this being one of very few published précis of the Infirmary's annual general meetings in the 1860s – revealed that the financial situation was impacting upon the Institution's charitable work. The columnist intimated that 'Owing to the smallness of the funds, it was impossible to receive 15 applicants who were waiting'. The Mesmeric Infirmary had, at least, increased its available balance to £70 12s 8d in the intervening five years, though this was hardly a capital sum that could be relied upon in the long term.[155] Advertisements placed in order to publicise the Committee's regular meetings routinely advised (or emphasised) that 'SUBSCRIPTIONS are earnestly SOLICITED'.[156] Finally, in June 1867, the Committee was forced to be publicly frank regarding the prospects of the Mesmeric Infirmary. An advertisement on the front page of the *Standard* announced:

> The Council regret to be compelled, in consequence of the death of many of the chief patrons, viz., the Archbishop of Dublin, the Earls of Ducie and Carlisle, the Baron de Goldsmid, and many others, to SOLICIT for further ASSISTANCE.
>
> Since the opening of the Infirmary in 1849 several thousands of patients have been admitted. The majority have derived great benefit, numbers have been entirely cured; although most of them only sought mesmerism after being pronounced incurable by their medical attendants. It is therefore hoped that such an invaluable Institution will not be allowed to languish for want of public support.[157]

Some sizeable donations were made, even in the declining years of the Infirmary's fortunes – an announcement in the *Morning Post* dated 26 October 1869 thankfully acknowledged 'the liberal DONATION of £100 from A. Z.' – but the situation was clearly untenable.[158] The disappearance of the Infirmary's business from the columns of the London newspapers seems to have paralleled, if it did not actually prompt, a corresponding decline in its public presence.[159] An advertisement placed in *The Times* for 2 June 1869 advises that consultations are still given daily (except on Sundays) on a gratis basis, before informing the reader that 'Numerous cases which were considered incurable have been successfully treated at this useful though little known Institution, for which funds are much required'.[160] By the 1870s, though, it appeared that the fortunes of British mesmerism

had declined in parallel with those of its most dedicated and persistent
charitable institution. An index of both might be gauged by the success of a
series of three lectures delivered in November 1875 by 'Professor Meredith,
late of the Mesmeric Infirmary, London' regarding which, a columnist
for the *Blackburn Standard* noted drily, 'There were not large audiences'.[161]
The Mesmeric Infirmary appears to have published its final annual report
in 1869, a year after Elliotson's death.[162] The Superintendant, Thomas
Chandler, however, was still in residence at Weymouth Street as late as 18
January 1870.[163] With the *Zoist* having ceased publication in 1856, there was
no specialist journal to mourn the Mesmeric Infirmary's apparently silent
passing, and no interest, either, from the popular press.

The quiet death of mesmerism in Britain in the 1870s has, quite rightly,
been associated with the rise of chemical anaesthesia.[164] Elliotson and his
associates were undoubtedly wary of the potential threat to the exclusivity
of their claim to painless surgery posed by ether and chloroform.[165] They
were less aware, though, of the change to medical culture that would
come with the widespread introduction of chemical anaesthetics and
the accompanying publicity which made such advances commonplace
knowledge in the public mind.[166] This was no minor revolution in
thought. The introduction of chloroform, notably, was regarded as making
ether − rather than mesmerism − redundant.[167] Queen Victoria's (at the
time disputed) endorsement of chloroform as an analgesic in childbirth
in 1853 was thus almost an afterthought.[168] Again, the chemical nature
of the substances literally introduced into the economy of the human
body in the pursuit of analgesic unconsciousness necessitated those who
administered them to enjoy a status which, if it was not as prestigious
as that of a surgeon or a physician, aspired to rank them alongside such
regulated professionals as apothecaries and pharmacists.[169] This was an age,
after all, acutely aware of the adulteration of foodstuffs and the dubious
content of quack medicines.[170] The day of the lay mesmerist was over,
and the seemingly utter reliability of chemically induced unconsciousness,
even taking account of the occasional fatalities which occurred under
chloroform, far exceeded the apparently variable analgesia produced by the
waving of hands or the strained ocular gaze. With interest in clairvoyance
and mesmeric diagnosis likewise in decline, there was seemingly no longer
a viable place for mesmerism in the national consciousness.

Notes

1 Anon., 'Hypnotism', *The Leisure Hour*, July 1887, pp. 454–6, at p. 454, col. 1.

2 See, for example, the advertisement for the *Journal of Psychological Medicine*, in *John Bull and Britannia*, 40 (29 September 1860), p. 609, col. 3. Reviewing the latter work in another issue of *John Bull*, an anonymous writer jokingly noted the ambiguity of the term as a consequence of the popularity of an actor by the same surname. See Anon, 'The Quarterlies', *John Bull*, 40 (27 October 1860), p. 684, col. 1.

3 See Anon., 'Mr Braid's Lectures on Animal Magnetism', *The Manchester Times and Gazette*, 11 December 1841, p. 3, cols 4–6, at col. 5.

4 See James Braid, 'On Neuro-Hypnotism', *The Medical Times* 6/146 (1842), reprinted in *The Discovery of Hypnosis: The Complete Writings of James Braid, the Father of Hypnotherapy*, ed. Donald Robertson (London: National Council for Hypnotherapy, 2009), pp. 368–9.

5 See advertisement ['Just published'], *The Lady's Newspaper*, 3 July 1852, p. 414, col. 1.

6 Anon., 'Mr Braid's Lectures on Animal Magnetism', p. 3, col. 4, original italics.

7 Anon., 'Mesmerism and Somnambulism', *The Morning Chronicle*, 1 December 1841, p. 2, col. 4; Anon., 'Mr Braid's Lectures on Animal Magnetism', p. 3, col. 4, original italics.

8 Anon., 'Mr Braid's Lectures on Animal Magnetism', p. 3, col. 4, original italics.

9 James Braid, *Neurypnology, or the Rationale of Nervous Sleep, Considered in Relation with Animal Magnetism* (London: John Churchill, 1843), pp. 16, 35–6. A correspondent of the *Worcester Journal* suggested that hypnotism by way of ocular exhaustion had been discovered prior to 1841, and that Braid's theory may have been derivative: see Anon., 'Mesmerism: To the Editor of the *Worcester Journal*', *Berrow's Worcester Journal*, 16 December 1841, p. 4, col. 2.

10 Braid, *Neurypnology*, p. 36.

11 Braid, *Neurypnology*, pp. 36–7.

12 Anon., 'Mr Braid's Lectures on Animal Magnetism', p. 3, col. 4.

13 Anon., 'The Mystery of Mesmerism and Somnambulism Explained', *Preston Chronicle*, 24 December 1841, p. 4, col. 6.

14 Anon., 'Mr Braid's Lectures on Animal Magnetism', p. 3, col. 4.

15 Anon., 'The Story of Hypnotism', *Pall Mall Gazette*, 19 July 1898, p. 3, col. 2; cf. the explanation given in Anon., 'Mesmerism and Somnambulism', p. 2, col. 4.

16 Anon., 'Mr Braid's Lectures on Animal Magnetism', p. 3, col. 4, original italics. Braid, however, was to caution that the deployment of hypnotism 'ought to be left in the hands of professional men, and of them only': see Braid, *Neurypnology*, p. 12.

17 Indeed, whilst Braid was conducting his experiments, 'Attention was called ... to a gentleman sitting in the gallery, who had been experimenting on himself, and fallen into a complete state of somnolency': Anon., 'Mr Braid's Lectures on Animal Magnetism', p. 3, col. 5.

18 Anon., 'Mr Braid's Lectures on Animal Magnetism', p. 3, col. 5. Further variations on Braid's use of the cork as a focus for the gaze may be found in Anon., 'Mesmerism and Somnambulism', p. 2, col. 4, and in Braid, *Neurypnology*, pp. 27–8, where the author also records how, in later experiments, he deployed a lancet case in the place of the cork.

19 This is not to say that Braid disregarded the restorative possibilities associated with hypnotically induced deep sleep in cases of excessive respiration or rapid heartbeat: see Braid, *Neurypnology*, pp. 76–7.

20 See Anon., 'Mesmerism and Braidism', *The Leicester Chronicle: or, Commercial and Agricultural Advertiser*, 2 April 1842, p. 4, cols 2–3, at col. 3.

21 Anon., 'Mr Braid's Lectures on Animal Magnetism', p. 3, col. 5.

22 Anon., 'Mr Braid's Lectures on Animal Magnetism', p. 3, col. 5.

23 Braid did, however, note a specific case where the clairaudient capabilities of hypnotism had been deployed in his own practice to counteract deafness. Anon., 'Mr Braid's Lectures on Animal Magnetism', p. 3, col. 5.

24 Anon., 'Mr Braid's Lecture on Animal Magnetism at The Athenaeum', *The Manchester Times and Gazette*, 31 December 1841, p. 3, cols 2–3, at col. 2. One wonders what Dr Herbert, 'the Hon. and Very Rev., The Dean of Manchester', who was present at the lecture, thought of Braid's free adoption of the Biblical rhetoric of the miraculous. His phrasing certainly resembles the Gospel of St Matthew, 11: 5. Braid, notably, was later chastised from the pulpit in apocalyptic tones by a Liverpool clergyman, prompting the doctor's own response *Satanic Agency and Mesmerism Reviewed, in a Letter to the Reverend H. McNeile, A.M., of Liverpool, in Reply to a Sermon Preached by Him in St Jude's Church, Liverpool, on Sunday, April 10, 1842* (Manchester: Simms and Dinham, and Galt and Anderson, 1842).

25 Anon., 'Mr Braid's Lecture on Animal Magnetism at The Athenaeum', p. 3, col. 2.

26 The British Association became the British Association for the Advancement of Science and was renamed the British Science Association in 2009.

27 Anon., 'Second Edition' [editorial], *The Manchester Times and Gazette*, 25 June 1842, p. 2, cols 4–5, at col. 4.

28 James Braid, 'The Editors of *The Manchester Times*', *The Manchester Times and Gazette*, 25 June 1842, p. 2, col. 4, original italics and capitalisation.

29 Anon., 'Second Edition', p. 2, cols 4–5, at col. 4, original italics.

30 Anon., 'Extraordinary Conduct of the Medical Section towards Mr Braid', *The Manchester Times* and Gazette, 2 July 1842, p. 3, cols 4–6, at col. 4.

31 Anon., 'Extraordinary Conduct of the Medical Section towards Mr Braid', p. 3, col. 6.

32 Anon., 'Extraordinary Conduct of the Medical Section towards Mr Braid', p. 3, col. 5.

33 Anon., 'Amputation without the Knowledge of the Patient', *The Standard*, 26 November 1842, p. 4, cols 3–4, at col. 3.

34 Elliotson's emphases are frequently associated with his polemical drive, and signify the rhetorical adaptation of evidence derived from the observation of others. Here, the apparently ready acceptance of *this* paper by the Royal Medical Society is regarded by Elliotson as evidence of the partial and unfavourable treatment of his own experimental findings by the same body.

35 Anon., 'Amputation without the Knowledge of the Patient', *The Standard*, 26 November 1842, p. 4, cols 3–4

36 Anon., 'Amputation without the Knowledge of the Patient', *Derby Mercury*, 30 November 1842, p. 4, cols 1–2; Anon., 'Amputation without the Knowledge of the Patient', *The Ipswich Journal, and Suffolk, Norfolk, Essex and Cambridgeshire Advertiser*, 3 December 1842, p. 1, cols 6–7; Anon., 'Extraordinary Case – Amputation without the Knowledge of the Patient', *Belfast News Letter*, 2 December 1842, p. 1, col. 1.

37 John Elliotson, *Numerous Cases of Surgical Operations Without Pain in the Mesmeric State, With Remarks Upon the Opposition of Many Members of the Royal Medical and Chirurgical Society and Others to the Inestimable Blessings of Mesmerism* (Philadelphia: Lea and Blanchard, 1843), p. 3.

38 Elliotson, *Numerous Cases*, p. 4, Elliotson's italics. Elliotson's account departs slightly from Topham's words as reproduced in Anon., 'Amputation without the Knowledge of the Patient', *The Standard*, 26 November 1842, p. 4, col. 3.

39 Elliotson, *Numerous Cases*, p. 4. In the *Derby Mercury* column, these words form part of Ward's rather than Topham's account: Anon., 'Amputation without the Knowledge of the Patient', *The Standard*, 26 November 1842, p. 4, col. 4.

40 Elliotson, *Numerous Cases*, pp. 4–5.

41 Anon., 'Amputation without the Knowledge of the Patient', *The Standard*, 26 November 1842, p. 4, col. 3.

42 Elliotson, *Numerous Cases*, p. 5. Elliotson's account differs from that of the *Standard* in some small details of punctuation.

43 Elliotson, *Numerous Cases*, p. 5, Elliotson's italics and emphasis; Anon., 'Amputation without the Knowledge of the Patient', *The Standard*, 26 November 1842, p. 4, col. 3.

44 Elliotson, *Numerous Cases*, p. 6. Elliotson's italics do not appear in the earliest extant account, rendered by *The Standard*, but *are* to be found in at least one derivative and edited version of the story in the provincial press: see Anon., 'Amputation during the Mesmeric State', *Preston Chronicle and Lancashire Advertiser*, 24 December 1842, p. 4, col. 5.

45 Anon., 'Amputation without the Knowledge of the Patient', *The Standard*, 26 November 1842, p. 4, col. 4.

46 Anon., 'Mesmerism: Amputation without the Knowledge of the Patient', *The Essex Standard, and General Advertiser for the Eastern Counties*, 2 December 1842, p. 4, col. 1.

47 Anon., 'Amputation without the Knowledge of the Patient', *The Standard*, 26 November 1842, p. 4, col. 3.

48 Anon., 'The Literary Examiner', *The Examiner*, 18 July 1846, p. 452, cols 1–2, at col. 1.

49 David Esdaile, 'Editor's Preface' to James Esdaile, *Mesmerism in India, and its Practical Application in Surgery and Medicine* (London: Longman, Brown, Green, and Longmans, 1846), pp. ix–xx, at p. ix.

50 James Esdaile, *Mesmerism in India, and its Practical Application in Surgery and Medicine* (London: Longman, Brown, Green, and Longmans, 1846), p. 8.

51 Esdaile, *Mesmerism in India*, p. 9.

52 Esdaile, *Mesmerism in India*, p. 59

53 Esdaile, *Mesmerism in India*, pp. 262, 263.

54 Esdaile, *Mesmerism in India*, p. 43, cf. 51. The account given here is rendered more or less verbatim in *The Zoist*, 4 (1846–7), 25–8, passim.

55 Esdaile, *Mesmerism in India*, p. 44.

56 Esdaile, *Mesmerism in India*, p. 45.

57 The use of a language unintelligible to the entranced subject is, of course, conventional in such experiments: see Anon., 'Animal Magnetism', *The Morning Post*, 7 November 1829, p. 4, col. 3.

58 Esdaile, *Mesmerism in India*, p. 45.

59 Esdaile, *Mesmerism in India*, pp. 45–6.

60 Esdaile, *Mesmerism in India*, p. 46.

61 Esdaile, *Mesmerism in India*, pp. 47–8.

62 Esdaile, *Mesmerism in India*, p. 55.

63 Esdaile, *Mesmerism in India*, pp. 56–7.

64 Esdaile, *Mesmerism in India*, p. 95.

65 Esdaile, *Mesmerism in India*, pp. 96–108.

66 Esdaile, *Mesmerism in India*, p. 15.

67 Esdaile, *Mesmerism in India*, p. 17.

68 Esdaile, *Mesmerism in India*, p. 20.

69 See, for example, J. Milne Bramwell, *Hypnotism: Its History, Practice and Theory* (London: Alexander Moring, 1906), p. 158; Derek Forrest, *Hypnotism: A History* (London: Penguin, 2000), pp. 181, 187 and 305–6, notes 33–6, 39, 40, 44–8.

70 John Elliotson, 'Report by Dr Elliotson upon *A Record of Cases Treated in the Mesmeric Hospital, from November 1846, to May, 1847, with the Reports of the Official Visitors …*', *The Zoist*, 21 (April 1848), 1–41. This is far from the only derivative

account featured in *The Zoist*. See also, for example, 'Mesmeric Cases by Dr Esdaile, Communicated by Dr Elliotson', *The Zoist*, 12 (1854–5), 74–80; 'Some Rapid Cures by Dr Esdaile, Communicated by Dr Elliotson', *The Zoist*, 12 (1854–5), 413–15.

71 Elliotson, 'Report by Dr Elliotson', pp. 15, 20. Regarding Elliotson's use of medical Latin, see *The Zoist*, 4 (1846–7), p. 50.

72 Elliotson, 'Report by Dr Elliotson', pp. 4, 28, 30.

73 Indeed, even where Esdaile's own words are represented more or less verbatim, there is still a tendency in *The Zoist* to deploy these in order to justify the policy of its editor in asserting the efficacy of mesmerism in a hostile medical environment, or in later years in establishing its primacy as an effective anaesthetic before, and equal to, ether and other chemical substances. See, for example, James Esdaile, 'The Protest and Petition of James Esdaile, MD, Surgeon, HEICS, to the Members of the American Congress', *The Zoist*, 9 (1853–4), 294–7.

74 Esdaile, *Mesmerism in India*, p. 15.

75 Pye Henry Chavasse, *Advice to a Wife on the Management of Her Own Health* (London: John Churchill and Sons, 1870), p. 84.

76 Esdaile, *Mesmerism in India*, pp. 14–15.

77 Esdaile, *Mesmerism in India*, p. v. To travel by dâk was to utilise a formal relay system of horses (and, occasionally, of human-powered palanquins also). The dâk system was later to involve not merely the mode of transport but also government administered bungalows which provided rudimentary shelter to the colonial traveller.

78 For further miscellaneous references regarding Esdaile's work see, for example, Anon., 'To the Worshipful, the Mayor of Liverpool', *Liverpool Mercury*, 24 April 1846, p. 3, col. 6; Anon., 'Local Intelligence', *Sheffield and Rotherham Independent*, 20 June 1846, p. 8, col. 3; Anon., 'Miss Martineau on Mesmerism', *Hampshire Telegraph and Sussex Chronicle*, 8 August 1846, p. 3, cols 3–4 at col. 3.

79 Anon., 'Mesmerism in India', *Newcastle Courant*, 6 November 1846, p. 2, col. 5. Given the tenor of the soldier's remarks, one wonders whether he might not have been clinically delirious.

80 Esdaile, *Mesmerism in India*, p. 12.

81 Esdaile, *Mesmerism in India*, pp. 6–7.

82 Anon., 'Mesmerism in India', *Newcastle Courant*, 6 November 1846, p. 2, col. 5.

83 Anon., 'Mesmerism in India', *Newcastle Courant*, 6 November 1846, p. 2, col. 5.

84 Anon., 'Mesmerism in India', *Daily News*, 5 January 1847, p. 3, col. 2. This article was reproduced verbatim in a supplement to the *Leeds Mercury*, 9 January 1847, p. 11, col. 6. An even more laconic account appears in *The Morning Chronicle*, 4 January 1847, p. 6, col. 1.

85 Anon., 'Mesmerism in India', *The Essex Standard, and General Advertiser for the Eastern Counties*, 25 December 1846, p. 4, col. 4.

86 Anon., 'Mesmerism in India', *The Essex Standard, and General Advertiser for the Eastern Counties*, 4 December 1846, p. 4, col. 2.

87 Anon., 'Mesmerism', *Geelong Advertiser and Squatter's Advocate*, 23 April 1847, p. 1, cols 3–5, at col. 4. This Australian newspaper reproduces what is apparently the only plan of the building published at the time.

88 Ernst Waltroud, 'Esdaile, James (1808–1859)', *Oxford Dictionary of National Biography*, available online at www.oxforddnb.com/view/article/8882 [accessed 27 February 2013].

89 Anon., 'Mesmerism in India', *The Essex Standard, and General Advertiser for the Eastern Counties*, 4 December 1846, p. 4, col. 2. This item was reproduced in part in a number of other provincial newspapers including the *Liverpool Mercury*, 4 December 1846, p. 582, col. 1, and the London *Era*, 6 December 1846, p. 7, col. 3. The almost simultaneous announcement across the provinces suggests not merely a common but most likely a telegraphic source originating in India.

90 Anon., 'Foreign News', *The Essex Standard, and General Advertiser for the Eastern Counties*, 1 October 1847, p. 4, col. 1.

91 Indeed, Dalhousie did *not* endorse mesmerism himself, though he *was* prepared to testify as to the insensibility produced by Esdaile's practice in India. See Anon., 'Lord Dalhousie on Mesmerism', *Daily News*, 11 August 1856, p. 6, col. 6.

92 Anon., 'Mesmerism', *Geelong Advertiser and Squatter's Advocate*, 23 April 1847, p. 1, cols 3–5, at col. 4. The source for at least part of the article would appear to be a Calcutta newspaper, the *Bengal Hurkaru*.

93 Anon., 'Mesmerism', *Geelong Advertiser and Squatter's Advocate*, 23 April 1847, p. 1, col. 4.

94 Anon., 'Mesmerism', *Geelong Advertiser and Squatter's Advocate*, 23 April 1847, p. 1, col. 5.

95 Anon., 'Mesmerism', *Geelong Advertiser and Squatter's Advocate*, 23 April 1847, p. 1, col. 5.

96 Anon., 'Mesmerism', *Geelong Advertiser and Squatter's Advocate*, 23 April 1847, p. 1, col. 5.

97 Anon., 'Mesmerism', *Geelong Advertiser and Squatter's Advocate*, 23 April 1847, p. 1, col. 5.

98 Esdaile, *Mesmerism in India*, pp. 45–6.

99 Anon., 'Mesmerism', *Geelong Advertiser and Squatter's Advocate*, 23 April 1847, p. 1, col. 5.

100 This is almost certainly Henry Storer, author of *Mesmerism in Disease* (1843), who practised mesmerism at the Bristol Mesmeric Institute. See Alison Winter, *Mesmerized: Powers of Mind in Victorian Britain* (Chicago: University of Chicago Press, 1998), p. 379, n. 54.

101 Anon, 'Mesmerism', *Bristol Mercury*, 25 September 1847, p. 8, col. 2. The institution projected here by Storer was ultimately established in 1849. See

Anon., 'Bristol Mesmeric Institute', *The Bristol Mercury, and Western Counties Advertiser*, 2 June 1849, p. 3, cols 2–3.

102 Anon., 'Mesmerism in India', *Dundee Courier*, 7 June 1848, p. 3, col. 4.

103 Anon., 'Hypnotism and Healing by Suggestion', *The Times*, 2 January 1914, p. 3, col. 1.

104 Harriet Martineau [attrib.], 'An Egyptian Magician', in 'Miscellaneous Extracts', Supplement to the *Manchester Examiner*, 1 July 1848, p. 4, col. 3.

105 See, for example, the practice of Mr Barth, 'mesmerist and medical galvanist' of '7, Eversholt-street, Mornington-crescent', who advertised in the dentistry columns of *The Times*, 21 September 1849, p. 12, col. 2; and the amputations under mesmeric trance performed in a Leicester infirmary described in detail in Anon., 'More Successful Cases of Mesmerism, in Connection with Surgical Operations in Leicester', *The Leicester Chronicle; or, Commercial and Agricultural Advertiser*, 9 November 1844, p. 3, col. 5.

106 Anon., 'Mesmeric Infirmary', *The Morning Post*, 7 May 1850, p. 6, cols 2–3, at col. 2.

107 Anon., 'Mesmeric Infirmary', *The Sheffield and Rotherham Independent*, 25 July 1846, p. 8, col. 3.

108 *The Times*, 27 June 1849, p. 7, col. 2, and widely syndicated: see Anon., 'Lord Ducie on Mesmerism', *The Aberdeen Journal*, 11 July 1849, p. 7, col. 2.

109 Anon., 'Mesmerism', *The Bristol Mercury*, 18 July 1846, p.3, col. 2. An identical announcement appeared in the *Leeds Mercury*, 25 July 1846, p. 12, col. 2.

110 Anon., 'Stow-on-the-Wold and Chipping Norton Agricultural Meeting', *Jackson's Oxford Journal*, 18 September 1847, p. 2, cols 1–2.

111 Anon, *The Missionary Register for MDCCCXXII* (London: Richard Watts, 1822), p. 143.

112 Anon., 'Mesmeric Infirmary', *The Morning Post*, 7 May 1850, p. 6, col. 2, original punctuation.

113 The donor of the estate is listed simply as 'P. Baume, Esq.', and this may well be the eccentric radical thinker Pierre Henri Joseph Baume, once reviled as 'the Islington Monster' for having donated his half-sister's body to University College for dissection in December 1832. On his death, the apparently penurious Frenchman was discovered to be the owner of two English estates, plus investments totalling some £50,000.

114 Anon., 'Mesmeric Infirmary', *The Morning Post*, 7 May 1850, p. 6, col. 2. The Secretary and Resident Superintendant of the Mesmeric Infirmary' was, from 17 November 1850, Thomas Capern, author of *The Curative Power of Mesmerism*: see Anon., 'Mesmeric Infirmary', *The Morning Post*, 9 May 1851, p. 3, cols 5–6, at col. 5.

115 Anon., 'Mesmeric Infirmary', *The Morning Post*, 7 May 1850, p. 6, col. 2.

116 Anon., 'Mesmerism', *The Bury and Norwich Post, and Suffolk Herald*, 29 May 1850, p. 3, col. 2.

117 Anon., 'Mesmeric Infirmary', *The Morning Post*, 7 May 1850, p. 6, col. 3. A commitment to the poor is also explicitly enshrined in the preface to the Infirmary's formal table of rules and statutes.

118 Anon., 'Mesmeric Infirmary', *The Morning Post*, 7 May 1850, p. 6, col. 2; Anon., *Report of the Sixth Annual Meeting of the London Mesmeric Infirmary*, 36 Weymouth Street, Portland Place (London: Walton and Mitchell, 1855), p. 1, paragraph 1.

119 Anon., 'Mesmeric Infirmary', *The Morning Post*, 7 May 1850, p. 6, cols 2–3.

120 Anon., 'Mesmeric Infirmary', *The Morning Post*, 7 May 1850, p. 6, col. 2.

121 'Mesmeric Infirmary' [advertisement], *The Morning Post*, 24 May 1850, p. 1, col. 2.

122 Anon., 'Mesmeric Infirmary', *The Morning Post*, 7 May 1850, p. 6, col. 2.

123 'Births', *The Times*, 2 February 1848, p. 7, col. 6.

124 Anon., 'Amputation Performed During Mesmeric Sleep', *The Times*, 30 March 1844, p. 8, col. 4.

125 Anon., 'Mesmeric Trance', *The Times*, 2 May 1854, p. 12, col. 4. The report is acknowledged as being derived from one previously published in the *Examiner*.

126 Anon., 'The Mesmeric Infirmary', *The Morning Post*, 8 June 1854, p. 3, cols 2–3, at col. 2.

127 Anon., 'A Severe Surgical Operation Performed Upon a Patient under the Mesmeric Trance, Without Pain', *The Standard*, 2 May 1854, p. 4, col. 6.

128 See, for example, Anon., 'Facts and Scraps and Summary of General News', *Berrow's Worcester Journal*, 6 May 1854, p. 6, col. 4; Anon., 'Painless Surgical Operation in Mesmeric Trance', *The Leicester Chronicle: or, Commercial and Agricultural Advertiser*, 6 May 1854, p. 1, col. 7.

129 Anon., 'Painless Operations in the Mesmeric State', *The Examiner*, 11 September 1852, p. 587, col. 2.

130 Anon., 'Mesmeric Infirmary', *The Morning Post*, 9 May 1851, p. 3, cols 5–6, at col. 5.

131 Anon., 'Mesmeric Infirmary', *The Morning Post*, 9 May 1851, p. 3, col. 5.

132 Florence Nightingale, who had been courted by Monckton Milnes, did not establish a school of nursing on British soil until 1860, though her involvement with the systematic training of nurses dates from the mid-1850s. See Monica E. Baly and H. C. G. Matthew, 'Nightingale, Florence (1820–1910)', *Oxford Dictionary of National Biography* (Oxford: Oxford University Press, 2004; online edition, January 2011) at www.oxforddnb.com/view/article/35241 [accessed 12 February 2014].

133 Anon., 'Mesmeric Infirmary', *The Morning Post*, 9 May 1851, p. 3, col. 5.

134 Anon., 'Mesmeric Infirmary', *The Morning Post*, 9 May 1851, p. 3, col. 5.

135 'Mesmerism' [advertisement], *The Morning Post*, 11 September 1858, p. 1, col. 2.

136 Elizabeth Garrett Anderson was the first woman to effectively qualify as

a doctor in the United Kingdom, becoming a Licentiate of the Society of Apothecaries in 1865, and an MD of the University of Paris in 1870. Louisa Brandreth Aldrich-Blake was almost certainly the first formally appointed female anaesthetist in the British Isles, being appointed as such to the Royal Free Hospital in 1895: see M. A. Elston, 'Blake, Dame Louisa Brandreth Aldrich- (1865–1925), *surgeon*', *Oxford Dictionary of National Biography* (Oxford: Oxford University Press, 2004; online edition, January 2011) at www.oxforddnb.com/view/article/30367 [accessed 12 February 2014].

137 Anon., 'Mesmeric Infirmary', *The Morning Post*, 9 May 1851, p. 3, col. 6.

138 Anon., 'Mesmeric Infirmary', *The Morning Post*, 28 May 1852, p. 6, cols 1–2, at col. 2.

139 Anon., 'The Mesmeric Infirmary', *The Morning Post*, 18 June 1853, p. 7, col. 2.

140 'Mesmeric Infirmary' [advertisement], *The Morning Post*, 27 May 1854, p. 1, col. 2.

141 Anon., 'The Mesmeric Infirmary', *The Morning Post*, 8 June 1854, p. 3, col. 1.

142 Anon., 'The Mesmeric Infirmary', *The Morning Post*, 8 June 1854, p. 3, col. 1.

143 Anon., 'The Mesmeric Infirmary', *The Morning Post*, 8 June 1854, p. 3, col. 1.

144 Anon., 'The Mesmeric Infirmary', *The Morning Post*, 8 June 1854, p. 3, col. 2.

145 Anon., 'The Mesmeric Infirmary', *The Morning Post*, 8 June 1854, p. 3, col. 2.

146 'Mesmeric Infirmary' [advertisement], *The Examiner*, 14 April 1855, p. 239, col. 3.

147 One very noteworthy exception to this is the discussion of the treatment of an epileptic youth, the son of a casualty of the Crimean War, whose case may well have been described at length for patriotic reasons. See Anon., 'Mesmeric Infirmary', *The Morning Post*, 22 June 1857; p. 2, cols 4–5.

148 Anon., 'Mesmeric Infirmary', *The Morning Post*, 11 June 1855, p. 2, col. 3. This meeting was briefly reported in *The Liverpool Mercury*, 12 June 1855, p. 5, col. 6.

149 Anon., 'Mesmeric Infirmary', *The Morning Post*, 13 June 1856, p. 3, col. 6.

150 Anon., 'Mesmeric Infirmary', *The Morning Post*, 22 June 1857, p. 2, col. 4.

151 Anon., 'Mesmeric Infirmary', *The Morning Post*, 21 June 1858, p. 6, col. 3.

152 'Mesmeric Infirmary' [advertisement], *The Morning Post*, 8 June 1861, p. 1, col. 2; 'Mesmeric Infirmary' [advertisement], *The Morning Post*, 9 June 1862, p. 1, col. 3.

153 These were, likewise, advertised in *The Morning Post*: see 'Mesmeric Infirmary' [advertisement], 6 June 1863, p. 1, col. 2.

154 Anon., 'Mesmeric Infirmary', *The Morning Post*, 13 June 1856, p. 3, col. 6.

155 Anon., 'The Mesmeric Infirmary', *The Morning Chronicle*, 19 June 1861, p. 6, col. 1.

156 'Mesmeric Infirmary' [advertisement], *The Morning Post*, 8 June 1863, p. 1, col. 3, original emphasis.

157 'Mesmeric Infirmary' [advertisement], *The Standard*, 25 June 1867, p. 1, col. 4, original emphasis.

158 'Mesmeric Infirmary' [advertisement], *The Morning Post*, 26 October 1869, p. 1, col. 3, original emphasis.

159 A report in the *Morning Chronicle*, published as early as 1860, notes that the existence of the Infirmary is 'not generally known': see Anon., 'Mesmeric Infirmary', *The Morning Chronicle*, 15 June 1860, p. 6, col. 6.

160 'The Mesmeric Infirmary' [advertisement], *The Times*, 2 June 1869, p. 4, col. 2.

161 Anon., 'Mesmerism', *The Blackburn Standard and North East Lancashire Advertiser*, 20 November 1875, p. 3, col. 2.

162 This, certainly, is the nominal extent of the run at the Library of the University of Cambridge, which is the most substantial one listed in the United Kingdom. See http://search.lib.cam.ac.uk/?itemid=|cambrdgedb|2170278 [accessed 12 February 2014].

163 Thomas Chandler, 'To the Editor of the *Morning Post*', *The Morning Post*, 18 January 1870, p. 7, col. 5. Derek Forrest incorrectly dates the closure of Weymouth Street to 1868: see *Hypnotism: A History* (London: Penguin, 2000), p. 190.

164 Robin Waterfield, *Hidden Depths: The Story of Hypnosis* (London: Pan, 2004), pp. 156, 189; Forrest, *Hypnotism*, p. 188.

165 Anon., 'The Mesmeric Infirmary', *The Morning Post*, 18 June 1853, p. 7, col. 2; Anon., 'The Mesmeric Infirmary', *The Morning Post*, 8 June 1854, p. 3, col. 1.

166 R. H. Collyer, 'Surgical Operations Without Pain', *The Morning Post*, 12 January 1846, p. 6, col. 4.

167 Anon., 'New Anaesthetic Agent – Ether Superseded', *Caledonian Mercury*, 15 November 1847, p. 3, col. 2. This article was widely syndicated: see *Freeman's Journal and Daily Commercial Advertiser*, 19 November 1847, p. 3, col. 4; *The Morning Post*, 19 November 1847, p. 7, col. 2.

168 Anon., 'France', *The Standard*, 22 April 1853, p. 3, col. 1.

169 Formal academic recognition did not come immediately, however, and if British medicine was slow in institutionalising anaesthetics as a discrete clinical discipline, India was once again refreshingly far-sighted, both in the pursuit of potential new techniques and in opening medicine to female as well as male professionals. See: Nara Alayana et al., 'Dr (Miss) Rupa Bai Furdoonji: World's First Qualified Lady Anaesthetist', *Indian Journal of Anaesthesia*, 54/3 (2010), 259–61, *passim*.

170 Anon., 'The Mesmeric Infirmary', *The Morning Post*, 18 June 1853, p. 7, col. 2.

Conclusion

'This is that devil's trick – hypnotism!'

SVENGALI (*crosses to sofa*) Sit down – I will show you something that will cure your pain better than music.

> *Trilby sits on divan – Svengali brings chair forward and sits facing her*

Look me in the white of the eyes.

> *She does so – he fixes his eyes on hers, then passes his hand across her forehead and temples. Billee comes down above sofa. All watch intently – Svengali turns to them – gesture outstretched hands*

She sleeps not. But she shall not open her eyes.

> *Trilby sits rigid*

(To Billee) Ask her.

BILLEE (*head of sofa*) Speak to me, Trilby.

> *Trilby with effort*

SVENGALI (*folded arms*) She shall not rise from the sofa.

(To Billee) Ask her.

BILLEE Can you rise, Trilby?

> *Trilby makes an effort to rise. After a pause Svengali rises – Billee gets between him and Trilby – Svengali seizes Billee by the elbows – Taffy crosses to Svengali*

TAFFY This is that devil's trick – hypnotism. (*Angry*)

Paul Potter, *Trilby*, Act 1, ll. 380–96[1]

IF THE MESMERIC INFIRMARY made any substantial contribution to popular culture in its relatively short existence, it was in the underwriting – for a time at least – of a plausible connection between mesmerism and analgesia in the British imagination. Paul Potter's *Trilby* (1895), a dramatised version of George du Maurier's 1894 novel of the same name, could never have been acted had the popular *fin de siècle* currency of mesmerism been based not just upon an identifiable technique – Svengali's manual passes and his 'hypnotic' eyes – but also upon its specific application in the relief of pain. In *Trilby*, Svengali employs 'that devil's trick' specifically to relieve the heroine of a painful 'Neuralgia in the eyes, or something'.[2] Beyond this recollection of an analgesic remedy that had passed out of fashion some twenty-five years previously, the established mesmeric clichés that mobilise Svengali's menacing presence on stage – his ability to control a subject, dubious sexual motives, mysterious or foreign origins and those peculiarities of diction which are stressed more in the novel than the play – are, indeed, present and potent. As components of an enduring myth of what a mesmerist could and should look like, these latter can be traced back to eighteenth-century farce, have their equivalents in 1830s popular reportage and enjoy a currency such that their sporadic appearances across the nineteenth century could be received with a type of recognition. Readers and audiences *knew* what a mesmerist or a hypnotist *meant*, even when the press – or the mesmerists themselves – were desperate to tell them otherwise.

The popularity of *Trilby*, though, at a time at which *British* mesmerism was itself apparently in abeyance, seems surprising. The only other play with a significant mesmeric content which was substantially reprised during this period was Leopold David Lewis's Alsatian melodrama *The Bells* (1871), which depicts a murderer who is unmasked by both personal guilt and the relaxed reticence often associated with the entranced. Its periodic revivals in London and the British provinces are primarily associated with the acting of Henry Irving, as advertisements for the various reprises of *The Bells* intimate.[3] The longevity of Lewis's play is thus surely associated with its status as an enduring vehicle for the celebrity actor rather than with any topicality associated with its comparatively muted mesmeric content: Irving was reputed to have taken the role of the play's central protagonist, the murderer Matthias, some eight hundred times between 1871 and 1905, and the celebrity actor, rather than mesmerism, was arguably the topical focus of any performance of *The Bells*, irrespective of whether or not he was actually part of the company reprising Lewis's play.[4]

As the British press was inclined to point out, in those comparatively few references made to the topic in the closing decades of the nineteenth century, mesmerism was now apparently little more than a curiosity well beyond the boundaries of medical respectability – albeit one which was still associated with some mystery, as a columnist in the *Sheffield & Rotherham Independent* acknowledged:

> whatever the explanation may be, there is no doubt of the fact that, while at one time there were mesmeric hospitals in London, Calcutta, and elsewhere, there are now none. There are still unlicensed practitioners who use mesmerism as a means of cure; but few regular physicians rely on it to any great extent, although willing to admit that in exceptional cases it has led to alleviation of pain, and sometimes to what looks like complete cure. The mode of operation in these successful cases remains a mystery.[5]

Those accounts of British analgesic and anaesthetic mesmerism published at the *fin de siècle* are few in number, relatively short in length and tend to be associated with the rather unglamorous world of dentistry.[6] Reports of amputations carried out on the Continent under trance conditions occasionally appeared in the British press as well, but these, again, functioned as a sort of curiosity, and displayed for the most part an editorial inclination to dwell upon the ludicrous or grotesque behaviour of the entranced patient rather than the technique of the hypnotist.[7] The implicit and dismissive quack status accorded to those anachronistic and 'unlicensed practitioners' still active in Britain, likewise, lacks the polemical vigour of the imputations sporadically brought against Dupotet and his contemporaries. These later pretenders to the mesmerist's art seem to have been perceived as no substantial sexual threat, no subtly controlling force to be feared. There is no sense of outrage in *fin de siècle* reportage upon the topic, no righteous indignation, no agonising over morals threatened or bodies violated. *British* mesmerism at the *fin de siècle*, surely, was thus insufficiently newsworthy to underwrite the monumental popularity of *Trilby*, a work that was 'parodied, pirated and trivialized' but which also motivated so-called 'Trilby-mania', a marketing phenomenon which, L. Edward Purcell argues, initiated the commercial culture of the modern bestseller.[8]

If British mesmerism could no longer supply sufficiently spectacular copy for the popular press, its Continental equivalent still, on occasions, could – if only for the decade immediately preceding the London production of du Maurier's *Trilby*. This was the decade, once more, of Continental savants – specifically, of Jean-Martin Charcot, whose work at the Parisian Salpêtrière was sporadically reported in Britain from the 1880s through to the neurologist's death in 1893. Mesmerism, it seemed, had finally turned full circle in a mere hundred years. It was a Continental activity once more, undertaken by charismatic foreigners, reported from a distance, and spectacularly demonstrated under the control of the presiding operator. Its specifically medical attributes, painstakingly stressed under the cultural regime generated and maintained by the London Mesmeric Infirmary, were once again compromised by the nature and implications of those public displays of entranced – and mostly female – bodies. Charcot himself, for all his conventional training, appears to have embodied some of the commanding demeanour of Mesmer, who was active almost exactly a century earlier. British reportage, therefore, swung rhetorically away from its earlier indulgent – and, indeed, at times almost respectful – attitude towards the systematic practices of the London Mesmeric Infirmary, and once more tantalised its readers with drama, clairvoyance and vulnerable women.

This much is vouchsafed in an account of a visit to the Salpêtrière, published in the *Leeds Mercury* in 1883. The writer, 'Our Own Correspondent', notes:

> Within the last few years the hospital La Salpêtrière has been much before the public. The course of lectures, with demonstrations by Professor Charcot, has attracted the attention of the therapeutic world as well as the crowd of scientific triflers who abound in every great city. The sensational character of these performances has afforded a rich field of observation for the novelist, dramatist and moralist.

If French novelists were indeed in attendance at the demonstrations given by Charcot and his associates – Dumas was one such name associated with the exhibitions[9] – British readers and writers were still more likely to access the subject by way of press reports.[10] These latter, of course, maintained their own freighting of strident morality. What disturbs 'Our Own Correspondent', in this respect, is the apparent immodesty implicit in the public exhibiting of what are apparently insane subjects – the Salpêtrière's reputation at the time being especially associated with nascent clinical psychiatry rather than interventive surgery. The columnist continues:

> For a poor girl to have to give proof that she was totally devoid of all sense of shame, before a mixed audience, is one of those hardy

notions of which only the French mind is capable. These theatrical exhibitions at the Salpêtrière have now ceased, having yielded an abundant crop of results which it will take some time to digest. The work has fallen back on more sober and severe lines, which perhaps is no loss to anybody.[11]

If the rhetoric here might possibly recall the excesses associated with Dupotet's London demonstrations and the verbal immodesty of the O'Key sisters, other commentators were quick to distance the English (rather than Continental) subject from susceptibility to the potentially humiliating and predatory manipulations of the mesmeric operator. A correspondent for the London *Daily News*, for example, noted in 1887 that incidences of hypnotic insensibility 'occur not infrequently in France, and more often with women than with men'.[12] Du Maurier's Trilby O'Ferrall, intriguingly, is the daughter of an alcoholic Irishman, 'a gentleman, the son of a famous Dublin physician', and a Scottish mother, 'a most beautiful highland lassie of low degree', a *demoiselle de comptoir* at the Montagnards Écossais in Paris's tenth arrondissement.[13] Trilby's susceptibility to hypnotic suggestion, and the sexual abuse that implicitly forms part of her relationship with the leering Svengali, an eastern European domiciled in bohemian Paris and, like her, speaking both French and English, would perversely seem to prove the rule voiced by the correspondent in the *Daily News*. Paris, as it were, is the problem, its morals, manners and fashions corrupting those who travel or make their homes there. If du Maurier's trio of British heroes – nick-named so as to suggest an Englishman, a Welshman and a Scot, living together in perfect harmony – are able to resist the temptations of bohemian life in the French capital, the wholly Celtic Trilby, a posthumous female child with an Irish surname, has been brought up in intimacy with Parisian morals. If Svengali, like Mesmer, is an exile in Paris rather than a child of that city, he has likewise adopted, and adapted himself to, the morality of La Ville-Lumière as perceived by late Victorian British prejudice. In a sense, fictions such as *Trilby*, and Francophobic assertions, such as that tendered by the *Daily News*' correspondent, serve to rhetorically keep the hypnotic threat upon the European Continent, even where they appear to testify to its profound effect upon selected – and racially differentiated – human bodies. The rhetoric of both the novel and the newspaper, indeed, might profitably be considered as a parallel debate to that other Parisian vice apparently threatening the unwary British at the *fin de siècle*, absinthe.[14]

This is not to say that no serious British reportage was associated with Charcot's work. The Professor's inductive technique – which on occasions acknowledged the methods popularised by both Mesmer and Braid – was reported as much for its novelty as for its success. A columnist for the *Glasgow Herald*, for example, notes:

> Professor Charcot, of Paris, in treating hysterical patients, throws them into a cataleptic or trance-like condition by the sudden flashing of a light across the eyes, by the sound of a Chinese gong, by a sharp whistle, or by the hum and vibration of a tuning fork.[15]

The divisions between the hypnotic school of Paris (under Charcot) and Nancy (under Hippolyte Bernheim) were also briefly acknowledged in the *Daily News* as early as 1890, though the technical disagreements between Continental savants did not in any way dominate British reportage of the actual practice of mesmerism at the *fin de siècle*.[16] It was the work of the Paris School which dominated British writings on mesmerism at this time. The reporting of Charcot's practice may thus effectively represent the final word on mesmerism in popular British consciousness in the nineteenth century. With this last reflex of the reporting of hypnotic phenomena came a change of tone which, while maintaining the longstanding association between mesmerism and the induced control of a subject, narrowed the definition of those apparently most easily influenced by the mesmerist's eyes or hands. Effectively, at the end of the nineteenth century, mesmerism became something definitively associated with the *sick* rather than the merely susceptible, and its long-term effects became viewed as pathological rather than recuperative.

This, certainly, is the major connection between *Trilby* and the culture of mesmerism in *fin de siècle* Britain. Though fiction was still on occasions inclined to suggest that anyone, irrespective of their physical or mental health, might be brought unwillingly or unknowingly under the control of an unscrupulous mesmerist – as is the case in Conan Doyle's novella *The Parasite* (1894) or Richard Marsh's *The Beetle* (1897) – the British press was quietly concurring with Charcot's assertions regarding the intimacy of hysteria and hypnotic susceptibility. Charcot's practice is recorded as being deployed upon patients with hysteroid symptoms – including dumbness[17] – in 1889.[18] Other British newspapers unquestioningly elided the hysteroid and the hypnotic in their reporting of Charcot's experiments.[19] There is, seemingly, some reassurance in such things, as the *Glasgow Herald* intimated in an 1888 survey of historical and contemporary mesmeric practice:

> There would appear to exist ... a condition, natural or acquired, of the nervous constitution whereby certain persons are very readily mesmerised. If any choice be made in the matter, it is perhaps legitimate to suggest that the nervous, high-strung idealistic temperament is that on which the mesmerist operates with a fair chance of inducing the hypnotic condition. Contrariwise, it is the 'steady and stolidy' person, to quote Mr Gilbert's apt expression – the unimaginative, unimpressionable individual – who defeats all attempts to influence his existence outside of the sphere of his own will.[20]

If susceptibility to hypnotism would appear to be yet another likely decadent symptom of *fin de siècle* aestheticism in the eyes of the newspaper's columnist, his reading of Charcot's specific practice draws upon a more familiar gendered prejudice. The column continues:

> These remarks may illustrate how and why it is that Charcot's experiments on hysterical women and on others affected with the various neurotic ailments have been so productive of positive results. The first and primary condition for success in mesmerism, in other words, is a facile, pliable disposition.[21]

That 'facile, pliable disposition' may be ideal for the induction of suggestive hypnotic states, but it is also an abiding weakness which might facilitate a further degeneration of the subject's mental condition.

Another consideration of hypnotism, published five years later in the *Glasgow Herald* makes this clear. Delivering a eulogy in commemoration of Charcot's recent death, Professor Grainger Stewart, of the Medical Faculty of the University of Edinburgh, tendered some sage advice for the undergraduates gathered at the opening of the Winter Session. After informing the assembled cohort of his belief that 'the hypnotic conditions of all varieties were practically a diseased state of the nervous system, an artificial neurosis', albeit one that might on occasions produce 'results undoubtedly favourable', he cautioned:

> that in every case hypnotic treatment involved hazard to the nervous system, that those who were most susceptible to its influence were the most apt to suffer, and that though it might free the patient from one set of symptoms it was apt to make him the victim of many others. Therefore, he recommended the students to employ hypnotism very rarely, to a very moderate extent, and only after careful study of the patient's condition. (Loud applause)[22]

Stewart's words here are significant. If the physician is unusually undogmatic in his endorsing of the work of Charcot, he is none the less wary as to the present and future state which might be enjoyed by the hypnotic subject. Hypnotism, at the close of the nineteenth century, was a dangerous business, though the perceived risks were apparently of a quite different order to those associated with the practice in the past. As far as medicine was concerned, it seems that the perceived danger at the *fin de siècle* was one of further, profound mental disturbance rather than immediate bodily interference.

Stewart's address was delivered to a gathering of aspiring medical professionals, individuals who, if they were not always strictly confined by a personal ethical code, were at least regulated by formal bodies, colleges and societies. Such safeguards, however, do not apply to the 'unlicensed practitioners' briefly referenced by the *Sheffield & Rotherham Independent* in 1887. Indeed, as the *Pall Mall Gazette* pointed out seven years later, even creditable experts such as Charcot, Bernheim and their contemporary, Jules Bernard Luys of the Parisian Hôpital de la Charité, risked imperilling the mental integrity of their patients through the very treatments they applied in the cause of their compromised health. *The Pall Mall Gazette* columnist – who styles himself simply 'An Amateur' – notes of these named savants:

> But even these practitioners have carried their experiments too far, and many of their patients have developed nervous symptoms almost worse than the ills they suffered from before. As a conclusion, I should advise no one to play with hypnotism. In inexperienced hands it may result in the most serious consequences, and in several cases what began as a joke ended with a death.[23]

The concerns expressed in the *Pall Mall Gazette* are less a fear of some destructive control gained over the malleable mind and manipulable body of the patient, and more one of the mental anarchy that might arise as an unforeseen neurosis develops beyond the management of the hypnotic operator. When this aspect of the debate upon mesmerism at the *fin de siècle* is acknowledged, the implications of du Maurier's *Trilby* are perceptibly enhanced, its medical as well as sexual script emerging as a context which has been to date but partially perceived.

Trilby, of course, has been conventionally regarded in criticism as a narrative preoccupied with the sexual and financial exploitation of the heroine.[24] Svengali's mesmerism or hypnotism (for the terms are used almost interchangeably in the novel) is a means to an end – a means spectacular and suggestive, certainly, but one focused upon the living and much displayed body of Trilby O'Ferrall.[25] If the heroine is not obviously identifiable as hysterical in the sense associated with so many of Charcot's female patients, her final mental condition *is* reflective of the injudicious deployment of 'that devil's trick – hypnotism' by Svengali.[26] Trilby's conventionally tragic and pathetic demise at the termination of both novel and play – where Svengali's portrait, through its hypnotic eyes, exercises a directionless but still potent posthumous control – masks the utter debilitation of the afflicted heroine's physiological system and mental economy.[27] These latter, truly, are the key to du Maurier's *Trilby*.

The implications of Trilby's wasted body and distracted mind – which are more heavily emphasised in the novel than in the drama – have been somewhat eclipsed in criticism by the *doppelgänger* status imposed by Svengali's hypnotic intervention. As the musician Gecko, one of the heroine's early associates and an ardent admirer, confides 'There *were* two *Trilbys*' – one self-determined and confident, 'the Trilby you knew'; the other utterly in thrall to Svengali, '*his* Trilby', 'an unconscious Trilby of marble'.[28] Of the latter, Gecko significantly states that 'you might have run a red-hot needle into her and she would not have felt it', thereby recalling one time-honoured test for mesmeric insensibility.[29]

The real neurosis suffered by du Maurier's mesmerically scarred heroine is not manifested in her assumed physiological insensibility whilst entranced, or in her pathetic swan-song, the last moment at which she switches from the personality of the unfeigned Trilby O'Ferrall back to that of the diva, La Svengali. Rather, it is expressed as her mind wanders back to earlier days, and compels the financially independent protégée of Svengali to seek work as a humble washerwoman, 'her old clean trade' before her impresario manipulated her unconscious persona into the diva, La Svengali.[30] She writes first to a former Parisian associate in the laundry trade, before finally – with a boldness characteristic of the Trilby of the Quartier Latin – entering a London *blanchisserie de fin* in the company of her doctor, Sir Oliver Calthorpe and Svengali's aunt, Marta:

> The *patronne*, a genial Parisian, was much astonished to hear a great French lady, in costly garments, evidently a person of fashion and importance, applying to her rather humbly for employment in the business, and showing a thorough knowledge of the work (and of the Parisian workwoman's colloquial dialect). Marta managed to catch

the *patronne*'s eye, and tapped her own forehead significantly, and Sir Oliver nodded. So the good woman honoured the great lady's fancy, and promised abundance of employment whenever she should want it.

Employment! Poor Trilby was hardly strong enough to walk back to the carriage; and this was her last outing.[31]

Marta's gesture is sufficient an index of the heroine's perceived insanity – even though, of course, her wish is an expression of the return of Trilby's own, eclipsed, personality, ignorant of the intervening period in which she has been a musical and financial success. As the narrator notes in the coda to the encounter, though, Trilby's debilitation is not confined to her mental faculties. Her inability to comfortably return to her carriage is but one of several clear indications in the novel as to how her physicality has been compromised and drained of sustaining vitality. Her former associates 'had not failed to note how rapidly she had aged'; indeed 'all strength and straightness and elasticity seemed to have gone out of her with the memory of her endless triumphs'.[32] The narrator is emphatic that 'It was evident that the sudden stroke which had destroyed her power of singing had left her physically a wreck', and this much is confirmed subsequently by two presiding doctors of conventional medicine.[33] The first had been 'puzzled by her strange physical weakness'.[34] Sir Oliver Calthorpe, summoned as medical consultant, is equally mystified as to the slow but seemingly inevitable decline of Trilby:

He saw her three times in the course of the week, but could not say for certain what was the matter with her, beyond taking the very gravest view of her condition. For all he could advise or prescribe, her weakness and physical prostration increased, though no cause he could discover. Her insanity was not enough to account for it. She lost weight daily; she seemed to be wasting and fading away from sheer general atrophy.[35]

In both the novelistic and stage incarnations of *Trilby*, what began as a purported medical treatment incautiously deployed by an amateur has indeed concluded tragically in the recipient's death. The fear expressed by 'An Amateur' in the *Pall Mall Gazette* has been amply illustrated here, and with specific reference to the body as well as the mind. Indeed, Trilby's insanity is surely questionable: she is not mad, merely ignorant of events that have passed during her entranced interlude – this again being a classic convention of hypnotic sleep. It must be remembered, though, that hypnotism was first applied to Trilby because of a neuralgic rather than psychological disorder. Du Maurier's novel, and its dramatised descendant, are implicitly concerned as much with the body as they are with the mind.

It is surely significant, therefore, that 'An Amateur' contributed his warning to the *Pall Mall Gazette* less than a month after the opening of *Trilby* at the Haymarket Theatre on 30 October 1895.[36] If there is an evident fear of casual imitation in the article's rhetoric, there is likewise a suggestion that 'hypnotism' (as the anonymous columnist terms it) can effect no lasting cure when applied to bodily disorders. If the early years of mesmeric reportage were characterised by the debasement of the living, the final moments of the practice's presence in the nineteenth century were associated with a more conclusive finality. The 'devil's trick' of mesmerism, it seems, might very well display some temporary alleviation of symptoms, or an improvement, even, on the part of the patient, but its application apparently vouchsafed no lasting curative value. Firm reassurances of the latter, indeed, are what appear to be consistently missing from the public discourse on mesmerism and hypnotism from the eighteenth-century *fin de siècle* to its Victorian equivalent.

Notes

1 Paul Potter, *Trilby*, in George Taylor, ed., *Trilby and Other Plays: Four Plays for Victorian Star Actors* (Oxford: Oxford University Press, 1996), 199–271, at p. 216.

2 Potter, *Trilby*, Act 1, l. 263 in Taylor, ed., *Trilby and Other Plays*, p. 212; cf. George du Maurier, *Trilby: A Novel* (London: Osgood, McIlvaine & Co., 1895), p. 67.

3 See, for example, the bill-board poster for Irving's final tour, dated 9 October 1905 and reproduced at: www.arthurlloyd.co.uk/BradfordTheatres/Theatre-RoyalBradford.htm [accessed 27 February 2013].

4 Bram Stoker, *Personal Reminiscences of Henry Irving*, Revised and Cheaper Edition (London: Heinemann, 1907), p. 92.

5 Anon., 'Mesmerism versus Chloroform', *The Sheffield & Rotherham Independent*, 6 July 1887, p. 8, col. 4.

6 Anon., 'Hypnotism at Leeds', *The Speaker*, 12 April 1890, 395–6.

7 Anon., 'Mesmerism versus Chloroform', *The Sheffield & Rotherham Independent*, 5 June 1886, p. 4, col. 4.

8 L. Edward Purcell, '*Trilby* and Trilby-Mania: The Beginning of the Bestseller System', *Journal of Popular Culture*, 11/1 (1977), 62–76, at p. 62.

9 Anon., 'London and Paris Gossip', *Trewman's Exeter Flying Post, or Plymouth and Cornish Advertiser*, 30 June 1880, p. 8, cols 1–2, at col. 2.

10 This is not to say that French fiction concerned with hypnotism did not appear in translation in the popular press. Balzac's *Ursule Mirouet* was serialised in *The Lady's Newspaper*, chapter 10 – entitled 'Mesmerism' – appearing on 21 February 1863 on pp. 291–2.

11 Anon., 'A Visit to the Salpêtrière', *The Leeds Mercury*, 22 October 1883, p. 5, cols 1–2, at col. 1.

12 Anon., 'The Sleeping Frenchman', *The Daily News*, 1 April 1887, p. 6, col. 7.

13 Du Maurier, *Trilby*, pp. 51, 52, 400.

14 Consider here, for example, the polemical as well as novelistic interventions of Marie Corelli, a writer of similar stature to du Maurier at the time. See Marie Corelli, *Wormwood: A Drama of Paris* [1890], ed. Kirsten MacLeod (Peterborough, Ont.: Broadview, 2004), pp. 61–3.

15 Anon., 'Curiosities of Mesmerism II', *The Glasgow Herald*, 28 July 1888, p. 9, cols 4–5, at col. 4.

16 Anon., 'This Morning's News', *The Daily News*, 14 April 1890, p. 5, cols 5–6, at col. 6.

17 See, for example, Sigmund Freud and Joseph Breuer, *Studies on Hysteria* [1893–95], trans. James and Alix Strachey (London: Penguin, 1986), p. 77.

18 Anon., 'Fourth Edition', *Pall Mall Gazette*, 24 December 1889, p. 5, col. 2.

19 Anon., 'Curiosities of Mesmerism', *The Blackburn Standard, Darwen Observer, and North-East Lancashire Advertiser*, 28 July 1888, p. 3, cols 6–7, at col. 6.

20 Anon., 'Curiosities of Mesmerism II', *The Glasgow Herald*, 28 July 1888, p. 9, col. 4. The allusion is to W. S. Gilbert, *Patience* [1881] in *The Complete Annotated Gilbert and Sullivan*, ed. Ian Bradley (Oxford: Oxford University Press, 2001), pp. 265–353, at p. 345.

21 Anon., 'Curiosities of Mesmerism II', *The Glasgow Herald*, 28 July 1888, p. 9, col. 4.

22 Anon., 'Edinburgh University Medical Classes', *The Glasgow Herald*, 11 November 1893, p. 6, col. 7.

23 An Amateur [pseud.], 'Mesmerism: Its Uses and Abuses', *The Pall Mall Gazette*, 22 November 1895, p. 1, col. 3, and p. 2, cols 1–2, at p. 2, col. 2.

24 Witness, for example, Nina Auerbach's striking suggestion that 'In a key tableau of the nineties … three men lean hungrily over three mesmerized and apparently characterless women, whose wills are suspended by those of the magus/masters. The looming men are Svengali, Dracula, and Freud; the lushly helpless women are Trilby O'Ferrall, Lucy Westenra, and (as Freud calls her) "Frau Emmy von N., age 40, from Livonia".' Nina Auerbach, 'Magi and Maidens: The Romance of the Victorian Freud', *Critical Inquiry*, 8 (1981), 281–300, at p. 283.

25 Du Maurier, *Trilby*, pp. 72, 73.

26 Potter, *Trilby*, Act 1, l. 396, p. 216. The parallel scene in the novel does not conclude with the angry termination featured in Potter's play: see du Maurier, *Trilby*, pp. 67–8.

27 Du Maurier, *Trilby*, pp. 415–20.

28 Du Maurier, *Trilby*, pp. 440, 441, original italics. Of Svengali's Trilby, Gecko significantly states that 'you might have run a red-hot needle into her and she would not have felt it' (p. 441), recalling the time-honoured test for mesmeric insensibility.

29 Du Maurier, *Trilby*, p. 441; Anon., 'Mr Braid's Lectures on Animal Magnetism', *The Manchester Times and Gazette*, 11 December 1841, p. 3, cols 4–6, at col. 5.

30 Du Maurier, *Trilby*, p. 386.

31 Du Maurier, *Trilby*, pp. 387–8.

32 Du Maurier, *Trilby*, pp. 382, 383.

33 Du Maurier, *Trilby*, p. 383.

34 Du Maurier, *Trilby*, p. 386.

35 Du Maurier, *Trilby*, p. 387.

36 Herbert Beerbohm Tree first produced the play at the Theatre Royal, Manchester, probably for copyright reasons, opening there on 7 September 1895. See Anon., 'Day to Day in Liverpool', *The Liverpool Mercury*, 6 September 1895, p. 6, col. 6. Following provincial acclaim, the London production opened at the Haymarket and was greeted with both popular approval and some critical disdain, these being widely reported in the provinces: see Anon., 'Our London Letter', *Dundee Courier and Argus*, 31 October 1895, p. 3, col. 2. Parodies of *Trilby* were produced within days at the Opera Comique and the Strand Theatre: see Anon., 'Theatrical and Musical Notes', *The Morning Post*, 28 October 1895, p. 2, col. 7.

Bibliography

Books and articles

Ackroyd, Peter, *Dickens* (London: Sinclair Stevenson, 1990).

Alayana, Nara, et al., 'Dr (Miss) Rupa Bai Furdoonji: World's First Qualified Lady Anaesthetist', *Indian Journal of Anaesthesia*, 54/3 (2010), 259–61.

Albert, Dr, 'Regeneration of Mesmerism in France', *The Liverpool Mercury*, 17 November 1826, p. 158, col. 1.

Albert, Dr, 'Regeneration of Mesmerism in France', *The Kaleidoscope; or, Literary and Scientific Mirror*, 21 November 1826, p. 158, col. 3.

An Amateur [pseud.], 'Mesmerism: Its Uses and Abuses', *The Pall Mall Gazette*, 22 November 1985, p. 1, col. 3, and p. 2, cols 1–2.

Anon., *A Biographical Dictionary of the Living Authors of Great Britain and Ireland* (London: Printed for Henry Colburn, 1816).

Anon., *A Catalogue of the Entire and Valuable Library of the Late Rev. Michael Lort, DD, FRS, and AS, which will be Sold by Auction, by Leigh and Sotheby* (London: Leigh and Sotheby, 1791).

Anon., 'A Magnetising Mountebank', *The Satirist: or, The Censor of the Times*, 11 February 1838, p. 45, col. 2

Anon., 'A Severe Surgical Operation Performed Upon a Patient under the Mesmeric Trance, Without Pain', *The Standard*, 2 May 1854, p. 4, col. 6.

Anon., 'A Visit to the Salpêtrière', *The Leeds Mercury*, 22 October 1883, p. 5, cols 1–2.

Anon., 'Address Delivered at the Opening of the Medical Session in the University of London, October 1, 1832. By John Elliotson, MD Cantab., FRS, &c. &c.', *The Court Magazine and Belle Assemblée*, 1 December 1832, p. 309, col. 2.

Anon., 'Amputation during the Mesmeric State', *Preston Chronicle and Lancashire Advertiser*, 24 December 1842, p. 4, col. 5.

Anon., 'Amputation Performed During Mesmeric Sleep', *The Times*, 30 March 1844, p. 8, col. 4.

Anon., 'Amputation without the Knowledge of the Patient', *Derby Mercury*, 30 November 1842, p. 4, cols 1–2.

Anon., 'Amputation without the Knowledge of the Patient', *The Ipswich Journal, and Suffolk, Norfolk, Essex and Cambridgeshire Advertiser*, 3 December 1842, p. 1, cols 6–7.

Anon., 'Amputation without the Knowledge of the Patient', *The Standard*, 26 November 1842, p. 4, cols 3–4.

Anon., 'Animal Magnetism', *The Hull Packet*, 18 February 1842, p. 3, col. 4.

Anon., 'Animal Magnetism', *The Morning Post*, 16 June 1838, p. 6, cols 4–5.

Anon., 'Animal Magnetism' [poem], *The Satirist: or, The Censor of the Times*, 11 March 1838, p. 77, col. 2.

Anon., 'Animal Magnetism' in 'Reviews', *The Athenæum*, 16 June 1838, 417–21.

Anon., 'Animal Magnetism', *Cleave's London Satirist and Gazette of Variety*, 9 December 1837, p. 2.

Anon., 'Animal Magnetism', *Fraser's Magazine for Town and Country*, 1/6 (July 1830), 673–84.

Anon., 'Animal Magnetism', *Leigh Hunt's London Journal*, 3 September 1834, p. 182, col. 3.

Anon., 'Animal Magnetism', Supplement to *The Liverpool Mercury*, 24 November 1837, p. 1, col. 6.

Anon., 'Animal Magnetism', *The Derby Mercury*, 21 February 1844, p. 4, col. 4.

Anon., 'Animal Magnetism', *The Freeman's Journal and Daily Commercial Advertiser*, 26 February 1839, p. 3, cols 3–5.

Anon., 'Animal Magnetism', *The Lady's Newspaper*, 16 July 1853, p. 23, col. 3.

Anon., 'Animal Magnetism', *The Lancet*, 26 May 1838, 282–8.

Anon., 'Animal Magnetism', *The London Saturday Journal*, 1/15 (13 April 1839), 232–3.

Anon., 'Animal Magnetism', *The Morning Post*, 2 September 1828, p. 4, col. 2.

Anon., 'Animal Magnetism', *The Morning Post*, 7 November 1829, p. 4, col. 3.

Anon., 'Animal Magnetism', *The Morning Post*, 2 February 1838, p. 5, col. 4.

Anon., 'Animal Magnetism', *The Morning Post*, 2 March 1838, p. 6, col. 5.

Anon., 'Animal Magnetism', *The Morning Post*, 5 March 1838, p. 3, col. 1.

Anon., 'Animal Magnetism', *The Morning Post*, 5 May 1838, p. 3, col. 4.

Anon., 'Animal Magnetism', *The Morning Post*, 11 May 1838, p. 6, col. 5.

Anon., 'Animal Magnetism', *The Penny Satirist*, 9 September 1837, p. 2, cols 1–2.

Anon., 'Animal Magnetism', *The Periscope; or Circumspective Review*, 1 October 1838, 634–6.

Anon., 'Animal Magnetism', *The Satirist: or, The Censor of the Times*, 5 November 1837, p. 774, col. 3.

Anon., 'Animal Magnetism', *The Standard*, 1 September 1828, p. 4, col. 5.

Anon., 'Animal Magnetism', *The Times*, 1 November 1837, p. 3, col. 6.

Anon., 'Animal Magnetism', *The Times*, 25 June 1838, p. 7, col. 2.

Anon., 'Animal Magnetism', *The Times*, 2 July 1838, p. 3, col. 3.

Anon., 'Animal Magnetism', *The Times*, 6 September 1838, p. 2, col. 5.

Anon., 'Animal Magnetism: Experiments of Baron Dupotet', *The Lancet*, 2 September 1837, 836–40.

Anon., 'Animal Magnetism: Second Report of Facts and Experiments', *The Lancet*, 9 June 1838, 377–83.

Anon., 'Animal Magnetism: Conclusion of Second Report of Facts and Experiments', *The Lancet*, 16 June 1838, 400–3.

Anon., 'Animal Magnetism: Fourth Report – Remarks and Experiments', *The Lancet*, 7 July 1838, 516–19.

Anon., 'Animal Magnetism: Fifth Report of Experiments and Facts', *The Lancet*, 14 July 1838, 546–9.

Anon., 'Animal Magnetism: Sixth Report of Experiments and Facts', *The Lancet*, 21 July 1838, 585–90.

Anon., 'Animal Magnetism: Seventh Report of Experiments and Facts', *The Lancet*, 28 July 1838, 615–20.

Anon., 'Animal Magnetism; or Mesmerism', *The Lancet*, 1 September 1838, 805–11.

Anon., 'Another Mesmerian Mountebank', *The Satirist: or, The Censor of the Times*, 18 March 1838, p. 83, col. 3.

Anon., 'Art. III. On Vaccine Inoculation, by Robert Willan MD, FAS', *Edinburgh Review, or Critical Journal*, 9/17 (October 1806), 32–66.

Anon., 'Art. V. 1 *Histoire Critique de Magnétisme Animal*, par T. P. F. Deleuze', *Foreign Review*, 5/9 (January 1830), 96–124.

Anon., 'Art. XIII. Hints to the Public and the Legislature, on the Nature and Effect of Evangelical Preaching. By a Barrister', *Quarterly Review*, 4/8 (November 1810), 480–514.

Anon., 'Article VI. *Philosophical Transactions of the Royal Society of London* for the Year 1800', *Critical Review, or, Annals of Literature*, 32 (July 1801), 297–8.

Anon., 'Births', *The Times*, 2 February 1848, p. 7, col. 6.

Anon., 'Bristol Mesmeric Institute', *The Bristol Mercury, and Western Counties Advertiser*, 2 June 1849, p. 3, cols 2–3.

Anon., 'British Medical Association', *The Lancet*, 12 October 1839, 93–102.

Anon., 'Bury Mechanics' Institution', *The Bury and Norwich Post: Or, Suffolk and Norfolk Telegraph, Essex, Cambridge and Ely Intelligencer*, 18 April 1832, p. 2, col. 3.

Anon., 'Chit-Chat', *The Satirist: or, The Censor of the Times*, 25 February 1838, p. 61, col. 3.

Anon., 'Chit-Chat', *The Satirist: or, The Censor of the Times*, 28 January 1838, p. 29, col. 3.

Anon., 'Chit-Chat', *The Satirist: or, The Censor of the Times*, 18 March 1838, p. 85, col. 3.

Anon., 'Chit-Chat', *The Satirist; or, The Censor of the Times*, 9 September 1838, p. 285, col. 3.

Anon., 'College of Physicians: The Annual Celebration', *The Examiner*, 4 July 1846, p. 426, col. 3.

Anon., 'Curiosities of Mesmerism', *The Blackburn Standard, Darwen Observer, and North-East Lancashire Advertiser*, 28 July 1888, p. 3, cols 6–7.

Anon., 'Curiosities of Mesmerism II', *The Glasgow Herald*, 28 July 1888, p. 9, cols 4–5.

Anon., 'Day to Day in Liverpool', *The Liverpool Mercury*, 6 September 1895, p. 6, col. 6.

Anon., 'Deaths', *La Belle Assemblée; or, Bell's Court and Fashionable Magazine*, 1 May 1830, p. 230, col. 2.

Anon., 'Died', *London Packet or New Lloyd's Evening Post*, 22–4 March, 1797, p. 3, col. 4.

Anon., 'Died', *The Morning Post*, 29 March 1830, p. 4, col. 1.

Anon., 'Dr Elliotson', *The Morning Post*, 3 August 1868, p. 3, col. 5.

Anon., 'Drawing-Room Necromancy', *The Englishwoman's Domestic Magazine*, 1 August 1862, 156–63.

Anon., 'Dublin, March 24' [obituary], *The Morning Post* [London], 27 March 1830, p. 3, col. 4.

Anon., 'Early Irish Hypnotists and Mesmerists', *British Medical Journal*, 19 August 1933, p. 348, col. 2.

Anon., 'Edinburgh University Medical Classes', *The Glasgow Herald*, 11 November 1893, p. 6, col. 7.

Anon., 'Editorial', *Provincial Medical and Surgical Journal*, 31 July 1844, pp. 269–70.

Anon., 'Electrical Society', *The Morning Post*, 6 October 1838, p. 3, col. 5.

Anon., 'Electricity and the Electric Telegraph', *Cornhill Magazine*, 2/7 (July 1860), 61–73.

Anon., 'Emperor of the Quacks' [song], *Whitehall Evening Post*, 9–12 June 1781, p. 2, col. 4.

Anon., 'Experiments with the Metallic Tractors' [review], *The Oracle and Daily Advertiser*, 24 October 1799, p. 1, col. 4.

Anon., 'Extract of a Letter from Paris, April 23 [1787]', *The World and Fashionable Advertiser*, 4 May 1787, p. 4, col. 1.

Anon., 'Extraordinary Case – Amputation without the Knowledge of the Patient', *Belfast News Letter*, 2 December 1842, p. 1, col. 1.

Anon., 'Extraordinary Conduct of the Medical Section towards Mr Braid', *The Manchester Times and Gazette*, 2 July 1842, p. 3, cols 4–6.

Anon., 'Facts and Scraps and Summary of General News', *Berrow's Worcester Journal*, 6 May 1854, p. 6, col. 4.

Anon., 'Fashion and Varieties', *The Freeman's Journal and Daily Commercial Advertiser*, 10 October 1839, p. 2, col. 5.

Anon., 'Fashionable Mesmerism', *The Satirist; or, The Censor of the Times*, 5 September 1841, p. 287, col. 3.

Anon., 'Foreign News', *The Essex Standard, and General Advertiser for the Eastern Counties*, 1 October 1847, p. 4, col. 1.

Anon., 'Fourth Edition', *Pall Mall Gazette*, 24 December 1889, p. 5, col. 2.

Anon., 'Fracas at University College', *The Times*, 15 January 1839, p. 5, col. 5.

Anon., 'France', *The Standard*, 22 April 1853, p. 3, col. 1.

Anon., 'Further Particulars of Dr Jemmet Brown, Late Archbishop of Tuam', *European Magazine and London Review*, 34 (September 1798), 164–8.

Anon., 'Galvanism', *Hampshire Telegraph and Portsmouth Gazette*, 4 April 1803, p. 2, col. 4.

Anon., 'Haymarket Theatre – Amateur Performance', *Caledonian Mercury*, 22 May 1848, p. 4, cols 4–5.

Anon., 'Health of the Hon. Mrs Hare and Miss Martineau', *The Zoist*, 3 (1845–6), 535–7.

Anon., 'Hypnotism', *The Leisure Hour*, July 1887, 454–6.

Anon., 'Hypnotism and Healing by Suggestion', *The Times*, 2 January 1914, p. 3, col. 1.

Anon., 'Hypnotism at Leeds', *The Speaker*, 12 April 1890, 395–6.

Anon., 'Judicial Committee of the Privy Council', *The Morning Post*, 18 April 1840, p. 3, col. 4.

Anon., 'Lecture on Quackery', *The Hull Packet and East Riding Times*, 15 December 1848, p. 5, col. 3.

Anon., 'Literature', *John Bull*, 12 May 1839, p. 224, cols 1–3.

Anon., 'Local Intelligence', *Sheffield and Rotherham Independent*, 20 June 1846, p. 8, col. 3.

Anon., 'London and Paris Gossip', *Trewman's Exeter Flying Post, or Plymouth and Cornish Advertiser*, 30 June 1880, p. 8, cols 1–2.

Anon., 'London, January 1', *Jackson's Oxford Journal*, 5 January 1839, p. 4, col. 1.

Anon., 'Lord Dalhousie on Mesmerism', *Daily News*, 11 August 1856, p. 6, col. 6.

Anon., 'Lord Ducie on Mesmerism', *The Aberdeen Journal*, 11 July 1849, p. 7, col. 2.

Anon., 'Mechanics' Institution', *The Derby Mercury*, 29 October 1828, p. 3, col. 3.

Anon., 'Medical Delusions of the Past', *The Penny Satirist*, 20 May 1843, p. 1, col. 3.

Anon., 'Mesmeric Humbug', *The Age*, 9 September 1838, p. 285, col. 2.

Anon., 'Mesmeric Infirmary', *The Morning Chronicle*, 15 June 1860, p. 6, col. 6.

Anon., 'Mesmeric Infirmary', *The Morning Post*, 7 May 1850, p. 6, cols 2–3.

Anon., 'Mesmeric Infirmary', *The Morning Post*, 9 May 1851, p. 3, cols 5–6.

Anon., 'Mesmeric Infirmary', *The Morning Post*, 28 May 1852, p. 6, cols 1–2.

Anon., 'Mesmeric Infirmary', *The Morning Post*, 11 June 1855, p. 2, col. 3.

Anon., 'Mesmeric Infirmary', *The Morning Post*, 13 June 1856, p. 3, col. 6.

Anon., 'Mesmeric Infirmary', *The Morning Post*, 22 June 1857, p. 2, cols 4–5.

Anon., 'Mesmeric Infirmary', *The Morning Post*, 21 June 1858, p 6, col. 3.

Anon., 'Mesmeric Infirmary', *The Sheffield and Rotherham Independent*, 25 July 1846, p. 8, col. 3.

Anon., 'Mesmeric Phenomena', *The Times*, 10 September 1841, p. 3, col. 5.

Anon., 'Mesmeric Trance', *The Times*, 2 May 1854, p. 12, col. 4.

Anon., 'Mesmerism', *Bristol Mercury*, 18 July 1846, p. 3, col. 2.

Anon., 'Mesmerism', *Bristol Mercury*, 25 September 1847, p. 8, col. 2.

Anon., 'Mesmerism', *Geelong Advertiser and Squatter's Advocate*, 23 April 1847, p. 1, cols 3–5.

Anon., 'Mesmerism', *John Bull*, 13 January 1839, pp. 19–20.

Anon., 'Mesmerism', *Leeds Mercury*, 25 July 1846, p. 12, col. 2.

Anon., 'Mesmerism', *The Blackburn Standard and North East Lancashire Advertiser*, 20 November 1875, p. 3, col. 2.

Anon., 'Mesmerism', *The Bury and Norwich Post, and Suffolk Herald*, 29 May 1850, p. 3, col. 2.

Anon., 'Mesmerism', *The Satirist, or, The Censor of the Times*, 11 September 1842, p. 291.

Anon., 'Mesmerism: Amputation without the Knowledge of the Patient', *The Essex Standard, and General Advertiser for the Eastern Counties*, 2 December 1842, p. 4, col. 1.

Anon., 'Mesmerism and Braidism', *The Leicester Chronicle: or, Commercial and Agricultural Advertiser*, 2 April 1842, p. 4, cols 2–3.

Anon., 'Mesmerism and Hypnotism', *Quarterly Review*, July 1890, 234–59.

Anon., 'Mesmerism and Somnambulism', *The Morning Chronicle*, 1 December 1841, p. 2, col. 4.

Anon., 'Mesmerism at Deptford', *The Times*, 20 December 1843, p. 3, col. 3.

Anon., 'Mesmerism in India', *Daily News*, 5 January 1847, p. 3, col. 2.

Anon., 'Mesmerism in India', *Dundee Courier*, 7 June 1848, p. 3, col. 4.

Anon., 'Mesmerism in India', *The Essex Standard, and General Advertiser for the Eastern Counties*, 25 December 1846, p. 4, col. 4.

Anon., 'Mesmerism in India', supplement to the *Leeds Mercury*, 9 January 1847, p. 11, col. 6.

Anon., 'Mesmerism in India', *The Morning Chronicle*, 4 January 1847, p. 6, col. 1.

Anon., 'Mesmerism in India', *Newcastle Courant*, 6 November 1846, p. 2, col. 5.

Anon., 'Mesmerism: To the Editor of the *Worcester Journal*', *Berrow's Worcester Journal*, 16 December 1841, p. 4, col. 2.

Anon., 'Mesmerism Unmasked', *The Medical Times*, 9 (9 December 1843), 145–7.

Anon., 'Mesmerism versus Chloroform', *The Sheffield & Rotherham Independent*, 6 July 1887, p. 8, col. 4.

Anon., 'Miss Helen Faucit', *The Era*, 15 March 1840, p. 297, col. 4.

Anon., 'Miss Martineau on Mesmerism', *Hampshire Telegraph and Sussex Chronicle*, 8 August 1846, p. 3, cols 3–4.

Anon., 'Monthly Catalogue: Medical', *Monthly Review*, 74 (June 1786), p. 477.

Anon., 'More Successful Cases of Mesmerism, in Connection with Surgical Operations in Leicester', *The Leicester Chronicle; or, Commercial and Agricultural Advertiser*, 9 November 1844, p. 3, col. 5.

Anon., 'Mountebank Dupotet Again', *The Satirist: or, The Censor of the Times*, 11 March 1838, p. 75, col. 3.

Anon., 'Mr Braid's Lecture on Animal Magnetism at The Athenaeum', *The Manchester Times and Gazette*, 31 December 1841, p. 3, cols 2–3.

Anon., 'Mr Braid's Lectures on Animal Magnetism', *The Manchester Times and Gazette*, 11 December 1841, p. 3, cols 4–6.

Anon., 'New Anaesthetic Agent – Ether Superseded', *Caledonian Mercury*, 15 November 1847, p. 3, col. 2.

Anon., 'Notes on the Life of Augustus L. Egg', *Reader*, 44 (31 October 1863), p. 516.

Anon., 'Notice to Correspondents', *The London Dispatch and People's Political and Social Reformer*, 17 June 1838, p. 732, col. 3.

Anon., 'Obituary', *The Examiner*, 8 August 1868, 508–9.

Anon., 'Odds and Ends', *The Penny Satirist*, 29 August 1840, p. 4, col. 1.

Anon., 'Our London Letter', *Dundee Courier and Argus*, 31 October 1895, p. 3, col. 2.

Anon., 'Painless Operations in the Mesmeric State', *The Examiner*, 11 September 1852, p. 587, col. 2.

Anon., 'Painless Surgical Operation in Mesmeric Trance', *The Leicester Chronicle: or, Commercial and Agricultural Advertiser*, 6 May 1854, p. 1, col. 7.

Anon., 'Personal News', *The Examiner*, 6 January 1839, p. 8, col. 3.

Anon., 'Phrenological Society', *The Zoist*, 1 (1843–4), 134–7.

Anon., 'Poetry: A Song, Introductory to the Celestial Bed', *Morning Herald and Daily Advertiser*, 26 July 1781, p. 4, col. 1.

Anon., 'Police', *The Morning Chronicle*, 5 February 1825, p. 4, col. 3.

Anon., 'Police', *The Times*, 18 September 1837, p. 6, col. 6.

Anon., 'Police', *The Times*, 11 October 1837, p. 6, cols 5–6.

Anon., 'Police', *The Times*, 13 November 1838, p. 7, cols 2–4.

Anon., 'Police', *The Times*, 22 November 1838, p. 7, cols 1–5.

Anon., 'Police', *The Times*, 23 November 1838, p. 7, cols 3–5.

Anon., 'Police', *The Times*, 23 January 1839, p. 7, cols 3–4.

Anon., 'Popular Science: A Word or Two on Mesmerism, Epoch 1', *The Lady's Newspaper*, 30 January 1847, p. 102.

Anon., *Report of the Sixth Annual Meeting of the London Mesmeric Infirmary*, 36 Weymouth Street, Portland Place (London: Walton and Mitchell, 1855).

Anon., 'Royal College of Physicians', *The Times*, 29 June 1846, p. 8, col. 4.

Anon., 'Royal College of Physicians', *Trewman's Exeter Flying Post, or Plymouth and Cornish Advertiser*, 16 July 1846, p. 2, col. 1.

Anon., 'Royal Institution: Mr Davy's Lectures on the Elements of Chemical Philosophy', *The Morning Chronicle*, 17 February 1812, p. 3, col. 2.

Anon., 'Second Edition' [editorial], *The Manchester Times and Gazette*, 25 June 1842, p. 2, cols 4–5.

Anon., 'Somnambulism', *The Times*, 25 June 1844, p. 6, col. 6.

Anon., 'Startling Experiments', *The Satirist: or, The Censor of the Times*, 5 November 1837, p. 771, col. 2.

Anon., 'Stow-on-the-Wold and Chipping Norton Agricultural Meeting', *Jackson's Oxford Journal*, 18 September 1847, p. 2, cols 1–2.

Anon., 'Sunday's Post', *The Bury and Norwich Post: Or, Suffolk and Norfolk Telegraph, Essex, Cambridge, & Ely Intelligencer*, 7 April 1830, p. 1, cols 1–2.

Anon., 'The British Association', *The Belfast News-Letter*, 14 August 1835, p. 1, cols 4–5.

Anon., 'The College of Physicians and the Forthcoming Celebration', *The Morning Post*, 22 June, 1846, p. 5, col. 2.

Anon., 'The Humbug Called Mesmerism', *The Times*, 7 January 1838, p. 6, col. 6

Anon., 'The Humbug Called Mesmerism', *Hampshire Telegraph and Sussex Chronicle*, 14 January 1839, p. 2, cols 5–6.

Anon., 'The Lancet', *The Lancet*, 15 September 1838, 873–7.

Anon., 'The Late Dr Elliotson', *The Bury and Norwich Post, and Suffolk Herald*, 11 August 1868, p. 2, col. 5.

Anon., 'The Literary Examiner', *The Examiner*, 18 July 1846, p. 452, cols 1–2.

Anon., 'The Magnetism Charlatan', *The Satirist: or, The Censor of the Times*, 11 February 1848, p. 45, col. 3.

Anon., 'The Medical Adviser', *The Penny Satirist*, 1 July 1843, p. 4, col. 3.

Anon., 'The Mesmeric Infirmary', *The Morning Chronicle*, 19 June 1861, p. 6, col. 1.

Anon., 'The Mesmeric Infirmary', *The Morning Post*, 18 June 1853, p. 7, col.2.

Anon., 'The Mesmeric Infirmary', *The Morning Post*, 8 June 1854, p. 3, cols 1–3.

Anon., *The Missionary Register for MDCCCXXII* (London: Richard Watts, 1822).

Anon., 'The Mystery of Mesmerism and Somnambulism Explained', *Preston Chronicle*, 24 December 1841, p. 4, col. 6.

Anon., *The Power of Mesmerism: A Highly Erotic Narrative of Voluptuous Facts and Fancies* (Brussels?: Printed for the Nihilists, Moscow, 1891).

Anon., 'The Quack Dupotet', *The Satirist: or, The Censor of the Times*, 18 March 1838, p. 83, col. 1.

Anon., 'The Quarterlies', *John Bull*, 40 (27 October 1860), p. 684, col. 1.

Anon., 'The Sleeping Frenchman', *The Daily News*, 1 April 1887, p. 6, col. 7.

Anon., 'The Story of Hypnotism', *Pall Mall Gazette*, 19 July 1898, p. 3, col. 2.

Anon., 'The Todmorden Literary and Scientific Society', *The Manchester Times and Gazette*, 27 May 1837, p. 2, col. 7.

Anon., 'Theatres and Music', *John Bull*, 13 May 1848, 311–12.

Anon., 'Theatrical and Musical Notes', *The Morning Post*, 28 October 1895, p. 2, col. 7.

Anon., 'This Morning's News', *The Daily News*, 14 April 1890, p. 5, cols 5–6.

Anon., 'To Correspondents', *The Times*, 12 September 1838, p. 4, col. 1.

Anon., 'To the Worshipful, the Mayor of Liverpool', *Liverpool Mercury*, 24 April 1846, p. 3, col. 6.

Anon., 'Town Correspondents', *The Penny Satirist*, 26 January 1839, p. 4, col. 2.

Anon., 'University College London', *The Morning Chronicle*, 28 February 1839, p. 3, col. 7.

Anon., Untitled obituary, *The Caledonian Mercury*, 10 April 1830, p. 3, col. 2.

Anon., 'Varieties', *Berrow's Worcester Journal*, 15 February 1844, p. 4, col. 1.

Auerbach, Nina, 'Magi and Maidens: The Romance of the Victorian Freud', *Critical Inquiry*, 8 (1981), 281–300.

Baly, Monica E., and H. C. G. Matthew, 'Nightingale, Florence (1820–1910)', *Oxford Dictionary of National Biography* (Oxford: Oxford University Press, 2004; online edition, January 2011) at www.oxforddnb.com/view/article/35241, accessed 12 February 2014.

Balzac, Honoré de, 'Mesmerism' [chapter 10 of *Ursule Mirouet*], *The Lady's Newspaper*, 21 February 1863, 291–2.

——, *Ursule Mirouet* [1842], trans Donald Adamson (Harmondsworth: Penguin, 1976).

Bennett, Anthony, 'Rivals Unravelled: A Broadside Song and Dance', *Folk Music Journal*, 6/4 (1993), 420–45.

Binet, Alfred, and Charles Féré, *Animal Magnetism* (London: Kegan, Paul, Trench, 1887).

Blackmantle, Bernard (pseud.) and Isaac Robert Cruikshank (illus.), *The English Spy: An Original Work Characteristic, Satirical, and Humorous, Comprising Scenes and Sketches in Every Rank of Society, Being Portraits Drawn from the Life* (London: Sherwood, Jones and Co., 1825).

Boyle, Patrick, *The General London Guide; or, Tradesman's Directory for the Year 1794* (London: Patrick Boyle, 1794).

Braid, James, *Neurypnology, or the Rationale of Nervous Sleep, Considered in Relation with Animal Magnetism* (London: John Churchill, 1843).

——, 'On Neuro-Hypnotism', *The Medical Times*, 6/146 (1842), reprinted in *The Discovery of Hypnosis: The Complete Writings of James Braid, the Father of Hypnotherapy*, ed. Donald Robertson (London: National Council for Hypnotherapy, 2009), pp. 368–9.

——, *Satanic Agency and Mesmerism Reviewed, in a Letter to the Reverend H. McNeile, A.M., of Liverpool, in Reply to a Sermon Preached by Him in St Jude's Church, Liverpool, on Sunday, April 10, 1842, by James Braid, Surgeon, Manchester* (Manchester: Simms and Dinham, and Galt and Anderson, 1842).

——, 'The Editors of *The Manchester Times*', *The Manchester Times and Gazette*, 25 June 1842, p. 2, col. 4.

Brown, Theocritus, 'Animal Magnetism', *The Times*, 28 September 1837, p. 1, cols 4–6.

Burman, F. S., 'More Mesmeric Impostors', *Provincial Medical and Surgical Journal*, 4 November 1843, 101–2.

Chandler, Thomas, 'To the Editor of the *Morning Post*', *The Morning Post*, 18 January 1870, p. 7, col. 5.

Chavasse, Pye Henry, *Advice to a Wife on the Management of Her Own Health* (London: John Churchill and Sons, 1870).

Chenevix, Richard, 'On Mesmerism, Improperly Denominated Animal Magnetism', *The London Medical and Physical Journal*, 61 (1829), 219–30 and 491–501; 62 (1829), 114–25, 210–21 and 315–29.

Christmas, Henry, 'Essay on the Origin and Progress of Animal Magnetism', *Analyst: A Quarterly Journal of Science, Literature, Natural History, and the Fine Arts*, 10/30 (June 1840), 464–83.

Clarke, Charles and Mary Cowden, *Recollections of Writers* (London: Sampson Low, Marston, Searle & Rivington, 1878).

Collins, Philip, ed., *Dickens: Interviews and Recollections* (London: Macmillan, 1981), 2 vols.

Collins, Wilkie, 'Introductory Lines (Relating the Adventures and Transformations of *The Frozen Deep*)', in Wilkie Collins, *The Frozen Deep* and *Mr Wray's Cash-Box*, ed. William M. Clarke (Stroud: Alan Sutton, 1996), pp. 3–5.

Collyer, R. H., 'Surgical Operations Without Pain', *The Morning Post*, 12 January 1846, p. 6, col. 4.

Corelli, Marie, *Wormwood: A Drama of Paris* [1890], ed. Kirsten MacLeod (Peterborough, Ont.: Broadview, 2004).

Cosnett, J. E., 'Dickens and Doctors: Vignettes of Victorian Medicine', *British Medical Journal*, 305 (19–26 December 1992), 1540–2.

Dickens, Charles, *Little Dorrit*, ed. John Holloway (Harmondsworth: Penguin, 1980).

du Maurier, George, 'Hypnotism – A Modern Parisian Romance (In Four Chapters)', *Punch's Almanack for 1890* (5 December 1889), unpaginated.

——, *Trilby: A Novel* [1894] (London: Osgood, McIlvaine & Co., 1895).

Dupotet, Baron, 'Animal Magnetism: [A] Letter from Baron Dupotet', *The Lancet*, 2 September 1837, pp. 905–7.

Elliotson, John, *Cure of a True Cancer of the Female Breast*, reprinted from the last number (XXII) of *The Zoist*, with Introductory Remarks by Dr Engeldue, Fourth Edition (London: Walton and Mitchell, 1848).

——, 'Mesmeric Cases by Dr Esdaile, Communicated by Dr Elliotson', *The Zoist*, 12 (1854–5), 74–80.

——, 'Mesmeric Cure of a Cow by Miss Harriet Martineau', *The Zoist*, 8 (1850–1), 300–3.

——, *Numerous Cases of Surgical Operations Without Pain in the Mesmeric State, with Remarks Upon the Opposition of Many Members of the Royal Medical and Chirurgical Society and Others to the Inestimable Blessings of Mesmerism* (Philadelphia: Lea and Blanchard, 1843).

——, 'Report by Dr Elliotson upon *A Record of Cases Treated in the Mesmeric Hospital, from November 1846, to May, 1847, with the Reports of the Official Visitors ...*', *The Zoist*, 21 (April 1848), 1–41.

——, 'Some Rapid Cures by Dr Esdaile, Communicated by Dr Elliotson', *The Zoist*, 12 (1854–5), 413–15.

——, 'Surgical Operations Without Pain in the Mesmeric State', *The Zoist*, 3 (1845–6), 380–9.

——, *The Harveian Oration, Delivered Before the Royal College of Physicians, London, June 27th, 1846* (London: H. Baillière, 1846).

Elston, M. A., 'Blake, Dame Louisa Brandreth Aldrich- (1865–1925), surgeon', *Oxford Dictionary of National Biography* (Oxford: Oxford University Press, 2004; online edition, January 2011) at www.oxforddnb.com/view/article/30367, accessed 12 February 2014.

Esdaile, David, 'Editor's Preface' to James Esdaile, *Mesmerism in India, and Its Practical Application in Surgery and Medicine* (London: Longman, Brown, Green and Longmans, 1846), pp. ix–xx.

Esdaile, James, *Mesmerism in India, and Its Practical Application in Surgery and Medicine* (London: Longman, Brown, Green and Longmans, 1846).

——, 'The Protest and Petition of James Esdaile, MD, Surgeon, HEICS, to the Members of the American Congress', *The Zoist*, 9 (1853–4), 294–7.

Fancher, Raymond E., *Pioneers of Psychology* (New York: W. W. Norton and Co., 1979).

Foote, Edward Bliss, *Dr Foote's Home Cyclopedia of Popular Medical, Social and Sexual Science*, Twentieth Century Revised and Enlarged Edition (London: L. N. Fowler, 1901).

Forrest, Derek, *Hypnotism: A History* (London: Penguin, 2000).

Forster, John, *The Life of Charles Dickens* (London: Chapman and Hall, 1892).

Foucault, Michel, *The History of Sexuality: An Introduction*, trans. Robert Hurley (London: Penguin, 1984).

Freud, Sigmund, and Joseph Breuer, *Studies on Hysteria* [1893–95], trans. James and Alix Strachey (London: Penguin, 1986).

'G' [pseud.], 'Observations on Animal Magnetism', *Blackwood's Edinburgh Magazine*, 1/6 (September 1817), 563–7.

'G' [pseud.], 'Revival of Philosophical Quackery', *The Kaleidoscope; or, Literary and Scientific Mirror*, 21 November 1826, p. 158, col. 3.

'G' [pseud.], 'Revival of Philosophical Quackery', *The Liverpool Mercury*, 17 November 1826, p. 158, col. 1.

Gallo, David A., and Stanley Finger, 'The Power of a Musical Instrument: Franklin, the Mozarts, Mesmer and the Glass Armonica', *History of Psychology*, 3/4 (2000), 326–43.

Gape, Gregory [pseud.?], 'To the Printers' [letter], *Felix Farley's Bristol Journal*, 20 June 1789, p. 4, cols 4–5.

Gauld, Alan, *A History of Hypnotism* (Cambridge: Cambridge University Press, 1990).

Gilbert, W. S., *Patience* [1881] in *The Complete Annotated Gilbert and Sullivan*, ed. Ian Bradley (Oxford: Oxford University Press, 2001), pp. 265–353.

Gould, Stephen J., 'The Chain of Reason vs the Chain of Thumbs', *Natural History*, July 1989, 12–21.

Greenslade, Thomas B., Jr, 'Nineteenth Century Textbook Illustrations 40: Discovery of the Leiden Jar', *The Physics Teacher*, 32 (1994), 536–7.

Grimes, Hilary, 'Power in Flux: Mesmerism, Mesmeric Manuals and du Maurier's *Trilby*', *Gothic Studies*, 10/2 (2008), 67–83.

Haggard, Howard W., 'The First Published Attack on Perkinism: An Anonymous Eighteenth Century Poetical Satire', *Yale Journal of Biology and Medicine*, 9/2 (1936), 137–53.

Hamill, John, and Robert Gilbert, *Freemasonry: A Celebration of the Craft* (London: Angus Books, 2004).

Harris, Jack, *Harris's List of Covent Garden Ladies, or Man of Pleasure's Kalender for the Year 1793*, ed. Hallie Rubenhold (Stroud: Tempus, 2005).

Herfner, Irys, 'Mesmerism', *Dublin University Magazine*, 23 (January 1844), 37–53.

Herholdt, Johan Daniel, and Carl Gottlob Rafn, *Experiments with the Metallic Tractors in Rheumatic and Gouty Affections, Inflammations and Various Topical Diseases*, ed. B. J. Perkins, trans Tode and Kampfmuller (London: J. Johnson, 1799).

Hoblyn, Richard, *A Dictionary of Terms Used in Medicine and the Collateral Sciences*, Fourth Edition (London: Whittaker and Co., 1849).

House, Madeline, and Graham Storey, eds, *The Pilgrim Edition of the Letters of Charles Dickens* (Oxford: Clarendon Press, 1965–2002), 12 vols.

Humphreys, A. W., *The King of the Cannibal Islands* [song] (London: A. Hughes, [1830]).

Imlach, H., 'Animal Magnetism', *Provincial Medical and Surgical Journal*, 4 March 1843, p. 458, col. 2.

Inchbald, Elizabeth, *Animal Magnetism, A Farce in Three Acts, as Performed at the Theatre Royal, Covent Garden* (Dublin: P. Byron, 1777).

Kitton, Frederic George, *Charles Dickens by Pen and Pencil* (London: Frank T. Sabin, 1890), 3 vols.

Liégeois, Jules, *De la suggestion hypnotique dans ses rapports avec le droit civil et le droit criminal* (Paris: Picard, 1884).

Martineau, Harriet [attrib.], 'An Egyptian Magician', in 'Miscellaneous Extracts', Supplement to the *Manchester Examiner*, 1 July 1848, p. 4, col. 3.

Mayo, Herbert, *On the Truths Contained in Popular Superstitions, with an Account of Mesmerism* [1851] (Westcliff-on-Sea: Desert Island Books, 2003).

Mesmer, Franz Anton, 'Catechism on Animal Magnetism', in George Bloch, trans., *Mesmerism: A Translation of the Original Scientific and Medical Writings of F. A. Mesmer* (Los Altos: William Kaufmann, inc., 1980), pp. 79–86.

——, 'Letter from M. Mesmer, Doctor of Medicine at Vienna, to A. M. Unzer, Doctor of Medicine, on the Medicinal Usage of the Magnet' (1775), in George Bloch, trans., *Mesmerism: A Translation of the Original Scientific and Medical Writings of F. A. Mesmer* (Los Altos: William Kaufmann, inc., 1980), pp. 25–9.

——, *Mémoire sur la découverte du magnétisme animal* (1779), translated as 'Dissertation on the Discovery of Animal Magnetism', in George Bloch, trans., *Mesmerism: A Translation of the Original Scientific and Medical Writings of F. A. Mesmer* (Los Altos: William Kaufmann, inc., 1980), pp. 43–78.

——, 'Physical-Medical Treatise on the Influence of the Planets' in George Bloch, trans., *Mesmerism: A Translation of the Original Scientific and Medical Writings of F. A. Mesmer* (Los Altos: William Kaufmann, inc., 1980), pp. 1–22.

Miller, Jonathan, 'Mesmerism', *The Listener*, 90 (22 November 1973), 685–90.

Miller, Joseph, 'Remarkable Proof of the Truth of Animal Magnetism', *The Times*, 11 September 1838, p. 4, col. 5.

Milne-Bramwell, J., *Hypnotism: Its History, Practice and Theory* (London: Alexander Moring, 1906).

Milton, John, 'Il Penseroso' in L. D. Lerner, ed., *The Penguin Poets: Milton* (Harmondsworth: Penguin, 1953), pp. 71–6.

Overs, John, *Evenings of a Working Man, being the Occupation of His Scanty Leisure* (London: T. C. Newby, 1844).

Owen, A. R. G., *Hysteria, Hypnosis and Healing: The Work of J. M. Charcot* (London: Dennis Dobson, 1971), p. 172.

Peters, Catherine, *The King of Inventors: A Life of Wilkie Collins* (London: Secker and Warburg, 1991).

Pick, Daniel, *Svengali's Web: The Alien Enchanter in Modern Culture* (New Haven: Yale University Press, 2000).

Porter, R. S., 'The Sexual Politics of James Graham', *British Journal for Eighteenth-Century Studies*, 5 (1982), 199–206.

Potter, Paul, *Trilby* [1895], adapted by Herbert Beerbohm Tree, in George Taylor, ed., *Trilby and Other Plays: Four Plays for Victorian Star Actors* (Oxford: Oxford University Press, 1996), pp. 199–271.

Purcell, L. Edward, '*Trilby* and Trilby-Mania: The Beginning of the Bestseller System', *Journal of Popular Culture*, 11/1 (1977), 62–76.

Puységur, Le Marquis de, 'The Phenomena of Magnetism', *The Monthly Magazine, or British Register*, 16/96 (December 1833), 681–7.

Riquetti, Gabriel-Honoré, *The Secret History of the Court of Berlin* (London: S. Bladon, 1789), 2 vols.

Riskin, Jessica, *Science in the Age of Sensibility: The Sentimental Empiricists of the French Enlightenment* (Chicago: University of Chicago Press, 2002).

Rolleston, Humphry, 'Irregular Practice and Quackery', *The Canadian Medical Association Journal*, 17/5 (May 1927), 501–8.

Romer, Isabella F., *Sturmer: A Tale of Mesmerism, to Which Are Added Other Sketches from Life* (London: Bentley, 1841), 3 vols.

Ross, John M., ed., *The Illustrated Globe Encyclopædia of Universal Information* (London: Thomas C. Jack, 1882), 12 vols.

South, Christopher, 'The Humbug Mesmerism', *The Penny Satirist; A Cheap Substitute for a Weekly Newspaper*, 19 January 1839, p. 1, col. 1.

Stoker, Bram, *Personal Reminiscences of Henry Irving*, Revised and Cheaper Edition (London: Heinemann, 1907).

Storer, Henry, *Mesmerism in Disease: A Few Plain Facts, With a Selection of Cases* (London: Baillière, 1843).

Syson, Lydia, *Doctor of Love: Dr James Graham and His Celestial Bed* (Richmond: Alma Books, 2008).

Tatar, Maria M., *Spellbound: Studies on Mesmerism and Literature* (Princeton: Princeton University Press, 1978).

Waltroud, Ernst, 'Esdaile, James (1808–1859)', *Oxford Dictionary of National Biography*, available online at www.oxforddnb.com/view/article/8882, accessed 27 February 2013.

Waterfield, Robin, *Hidden Depths: The Story of Hypnosis* (London: Pan, 2004).

Winter, Alison, *Mesmerized: Powers of Mind in Victorian Britain* (Chicago: University of Chicago Press, 1998).

Wright, Franklyn, 'The Mesmerist's Spell', *The 'Halfpenny Marvel'*, 29 October 1895, pp. 1–13.

Advertisements

'American Metallic Tractors', *The Oracle and Public Advertiser*, 22 May 1797, p. 1, col. 3.

'Anatomical Preparations', *The Oracle and Daily Advertiser*, 11 June 1799, p. 4, col. 2.

'Animal Magnetism', *St James's Chronicle, or the British Evening Post*, 16 December 1784, p. 3, col. 4.

'Animal Magnetism', *The Morning Herald and Daily Advertiser*, 24 October 1785, p. 1, col. 2.

'Animal Magnetism', *The Morning Post*, 27 November 1837, p. 1, col. 2.

'Animal Magnetism', *The Morning Post and Daily Advertiser*, 6 February 1786, p. 1, col. 2.

'College for Instructing Pupils in Mesmer's Philosophy of Animal Magnetism', *The Morning Herald*, 7 June 1788, p. 1, col. 2.

'College for Instruction in Elementary Philosophy', *The World*, 26 June 1788, p. 1, col. 2.

'Curious Preparations', *The Oracle and Daily Advertiser*, 11 June 1799, p. 4, col. 2

'Dr de Mainaduc', *The World*, 17 June 1788, p. 2, col. 1.

'In the Press, and Will Speedily Be Published', *The General Evening Post*, 9–11 June 1785, p. 3, col. 4

'*Journal of Psychological Medicine*', *John Bull and Britannia*, 40 (29 September 1860), p. 609, col. 3.

'Just published', *The Lady's Newspaper*, 3 July 1852, p. 414, col. 1.

'Just published, price 2s 6d', *The Weekly Register*, 18 July 1798, p. 110, col. 3.

'Lectures', *The Morning Post and Daily Advertiser*, 10 November 1786, p. 1, col. 1.

'Literary Fund – The Anniversary Festival', *The Age*, 12 May 1833, p. 145, col. 3.

'Mesmeric Infirmary', *The Examiner*, 14 April 1855, p. 239, col. 3.

'Mesmeric Infirmary', *The Morning Post*, 24 May 1850, p. 1, col. 2.

'Mesmeric Infirmary', *The Morning Post*, 27 May 1854, p. 1, col. 2.

'Mesmeric Infirmary', *The Morning Post*, 8 June 1861, p. 1, col. 2.

'Mesmeric Infirmary', *The Morning Post*, 9 June 1862, p. 1, col. 3.

'Mesmeric Infirmary', *The Morning Post*, 6 June 1863, p. 1, col. 2.

'Mesmeric Infirmary', *The Morning Post*, 8 June 1863, p. 1, col. 3.

'Mesmeric Infirmary', *The Morning Post*, 26 October 1869, p. 1, col. 3.

'Mesmeric Infirmary', *The Standard*, 25 June 1867, p. 1, col. 4.

'Mesmerism', *The Morning Post*, 11 September 1858, p. 1, col. 2.

'Metallic Tractors', *The Star*, 1 December 1798, p. 1, col. 4.

'New System of the World', *The World*, 26 May 1788, p. 1, col. 2.

'*The Lancet*, Sept. 9', *The Morning Post*, 11 September 1837, p. 1, col. 3.

'The Mesmeric Infirmary', *The Times*, 2 June 1869, p. 4, col. 2.

'The Voluptuarian Cabinet', *The Satirist: or, The Censor of the Times*, 18 March 1838, p. 82, col. 3.

'University College Hospital', *The Times*, 21 May 1838, p. 1, col. 2.

'Verbeck, Piccadilly Hall', *The Standard*, 11 April 1887, p. 1, col. 5.

Index